The
Iranian Chronicles

*Unveiling the Dark Truths
of the Islamic Republic*

Ali Delforoush

iUniverse, Inc.
Bloomington

The Iranian Chronicles
Unveiling the Dark Truths of the Islamic Republic

iUniverse books may be ordered through booksellers or by contacting:

iUniverse
1663 Liberty Drive
Bloomington, IN 47403
www.iuniverse.com
1-800-Authors (1-800-288-4677)

ISBN: 978-1-4759-2911-9 (sc)
ISBN: 978-1-4759-2909-6 (hc)
ISBN: 978-1-4759-2910-2 (e)

Library of Congress Control Number: 2012912869

Printed in the United States of America

iUniverse rev. date: 7/31/2012

*Dedicated to Neda Agha-Soltan, Sohrab Aarabi,
Taraneh Mousavi, and everyone else who has lost his
or her life or suffered unjust imprisonment and torture
in the fight for democracy and human rights.
To my parents and grandparents for teaching
me to stand up for my beliefs.*

Contents

Introduction

―――〜〇〇〜―――

"I don't know why [people] say horses are noble creatures and doves are beautiful, but how come no one keeps vultures? ... What less does the clover flowers have from the red tulips? ... We need to cleanse our eyes ... We must see things differently." These are the eternal instructions and life lessons that renowned Iranian poet Sohrab Sepehri was reminding me of through the magic of YouTube.

The weather was mild for Ontario in late September, and so I was outside on the patio of my house enjoying the poetry along with the weak northern sunshine while reflecting on the past three years of my life. I sipped some scotch, feeling the fine blend warm my stomach as soon as I swallowed. I reached for my old *ghalyoon* (water pipe) next to me and inhaled the fragrant double-apple tobacco, sweet and satisfying and a powerful reminder of my former home in Tehran. It has been nearly two decades since my family and I came to Canada; in 1994, we fled the oppression of the Islamic Republic in favor of finding a better life. Since leaving my native land at the age of twelve, I have watched what is happening in Iran with growing alarm. The protests after the presidential election in 2009 instilled some hope that freedom and change could come to pass in Iran, but doubts still linger. In the last three years, I have reached out to more than four hundred brave and sometimes lost souls in Tehran and asked them to share their stories with me, all in the hope of painting in the blank spaces in my knowledge of what really goes on inside my former country, and with the notion that the much maligned people of Iran might be better understood if the West had a more accurate account of the realities the common man and woman face.

But before we dive into the state of life in Iran, please allow me to tell you a little about myself. My name is Ali Delforoush, and yes, for all the Farsi speakers, my last name is in fact Delforoush, which translated into English literally means "heart seller" (or, the more poetic version, "conscience seller").

I was born in 1982 in Tehran, Iran, and now reside in Thornhill, Canada. I graduated with an honors double major in political science and law and society. In addition, I recently acquired my bachelor's in law and am currently pursuing a master's degree in law. I have also written a number of articles with regard to Iran's social, economic, and political environments and have discussed these issues live on the BBC and with the Associated Press. I would like to make it clear that this book is not the rants of a neo-con, a monarchist supporter, or a *mojahed* (MEK)—or, even worse, someone who wants to humiliate his country and his people just to make a name for himself. Quite the opposite: through writing this book, my intentions have been to describe the people of Iran as noble and compassionate while exposing life under the Islamic Republic as chaotic, oppressive, and extremely challenging. I have always considered myself a proud Iranian Canadian who has strong affections for Iran and Iranians everywhere. My aspirations are that through these stories, Western readers will gain further perspective about Iranians, sympathize with the struggles of the people of Iran, and support them in their quest for liberty.

I strongly believe that there is a unique, family-oriented value system and hospitality that exists in Iran that I have yet to experience anywhere else. Iranians are proud of their heritage and like to share their cultural values with non-Iranians every chance they get. I most certainly recommend for everyone to communicate with and befriend an Iranian, for the hospitality, sophistication, and sense of respect that you will receive from an Iranian will certainly be a pleasant surprise; it may even lead you to question the negative representation of Iranians that has been produced by the media. I certainly hope that readers of this book will grasp the nuances of repression that over the past thirty-three years has spilled onto nearly every aspect of common life by the Islamic Republic. This should help readers to separate Iranians from their government, which, in my opinion, is extreme, intolerant, vicious, and a very different entity than the overwhelming majority of Iranians.

I consider myself a liberal at heart and place human rights, due process, and equality (especially for women) at the center of my existence. But before envisioning a democratic Iran, and having grand gestures of an Iran free from the reign and terror of the mullahs and fundamentalism, we need to fully realize that there is something significantly wrong within the fabric of life in Iran and specifically in Tehran.

Like many others living in Tehran, from an early age I found myself almost constantly fearful of the government and its outfits. One of my early memories during the preliminary years of the revolution was traveling with my mother at the age of four to my grandparents' house, only to have a brutal female "morals" police officer stop my mother because several strands of her hair were exposed beneath her *hejab* (head scarf).

During the beginning years of the Islamic Republic, and under the recent presidency of Ahmadinejad, women who did not uphold the strict religious and clothing codes of the government would be placed under arrest, rounded up, and taken to a detention center. The woman who stopped my mother released her only because she felt remorseful and decided to show compassion once I, scared and terrified out of my mind, began to cry and scream.

Unfortunately, not all women are as lucky as my mother was, and women today are often arrested regardless of who they are with. The difference is that now almost all of the arresting officers are men, who show no mercy.

Another one of my early memories was going to family parties and weddings, where I witnessed the fear and anxiety in the voices and eyes of adults who were nervously deliberating that at any moment, bearded and burly men swinging blunt objects could raid the party and place innocent people under arrest, just because the wedding was a coed mixture of men and women or because there was alcohol or a video player in the house or a satellite dish up on the roof.

Once I entered school, the fear only increased. I remember before attending school, my parents gave me special advice to never question the government and especially be respectful of the leadership (Khomeini and, later on, Khamenei). In the second grade, as part of the yearly celebrations commemorating the revolution, I and several other students were given the task of painting a life-size American flag, which was to be burned in front of the students at the school; when I refused to do so, I was given fifty lashes from a ruler across my palms for being "insensitive and disrespectful to the sacrifices of the great leader and the troops" (I guess there was a lash for every star on the flag).

The corporal punishment continued. Just months before my family and I left Tehran in late 1994, a friend and I were caught at school listening to a Michael Jackson tape on his Walkman. As the owner of the tape, my friend was slapped twice in the face by the principal and given a three-day suspension; I, on the other hand, was "only" slapped. Both of our mothers were called in to the school, and the principal lectured them on how their sons' "inappropriate material" was the main factor in "corrupting the youth" and again an "insult to the sacrifices of our dear leaders."

In addition to the recent alarming events in Iran, my adolescent experiences under the Islamic Republic were the primary factors behind this book, which I began when I visited Tehran in the summer of 2008. This project was at first initiated mostly on the basis of my curiosity, but due to the dramatic nature of my observations and the shocking revelations that I learned through my interviews, shortly after returning from Iran I decided to continue my research and present my findings in a narrative.

As mentioned earlier, over the past three years, I have interviewed and surveyed over four hundred very different individuals living in Tehran about their lives under the Islamic Republic. Besides some of the initial interviews that I did in my twenty-six-day stay during the summer of 2008, most of my research and communication was conducted through telephone conversations, e-mails, Skype, and interaction through social media sites.

After conducting 420 actual interviews over a period of three years and obtaining compelling accounts of life in Iran based on many different perspectives, I created eight stories that are composites based on true journalistic reportage of real people and events; these stories have been elaborated to a small extent in order to make certain points and to flesh out dialogue about the difficulties and challenges that regular individuals belonging to different social, political, and economic backgrounds face as a direct result of living under the Islamic Republic. It is important to note that the names of the individuals appearing in the following eight stories have been changed in order to protect their privacy and identities. I have full consent from these 420 individuals to disclose their stories. Any story that resembles the lives of individuals other than the 420 that I interviewed is solely coincidental.

In addition, these 420 individuals willingly shared their experiences, stories, and criticisms about the negative impact of the regime on their lives; they should be applauded for their courage in an environment that is best described as a zone of censorship and oppression, ruled under the terrifying fists of the regime. Their sentiments display how strongly they dislike the regime. Before we go any further, I would like to take this time to express my appreciation for the bravery and selflessness of the 420 individuals who went out of their way in order to share their tales and make this project a reality.

One opinion that was shared by almost all of the 420 individuals was the belief that human rights, integrity, ethics, cultural values, and legal morality in Iran all have been dismantled piece by piece since the revolution. This notion is especially believed to have been associated with the presidency of the always controversial Mahmoud Ahmadinejad, who almost all of the 420 believed was elected for a second term through election fraud, supported by the supreme leader Ayatollah Khamenei.

In my interviews, the very first question that I asked was, "How would you summarize life in Iran in a few words or sentences?" Not surprising, the majority of the 420 opted for a popular Iranian metaphor, *"Khar too khar,"* which translated literally means "donkey in donkey," which can be further defined as chaos, lawlessness, and mass ignorance. One particular response that made a great impression on me came from a seventy-two-year-old former government worker who was desperately trying to pay his life expenses while relying on his insignificant retirement pension. When I interviewed him in person, his answer to the above question was, "We are desperately trying to do the right thing but we're caught up in a storm of inhumanity created by [the Islamic Republic]; the evil is in the system."

Besides asking each of the 420 to share their most compelling accounts of the difficulties in their lives as a direct result of the regime, I also asked them how they would picture an ideal Iran. Not surprisingly, almost all desired a secular, limited government that placed values on human rights and basic freedoms. Every single person wanted credibility from their regime and valued much stronger electoral systems and social networks that provided subsidized health care, agriculture, and the promotion of a strong private sector with an emphasis on advancing domestic industries. While most were critical of various policies of Western nations, everyone that I spoke to would prefer closer relations with the West (including the United States) and even valued an open dialogue with Israel. The overwhelming desire among the 420 was for credibility to return to their nation and for Iran to play a responsible role on the global stage while refraining from such rhetoric that has led to Iran being labeled a rogue state.

Whether the person being interviewed was Omid, the young hip-hop artist struggling with censorship, or Nahid, the student activist who was unjustly imprisoned and tortured in the aftermath of the 2009 uprisings, or Rasul, the wealthy merchant lost in between the lines of love and lust, or Parisa, the prostitute who was forced into a temporary marriage with a cleric, or Siavash, the homosexual man living in secrecy while being forced into marriage by his orthodox parents, or Mohammad, the white collar employee who was forced to take on two additional jobs and work seven days a week just to keep a roof over his family's head, or Nasrin, the woman who desperately wanted recognition for females from the male-dominated system sponsored by the regime, or Shahram, the drug addict whose only remaining outlet became heroin, everyone I spoke with blamed Iran's social, economic, and political shortcomings on the Islamic Republic and the ruling clerics.

Further, the overwhelming majority believed that the Islamic Republic revolved around violence, propaganda, and the creation of fabricated fear and chaos in the hearts and minds of Iranians in order to maintain control and abuse their power. Many also indicated that the regime has recently recognized that the majority of the masses are no longer intimidated by fear, and thus, in order to continue their scheme, the regime has tried to insert its own corrupt behavior along with greed, dishonesty, and swindling onto the population so as to legitimize its own actions and spread its behavior onto the fabric of society as the norm.

Almost every single person I interviewed who took part in the 1979 uprisings, which led to the revolution, had major regrets and shared the popular belief that not only has the Islamic Republic failed to bring Iran into the twenty-first century, but they have managed to drag one of the planet's largest oil and petroleum producers into the top ten worst economies around—not to mention being among the most flagrant violators of fundamental human rights, along with having a notorious reputation for sponsoring international terrorism.

Although those who experienced life in Iran before the 1979 revolution believed their standards of living were higher under the shah and drew many comparisons between life now and life then, nevertheless my goal throughout this project was to get the perspective of individuals who were under the age of thirty-three, as I wanted to focus on those born after the revolution and only had experiences of life under the current regime. I feel they are best suited to provide uniform perspectives and criticisms of the Islamic Republic. Further, I selected the 420 individuals I interviewed based on the social ills that I wanted to address in writing this book. The following eight true stories are hence designed to portray the foul relationship that exists between the Islamic Republic and its people, with specific regard to issues such as censorship and the lack of freedom of speech, unjust political imprisonment and torture, association in public, women's rights, homosexuality, prostitution, unemployment, and drugs.

Despite all of the stories taking place in Tehran, the title of the book is *The Iranian Chronicles,* based on the fact that not only is Tehran the capital of Iran and the country's pulse, it is also a rich display of multiculturalism among Iran's ethnic population and thus provided me with a unique frame with regard to overall life in Iran. For a better understanding of Iran as a nation and Tehran as its capital, be sure to look at the appendix in this book, which discusses the "numbers behind Iran." The appendix also provides valuable statistics about each of the eight following stories.

Before we begin, as the introductory lines of poetry reveal, beauty can exist everywhere. Despite the extreme oppression of the Islamic Republic and the darkest hours of life in Iran, my homeland will always be beautiful as long as there is hope, an aspect of humanity onto which Iranians can proudly hold. The rays of hope began in June of 2009, when the people of Iran decided to stand up to tyranny, trusting that they would be successful in their struggle for democracy. Any attack by foreign forces on Iran would crush this hope and reinforce the stereotypes of the West that the Islamic Republic has been encouraging since the beginning of the revolution.

Chapter 1.
Omid: Lost Dreams

O ut of Iran's seventy-eight million people, two thirds of the population consists of individuals who are under the age of thirty-one. More importantly, most of these people were born after the 1979 revolution. Another quarter of the entire population are below the age of fifteen, and the nation's senior citizens (sixty-five years and over) make up only 5 percent of the population.[1] In contrast with Iran, according to the *CIA Fact Book*, the senior population of the United States stands at 13.1 percent of the entire population, while in Canada, nearly 16 percent of the population is over sixty-five. Accordingly, the spike in the population of youths is more evident in Iran than in any other county, as the median age is estimated at only twenty-six years.[2] With regard to Tehran, official numbers indicate a population figure of roughly eight million.[3] However, the majority living in Tehran believe the official figure to be much higher, as much as eighteen million.

While speaking mostly to individuals from eighteen to thirty-one in the course of writing this book, the overwhelming

---

1   https://www.cia.gov/library/publications/the-world-factbook/geos /ir.html.

2   Ibid.

3   Ibid.

response that I received was that the regime—along with its ultra conservative nature, has not only turned its back completely on the demands of the youth, but through oppressive policies and draconian measures, it has nearly criminalized the welfare of the youth. The regime's policies not only affect significant issues such as fundamental rights, freedom of expression, and association, they control trivial matters like clothing, hairstyle, music, dancing, and even dating, which directly affect the lives of the young and the growing population of Iran.

Our first story took place just a few days before the 2009 elections. This was the era when Iran's youth, especially the young boys and girls of Tehran, came into the spotlight as waves of green shirts, flags, and scarves marched into the streets in support of reformer candidate Mir Hossein Mousavi, whose campaign featured policies of reform along with a redefined sense of accountability and decency that was missing from the Ahmadinejad administration.

The need for reform was also shared by Omid, a very talented twenty-three-year-old musician who belonged to a new wave of hip-hop artists. Omid performed underground music for young listeners with a similar taste in music. He recently graduated from the University of Yazd with a degree in textile engineering and fabric production. However, his true passion is music, and his goal is to produce and write music for a living. At the age of eight, Omid began playing piano and showed a great deal of potential. By the age of twenty, Omid began writing lyrics and producing music at underground studios. Shortly after, Omid found himself among Tehran's underground hip-hop and music scene and began to line up gigs and performances at raves, concerts, and parties. Omid's music has an up-tempo style, which resembles most American hip-hop acts, while his lyrics embody the so-called "party lifestyle"; he has carefully tried to stay away from political rap in the hopes of one day getting a license from the Ministry of Culture and hence producing legal music and putting on performances.

-----\\\-----

As the warm June sun began to make its descent, Omid made his way toward the gates of the apartment complex he and his family lived in; casually, he walked out the gate. Standing on the edge of the street, he lifted his broken right hand, which was encased in a white chalky cast, and with some discomfort struggled to reach for his cigarettes in the left breast pocket of his designer blazer. Having a broken right hand was still new to him; he was still trying to shake the lifelong habits of a right-handed man placing his belongings in the left side of his jackets.

Nearly crushing the contents of his pocket with the cast, Omid grabbed the package of cigarettes with the tips of his fingers sticking out of the cast and lit one of the cigarettes before shaking off the effects of discomfort. The latest strains of pain and irritation of his broken hand took Omid back to the dark memories of only a few nights ago, when he was getting ready to perform in an underground concert. But just before he could start one of his more popular hip-hop songs, members of Tehran's disciplinary forces crashed the concert and began to arrest the attendees, smashing any paraphernalia they deemed immoral and illegal. This included Omid's new vinyl record, which led to him lashing out and hitting one of the officers. Other members of the disciplinary forces proceeded to hold Omid down and broke his right hand with a club, repeatedly striking his hand. After the beating, Omid was placed under arrest.

He nearly bit through the filter of his cigarette as the memories of the rest of that night crept back into his head. He felt the murderous rage return to his temple as he reminisced about spending that excruciating night in a crowded jail cell while his smashed knuckles and fingers lay in a makeshift cast, hastily administered by an officer at the precinct. Ironically, what hurt him the most that night was not his hand but the painful sight of watching his record get smashed into pieces. He tossed his cigarette to the ground next to him and stomped on it as he recalled the expression on the face of his father, who showed up to bail him out. Disappointed and irate, Omid's father paid the bail for his son's release, which included the property deed of his family apartment. No matter how hard he tried to explain himself, his father ignored him and gave him the silent treatment on the ride home and after his release.

He paced back and forth in his leather loafers over the demolished remains of the cigarette as he recalled that all throughout his life, he always wanted his father to be proud of him. Omid reflected on how everything he did with regard to his education was an attempt to satisfy his father, who persuaded him to obtain his degree in textile engineering and fabric production in the hopes that one day he could take over his father's successful rug and carpet store, located in Tehran's famous rug bazaar.

But this was not what Omid wanted to do, and deep down inside, he knew that soon he would have to confront his father and inform him that his true passion was writing and producing music. Nevertheless, this would have been easier had he not been arrested a few nights ago; ever since his father bailed him out, the mood around his house had been tense, and his parents more than ever have been trying to convince him to work in the bazaar store. In addition, his parents had forbade him from going to underground concerts and parties as part of the terms of his release imposed by the authorites; he was placed on probation and given the staunch warning that if he was arrested again within the next six months while performing or appearing at illegal concerts or immoral parties, he would be given an extended period of jail time. His father was also warned that should Omid be arrested again within the next six months, there would be a lien placed against their property by the authorities. While Omid fully understood the seriousness of his probation and the concerns of his parents, he left his home that night in order to attend a party along with his best friend, Babak. Deep down inside, he really was concerned about his father losing the family home, but at the same time, he wasn't worried about getting arrested again, as his hopes of gaining a license to produce and perform music were shattered on the night that he was arrested and branded for behaving outside the moral confines of the regime.

Before any other thoughts entered his head, Babak pulled his car next to Omid, who opened the door with his only functioning hand and entered the Kia Pride, a shabby vehicle by automotive standards, but one that Babak bought with the proceeds of selling his nonlicensed alternative rock album. The two set their sights on a party in the upscale neighborhood of Tajrish; by government standards, this party was deemed illegal.

"How is your hand feeling?" Babak asked his friend as he turned the wheel toward the center of the street and drove while Omid rolled his eyes in response, reaching for Babak's CD binder located above the dashboard.

"God, do you have anything decent in here, or am I doomed to hearing dinosaur rock every time that I get in your car?" Omid asked as he resisted the urge to rub the itchy skin of his right hand under the cast; he fought back the anger that threatened to bubble up to the surface as he impatiently flipped through the CD binder on his lap.

"You need some help?" Babak asked, glancing away from the road ahead at Omid and then back again.

"I can do it myself!" Omid said. "No, of course you don't have anything but metal and rock; I'm a fool to ask," he quickly responded before tossing the binder in the backseat.

"Take it easy, we're almost there, and by the way, this is Pink Floyd you're listening to. So show a little respect!" Babak said, glancing back at his friend again before reaching for a cigarette.

"You still haven't told me how your buddy Javid gets away with throwing all these parties," Omid said, referring to the person whose party they were about to attend.

"He's a good guy; his parents are filthy rich and live most of the year in Dubai, so Javid and his brothers are left with bags of cash and a five-story complex all by themselves; what do rich kids with money and empty houses do? They throw parties and lots of them," Babak answered in between taking puffs from his cigarette.

"Isn't he worried about getting busted?" Omid asked. "I mean, don't get me wrong, I love a good party just like the next guy, but after getting the shit kicked out of me and having my right hand turned into ground beef, the last thing I want to do is get arrested again!" Omid lifted his wrist in the cast and rubbed it against the door of the passenger seat.

"Do you think I would go to a party that wasn't safe?" Babak asked as he glanced back at Omid, who stared back blindly. "Relax, bro! Javid is all rock and roll, plus his older brother paid off a top guy in the *niroye entezami* [disciplinary forces] in exchange for looking after them and letting them know in advance if there is going to be raid on their parties; even his neighbors are cool with him having parties," Babak further reassured his friend as Omid nodded his head slowly.

Silence fell between the two as they drove on, the song "Dark Side of the Moon" blaring through the speakers, until Babak slowed down and then parked among mostly luxury German automobiles, a few houses down from the posh, five-story party house. They walked up to the lookout, a large man Omid knew and could trust.

"Hey, Omid 2 p.m.! What's up, brother?" the lookout asked, calling Omid by his hip-hop name as the two men hugged and slapped each other on the back.

"Babak, I'd like you to meet Maziar, we met a few months ago at a midtown studio; he's a natural talent, a real music lover, he plays the piano, guitar, *setar* [a Persian musical instrument that resembles a guitar], and he even plays the harmonica from time to time," Omid said as the three shared a laugh.

"Please, you're embarrassing me, bro," Maziar responded with a smile on his face as the three chuckled some more. "So I see the rumors are true; those bastards really did bust up your hand," Maziar said, looking over at Omid's cast.

"Yeah, it's true. I just … I didn't want them to get my dad involved," Omid said, shrugging it off.

"Let me guess, they released you when your dad put up the house deed as bail," Maziar replied as Omid nodded, clenching his fist in his pocket before a few seconds of awkward silence fell between the three men.

"Enough about me; what are you doing here? I didn't take you as a doorman," Omid said; Maziar shrugged his broad shoulders and shook his head before lighting up a cigarette.

"What can I say, brother? A bachelor in mechanical engineering and years of music lessons, and I still have to use my size to make a little cash just so I can pay the fucking rent!" Maziar responded while he rested his head back and blew out smoke. Omid felt sorry for the man, who had a huge talent in music; he would have never pictured him handling security duties at a party in order to make a living.

"But at least you guys seem to be doing well; I guess it is true what they say, the best job in Tehran is having a rich daddy!" Maziar continued as the three of them once again broke out in laughter.

"Okay, you guys should head on in, I don't want to take your time any more than this ... everyone is inside having a good time. You guys have a good night; I'll try to catch up with you once the crowd dies down," Maziar said as he opened a small portion of the large metal gates while Omid and Babak walked into the parking area of the complex and headed toward the main entrance.

Upon opening the doors of the complex, they heard loud drums and bass sounds, which put a spring in their step. They entered the complex with a grin on their faces. The narrow hallway near the entrance of the complex was crowded with groups of young men and women in the latest fashion trends. Most of the people were smoking cigarettes, while smoke from a nearby smoke machine floated over the expensive granite flooring, hanging in a haze.

Omid and Babak went into the first unit of the complex, on the first floor, looking for a friendly face. Omid led the way as the two entered a dim and intimate unit where a smaller crowd gathered. Omid squinted his eyes in order to get a better look at the person who was singing slow songs while playing acoustic guitar. The two made their way toward the front of the unit and passed slow dancing couples, who mostly were making out while listening to the soft tunes of the acoustic guitar; the singer was familiar to both Omid and Babak. Having made their way toward the front, the two stood in the unfurnished unit in the hopes of sparking up a conversation with the performer.

As the song neared its end, Babak waved to the singer, who also began to notice the two of them. The familiar face was a young man named Ali, who was around the same age as Omid and Babak. Ali sang and played guitar in a band that performed at weddings and private parties. Ali was no stranger to dealing with the notorious disciplinary forces and Tehran's moral police, as he was arrested a few months before this story while practicing with his band.

"Nice set, my friend, you really had the crowd going!" Babak said as he walked up to where Ali was sitting; the small crowd in the room began to head out and toward the other units of the complex.

"Well, would you look at what the cat dragged in, I haven't seen you two for ages!" Ali replied with a smile on his face as he rested his guitar on the chair before hugging his old friends.

"I thought I'd never see you play music again, especially since what happened just two months ago," Omid said as Ali stood back, picked up his guitar, and clutched it tightly. Ignoring Omid momentarily, Ali adjusted the strings on his guitar while the smile on his face quickly faded.

"Why? What happened two months ago?" Babak asked after he witnessed Ali's response.

"If you really want to know about two months ago, then I should first tell you about what happened four months ago," Ali replied, putting his guitar back against the chair and reaching for a cigarette.

While taking deep drags from his cigarette, Ali explained that about four months ago, he and his alternative rock band were putting on an unlicensed show and had an experience similar to Omid's a few nights ago; they were raided by disciplinary forces, who placed Ali and his bandmates under arrest, confiscated their instruments, and released them on probation once their parents put up their house deeds as bail. While staying true to their passion, after their arrest Ali and the rest of his band put together enough cash and managed to get secondhand instruments, practicing in Ali's basement while getting ready for another gig. That was until two months ago, when one of the neighbors "ratted out" the band for playing loud music; the police arrested Ali and found CDs, DVDs, and a couple of half-empty bottles of vodka and whiskey.

Omid felt the pain behind Ali's voice; he looked visibly sad and then angry. He said, "They gave me twenty fucking days in jail for that shit, man, and ninety fucking lashes too!"

"Shit! I heard it was bad, but ninety lashes! Fuck, man, that must have been hell!" Omid said, gritting his teeth.

"Hell? I couldn't sleep on my back for a fucking month! And what's funny is that after the lashing, they told me that I passed out from the pain after the fortieth lash, and the fuckers had to stop. I guess I should send them a thank you card," Ali replied, hanging his head and squeezing his fists as silence took over the dim room. Omid began to picture the brutality that his friend Ali had gone through before looking at Babak, who stood glued to his spot while biting his lower lip.

"But I guess I'm not the only one with scars," Ali said, lifting up his head as he looked at the cast on Omid's hand.

"Better this than forty lashes and twenty fucking days in jail!" Omid responded.

"I'm really sorry to hear that, Ali; I had no idea what they did to you; so what are you doing now?" Babak asked.

Before he answered, Ali took another long drag from his cigarette and said, "What can I say? Life hasn't been easy. My dad kicked me out of the house once I was released from jail, and the bastards now have a lien against the house since I violated the terms of my probation. Right now I'm living with the drummer from my band, plus Javid hooks me up with gigs here and there and puts a little cash in my pockets."

The skin underneath Omid's cast began to itch again as every one of the details that Ali described took him back to the worst moments of his life. Clenching his fist tight in his pocket once again, Omid fought back the insatiable anger bubbling underneath the surface and reached for a cigarette, only this time he crushed the paper pack along with its contents.

"You all right?" Ali asked as he noticed the mess in Omid's hand.

"Yeah, just … my right hand aches a little, you know," Omid answered as he chucked away the crumpled-up litter in the palm of his hand.

"Fuck 'em! We're still gonna party, play rock, rap, and do what we want, and if they want to make me stop, then they better cut off both of my arms so I can't pick up my guitar again!" Ali declared with a goofy smile on his face, causing the other two to crack smiles of their own.

"Speaking of Javid, have you seen him around?" Babak asked Ali.

"Yeah, he should be up in the penthouse suite; that's where the party is at! I think I saw him behind the DJ booth before I came down here," Ali said; Omid and Babak exchanged temporary farewells with him and made their way through the crowd and up the loud stairwell to the fifth floor of the complex.

The two walked toward the large double doors of the penthouse and, before entering, passed a handful of beautiful girls wearing cocktail dresses and short skirts. The girls smiled as Omid and Babak walked past, only managing to respond with smiles of their own. The light inside the penthouse was dim, and the only source of light came from flashes of a blinking bulb hitting a disco ball and lasers that shot through the gyrating crowd, which danced in a trance to electronic music mixed by a DJ. Smoke from the same smoke machine hung over the crowd in a daze and provided a unique bit of ecstasy as the lasers began to make their way through the smoke.

Babak spotted his friend Javid and moved toward a large leather couch, which the DJ stood behind. Omid followed a few steps behind Babak as his friend greeted a ponytailed and sophisticatedly dressed man sitting among a group of women dressed like the girls they saw when entering the penthouse. There was also a large glass coffee table in front of the couch, crammed with assorted bottles of alcohol and water pipes that seeped more smoke into the setting. Javid, sitting in the center of couch, embraced Babak and indicated that he and Omid should follow him to the quieter rooftop of the complex.

"I'm glad you guys made it tonight; I've heard a lot of good things about you, Mr. Omid 2 p.m.!" Javid said.

"Thank you for inviting me," Omid replied. "I've heard a lot of good things about you too, and I have to say that this is probably the coolest party I've been to."

"Javid is thinking about throwing an underground concert, with multiple rock and rap acts," Babak said.

"Rock and rap acts? Under the same roof?" Omid asked, raising his eyebrows.

"People are getting tired of electronic music and bands that cover Iranian artists living abroad," Javid said. "They want something different, something unique and exciting; think of this as a large outdoor concert, only in some remote location, like a farm in the middle of nowhere, you know, way out of sight and away from the uniforms, their batons, and handcuffs."

Javid's answer played over and over in Omid's head as he reflected on what he had just heard. No one had ever imagined putting on a show this big, let alone actually going through with it. He badly wanted to picture it, but every time he tried, the skin underneath his cast began to itch again and the fear of what had happened to him (and worse to Ali) crawled back into his head. He clenched his left fist in his pocket again, so hard this time that he felt his skin crack.

"Are you listening to this, Omid?" Babak asked.

"Yeah, I was just ... picturing it all in my head," Omid answered as he slowly unclenched his fist.

"Like I was saying, I'm looking for the best talent ... male and female singers, it doesn't matter what style of music they play: rock, rap, jazz, punk, alternative ... whatever," Javid repeated his plans while Omid could see, based on the size of the grin on Babak's face, that his friend was impressed by their host's proposal.

"I want you both to be there and put on a show. Of course I'll be paying the acts handsomely from the proceeds that my partner and I make on the ticket sales, and who knows, if this thing takes off, we'll be doing a lot more business together, gentlemen," Javid continued while Omid remained motionless and quiet.

"Approximately when are you planning to put this show on? Cause I might have a couple of gigs coming up in the next couple of weeks," Babak explained.

"It wouldn't be until midsummer, you know, after the dust from the election has settled down," Javid answered.

"You sure no one's going to interfere? I mean, usually word tends to get out early when something as big as this goes down, and I'm on probation. I can't be involved in something like this and get arrested again," Omid declared, his eyes wide in alarm.

He felt fear slicing though his blood at that moment. Music was his passion, and he would have done whatever he could to get involved in a performance of the scale that Javid described, but nevertheless he wanted to be reassured that he wouldn't suffer the fate that had fell to his friend Ali, and although Babak had informed Omid earlier that Javid knew a trusted source within the establishment, Omid nevertheless wanted nothing short of a guarantee.

Javid once again reassured Omid that what he planned on doing would be more than safe. He explained that what he and his business partners envisioned was an event far away from Tehran; the location would be revealed to only a handful of people, which included performers and VIP members, plus the event was designed to be by invitation only. He then explained that those who were invited through instructions would gather in a public location and be chartered to the secret location by buses arranged and paid for by Javid and his partners.

"Trust me, it's going to be safe, plus my brother knows a top guy working for the *niroye entezami*. We pay this guy a few large stashes of cash here and there in return for protection," Javid further reassured Omid and Babak. As Omid listened carefully, the skin underneath his cast stopped itching and the clenched fist in his pocket straightened back to normal.

"Now, what do you gentleman say that we go back to the party and enjoy ourselves? I've got this beautiful jazz singer covering the works of Shamlou [a contemporary Iranian poet] on the third floor, you guys have to hear her sing, she is amazing," Javid said as the three headed toward the rooftop exit and down the stairwell.

Chapter 2.
Omid: The Heated Debate

O mid and Babak followed Javid down the stairs, but before they could reach the third floor, havoc erupted. Suddenly the front door of the complex smashed open as Maziar, the lookout from the front gates, entered the complex, frantically looked up the stairwell, and screamed, "*Niroye entezami!*" Terrified and stunned, the three quickly rushed over to a window in the stairwell and anxiously looked outside of the building at the gates, as military SVUs smashed through the gates and entered the complex while officers armed with batons rushed out toward the entrance of the complex.

"Javid! Get away from here; I'll try to hold them off!" Maziar screamed from below as he planted his large figure against the entrance door and desperately tried to block the uniforms from getting in while the crowds on the floors below begin to panic and scream at the revelations of a raid.

"Javid, we have to get out of here!" Omid shouted as a flabbergasted Javid stared out the window, silent and frozen to the spot he was standing on.

"Javid, come on, man, they're coming up the stairs! We gotta escape from the roof!" Omid shouted again as he peeked down the stairwell and noticed that the bearded men in uniform had managed to get through Maziar's last ditch efforts.

Omid's fear returned; he was surrounded by chaos as the crowds inside the complex began to clatter down the stairs, shouting and screaming. Women in short dresses and skirts began to desperately cover their exposed skin and hair, while the men frantically placed stacks of chewing gum in their mouths in attempts to mask the smell of alcohol. Standing in the stairwell between the fourth and third floor, Omid saw Babak anxiously heading up the stairs and toward the roof. With every step that Babak took, he would pause and look over the stairwell while shouting for his friends to join him in escape.

"I don't understand it," Javid said, "We paid off the guy! He was supposed to look after us; he was supposed to give us a heads-up for this kind of thing!" Javid and Omid both began to quickly move up the stairs; terrified, Omid peeked over the stairwell and saw a number of uniforms making their way up the stairs, arresting and hauling boys and girls out of the complex.

"Come on! Move it!" Babak shouted from the rooftop entrance as Omid and Javid quickly joined him on the roof. The three quickly proceeded toward the edge of the roof, nearly attached to the adjacent complex, and made the short jump over to the next rooftop.

"We've got to jump rooftop to rooftop," Babak said. "That way we'll be right on the main street, where we can walk down the fire escape and get into a cab!" Omid, Babak, and Javid quickly made their way toward the next jumping point.

"Wait a minute! This jump's nearly two fucking meters!" Javid shouted as they arrived at the edge of the second roof; their next jump was much wider and more difficult than the previous one.

"So what? We can make it, Javid!" Babak replied as he backed away a few meters from the edge in preparation for the long jump; dramatically, he jumped onto the next roof. But before Javid and Omid could jump, the rooftop door of Javid's complex smashed wide open as uniformed forces ran out, spotting the three on the next complex's roof.

"I can't make it, it's too fucking far!" Javid shouted, sweat running down his forehead while Omid looked back at the uniforms chasing after them before turning his attention toward the chilling gap that remained between the two roofs.

"Come on ... Jump!" Babak shouted, waving his right hand in the air.

With every step that the uniforms took toward them, Omid's heart beat louder. Time nearly stood still at that moment as images of his arrest from just a few nights ago began to flash right before his eyes. There he was, standing before a set of turntables while handing over his vinyl record to a DJ at the party. He thought that someone must have ratted out that party, because before he could begin, the door of the uptown penthouse came down as burly and bearded men in uniforms waged havoc on a crowd of sophisticated yet spoiled young professionals. Similar to what he just witnessed, men and women began to scream and panic on that haunting night as the uniforms ran through the crowd and smashed their batons against the knees and hips of men and women before placing them under arrest.

The sound of his album being smashed echoed in his head while the crackling of his bones screeched up his spine. Omid didn't want to go through something like that ever again, yet he felt powerless, frightened, and angry all at the same time. Images of his dad losing their apartment and kicking him out bounced in between his other thoughts. Ironically, whether he made the jump or died while attempting it, both options seemed like the perfect escape. Cold sweat began to run down the back of his neck as he noticed the uniforms making the short jump toward the roof that he and Javid stood on. The uniforms were closing down on them; only a handful of seconds remained between delight and disaster.

He swallowed his fears, closed his eyes, and envisioned himself making the difficult jump, which the taller and more athletic Babak barely made. The sound of his record being smashed rang in this head as he clenched his fist one more time, stared down the wide gap, and began to run toward the edge of the roof before taking the long leap. He made the difficult jump. Once on the other side, Omid and Babak paused momentarily in the hopes that Javid would follow too, but unlike them, a teary-eyed Javid surrendered with his arms stuck upward as the men in uniform tackled him down and placed handcuffs around his wrists.

Omid and Babak did not wait for the men in uniform to try to make the same long jump that they just made; without much deliberation, they continued with the plans of making it to the rooftop located next to the intersection of the main street. Just before the two left the last rooftop, Omid looked back to see if anyone was still chasing them, and to his surprise he discovered that no one was after them; it seemed that their assailants were satisfied with their catch. The two quickly made their way toward the main street, where Omid signaled for a taxi to take them home.

"My car is there!" Babak shouted. What if they run my plate numbers? I'll be fucked!"

"Nothing's gonna happen to your car, Babak. You didn't park it that close to Javid's place. I'm sure that they didn't even get a good look at your face," Omid replied before he got into the cab. "I promise you that nothing is going to happen to your car. I'll even drive you out here tomorrow so you can get it."

Babak remained silent, slowly shaking his head.

The ride home was fairly silent as the two sat nearly glued to their spot while trying desperately to get hold of their friends Ali, Javid, and Maziar through phone calls and text messages, which sadly proved to no avail.

The next day, Friday, Omid woke up in a pool of his own sweat. Before doing anything else, he rushed over to his cell phone and checked his messages, only to see that neither Ali nor Maziar had replied to the messages that he had sent them just hours before. Sad and fearing for the welfare of his friends, Omid decided to head to the kitchen, where his mother had been preparing their traditional weekend lunch, while his father was casually reading the sport pages as he sat at head of the kitchen table.

The scene at the kitchen table played out the same way as many other recent troubled conversations between Omid and his father. Omid took his usual seat opposite his father, who scolded him and said he looked like a bum, just like many of his friends.

"My friends aren't bums, Father," Omid said. "And I'm not a bum. I'm a musician." He gripped the cup of tea his mother had just placed in front of him. It was a familiar exchange, one repeated time after time, and every time it cut down a little more of Omid's self-esteem.

His mother, like usual, tried to intervene and ensure that there were no confrontations, at least not on that day. She pleaded with her husband to give her son a break, reminding him that their son had promised to forget about music and join his dad in their bazaar store.

"Woman, your son has been making promises ever since he graduated from university," Omid's father said. "Instead, he chooses to hang around a bunch of idiots, singing rap songs about girls and their short skirts!"

"When are you going to get it?" Omid replied, raising his voice. "My friends and I are musicians! It might seem hard for you to believe but my passion is in producing music and writing lyrics."

"And where is that going to get you? Where has it got you so far, Omid? Did you forget that just a few days ago, I had to bail you out of jail?" His father raised his voice in return, with the veins in his neck and forehead visible. "Do you think that your mother and I don't know that you have a passion for music? Do you think that we don't know how talented our son is?" his father continued while Omid sat quietly looking at his father.

Omid's father went on to ensure him that he and his mother wanted nothing but the best for their son. As a matter of fact, they loved having an artist and a musician as bright as Omid as a son; he actually said that he was proud to have such a talented son. However, his father warned him that because Iran was ruled by the tight iron fists of the mullahs, he had no other choice but to bite the bullet and stop his involvement in the world of underground music. Omid remained silent as his father lectured him more on how he and his mother could not bear to hear that their son had been arrested for doing what made him happy, let alone lashed or beaten so hard that his bones were encased in a cast.

The skin on his palm wrapped around the hot cup of tea began to burn. He wanted to scream and smash the cast on his hand against the kitchen table. He wanted to crush the burning cup of tea in his bare hands. He was frustrated and angry, and not just because of the predicament that had befallen him but for everything that he had gone through in the past few days. The sound of his album being smashed rang in his head again.

"If this was the ideal world and we lived in a free society where you could excel and make a living by producing music, then I'd be all for it, I'd even invest in your music, but we don't live in the ideal world, my son. We live in a prison with tall walls all around us, we live in a place where you need permission to scratch your ass. We live in the middle of censorship, lashes and batons, prisons, and executions, all used to scare us so we don't ever think about breaking these walls." As his father talked, Omid could still hear the sound of his record being smashed over and over in the background of his mind.

He wondered again what had become of Ali, Maziar, and Javid and the rest of people that were at the party. Surely most of them must have been arrested; they were probably being lined up for harsh punishments. His grip over the tea cup tightened; he wanted to ask why, why was it like this? But he already knew the answer. It was simple and had a lot to do with what his dad had just said. He felt those walls that his father mentioned close in on him. The air around his lungs squeezed into a narrow stream. Desperate for air, Omid felt like he was being choked.

"Just come by the store for a few hours tomorrow and see how you like it," his father continued. "I promise you that selling carpet is not as bad as you think it is; plus, if you think of other business idea, then let me know about them. Maybe we can put your ideas to use and get you on your own feet, son." Omid loosened his grip around the hot cup and began to nod. His father in return cracked a partial yet bright smile.

He returned to his room and sat on the messy, unmade bed. He looked around his room at the large posters of different hip-hop artists, which he had bought over the past few years from unlicensed sellers on the street. The faces went blank in his mind as the sound of his record being smashed returned to his head. He couldn't help staring at the cast on his hand, which lay on his lap. His father's speech was attached to nearly every one of the vivid memories he had had about the night before and the night that he was beaten and arrested. His father was right and not just about the hassles he was putting himself and his family through but about the state of life in Iran. The walls yet again began to close in on him. He didn't want to jump rooftops like a fugitive running away from the authorities or live in constant fear of a raid going down whenever he was at a party. Most importantly, he didn't want to end up like his friend Ali, who was nearly homeless after his parents kicked him out. Whatever it was, Omid knew that there wasn't a future for him in the music business while living in the Islamic Republic of Iran.

His father was not demanding the unreasonable. After all, like every other father, he wanted the best for his child and offered the next best solution for him, which was an honest living with a chance to improve and expand. The walls were no longer closing in on him. He glanced at his right hand and its cast and thought about what it represented. The youth of Iran were the country's right arm and its strongest tool for moving the nation forward, yet it was the youth that were in shackles and casts, stripped away from the very thing that made them young. The sound of smashing was gone, as was the tight-gripped fist lying on his lap.

Before he could take his metaphor any further, his phone rang. It was Babak, who informed Omid that he was not too far from his apartment; he asked if Omid would drive him to Javid's neighborhood in the hopes of retrieving his car. Omid and Babak headed back to Javid's neighborhood and spotted Babak's car; the vehicle had not been damaged or confiscated by the disciplinary forces.

The two then noticed Javid's complex; the mangled and dented gates had been locked with thick chains and a warning was attached, saying that the residence had been "seized by Tehran's disciplinary forces as a result of hosting anti-Islamic and decadent functions."

From a tiny crack in between the gates, Omid and Babak saw the smashed entrance to the complex, while most of the windows of the units were broken; the parking area was covered with broken glass. The entire neighborhood felt eerily quiet and abandoned as the two smoked and spoke quietly among themselves.

Babak informed Omid that late last night, Ali and one of Javid's brothers called him. The good news was that Ali managed to escape through one of the windows on the main floor, while the bad news was that others were not as lucky. Maziar, in the effort of barricading the main entrance, assaulted several of the forces and was beaten down and taken to a maximum penitentiary; he was rumored to be facing a sentence of four months. Javid was taken to the same penitentiary for being the proprietor of the immoral party, while having a large amount of alcohol and other illegal materials such as satellite television, Western music and movies, along with a handful of Ecstasy pills. According to Babak, Javid's doom was feared to be worse than Maziar's expected sentence. The news was bittersweet for Omid, who was happy to hear Ali had escaped but sad to learn the fates of Maziar and Javid. Javid's brother told Babak that the high-ranking member of the disciplinary forces who they bribed was the very same person who orchestrated the raid on their party.

Before leaving Javid's neighborhood, the two headed over to a local hangout for a late lunch and to meet with an old friend by the name of Saeed. Saeed had been Omid's university roommate. However, unlike Omid and Babak, Saeed never really got into music and instead dabbled in poetry and literature. Saeed also considered himself to be an activist, and at the time of this story, he volunteered for the reformer candidate Mir Hossein Mousavi.

For years, the three had congregated at the same local café and became good friends with the owner, who turned a blind eye whenever they would break into political debates and social arguments.

Omid and Babak arrived at the nearly empty coffee shop and approached the table where their friend had been sitting; they exchanged the usual greetings of handshakes and hugs. Saeed wore a green shirt with a picture of Mousavi on the front.

"So I take it that you're 100 percent committed to making sure that Ahmadinejad is not the president after next Friday's election," Babak said.

"It's about time we got that crook out of office and back to the gutters where he belongs," Saeed said, the conviction in his voice clear for the other two to hear.

"Mousavi ... Ahmadinejad, same shit, different toilet! Give it up, Saeed," Babak joked while Saeed rolled his eyes before signalling for the only server in the café. The three ordered nonalcoholic, fruit-flavored beers along with shawarma sandwiches before Saeed began lecturing them on why they should support Mousavi and how he was different from Ahmadinejad.

Mousavi had been Iran's prime minister from 1981 till 1989; during most of those years, Iran had been at war with Iraq. Saeed reminded his friends that Mousavi was far more qualified compared to Ahmadinejad, especially since he managed the difficult task of balancing the budget during the harsh years of the war. For Saeed, Mousavi was a revelation, a reformer, and a breath of fresh air compared to his opponent.

"Saeed, you really think that things are going to be different with Mousavi in charge?" Babak asked before taking a bite out of his sandwich.

"Of course I do," Saeed answered with the same conviction as before.

"You don't think that this is another so-called 'reformer,' brought in just to fool us and to buy this regime some more time, just like Khatami?" Omid asked before taking a swig of his nonalcoholic beer.

"You do remember Khatami, right? The guy your older brother and my cousin used to go to his rallies, put up his posters, and swear by his name that he was the best thing to happen to us since they allowed the sale of condoms?" Omid further asked before he looked around in order to make sure that the lone occupied table at the front of the café could not overhear their conversation.

"Mousavi is different from Khatami, Omid, he is not going to let us down like Khatami did," Saeed replied, setting aside his sandwich.

"How different? You mean different, like he's going to stop censoring the Internet and satellite channels? Is he going to loosen things a bit so that kids like Babak and I can expand our talents in music and maybe even get licenses to record and promote music without having to worry about bearded bullies and their batons?" Omid asked as he set aside his beverage and reached for his cigarettes.

The café was quiet; the couple occupying the table in the front were keeping to themselves, and the lone server conversed quietly with his boss near the cash register. Silence fell over the boys' table. Saeed didn't know what to say; Babak, on the other hand, was in the midst of enjoying his sandwich with his eyes slowly moving between his two friends.

"Is he going to give women the right to wear whatever they like without having to fear being snatched off the streets by the same bunch of bullies?" Omid asked before taking a deep drag and puffing the smoke over his head. "Is he going to give us freedom of expression? Cause that's what I really want to know, Saeed, not about some color that's going to be today's fad and tomorrow's epic yawn!" Omid followed up as the smoke over his head began to hang in a haze.

"We have to be realistic, Omid. How can the president do all of that when Khamenei [supreme leader] has the last word on all those matters?" Saeed replied, reaching for his beverage and taking a swig from the bottle.

"Well, that's the problem, isn't it?" Omid said before looking to the table in the front of the café again and making sure that they did not heard his assertions, while the other two quietly nodded their heads.

The three continued to talk about the upcoming elections and what really mattered to them. They all agreed that while the office of the supreme leader existed in its current capacity, social and political reforms could not be made. While each had their own visions of how Iran and the status of the youth could be improved, nevertheless each agreed that there should be a greater emphasis placed on religious and personal freedoms.

—⟶⟶⟵—

The last time I spoke to Omid, he said that he was working for his father, and they were on the verge of opening a new office that he was going to manage; this office was going to export rugs and carpets from Iran to neighboring nations. Although Omid clearly voiced his discontent about the controversial election results of 2009, its aftermath, and the growing oppressive policies, he indicated that he was also disenchanted with the opposition movement and no longer had hopes for a better Iran.

According to Omid, part of this disenchantment was due to the fact that he and his friends had tried desperately to have their voices heard by taking part in rallies and demonstrations that followed the election, only to face more forces and their batons and the sad reality that a positive change was unlikely to take place. In addition, Omid's enthusiasm for carrying on the fight for reform was reduced after Saeed was arrested just two weeks after this story for attending a mass demonstration. Saeed was imprisoned in Tehran's notorious Kahrizak detention center, where he was beaten daily for sixteen days before signing a forced confession and spending four months in jail for undermining the authority of the regime.

Omid also informed me that his friend Maziar was released on probation after serving his term and continued to struggle to find regular employment. Nearly the same was said about Omid's other friend, Ali, who was still trying to make a living as a musician.

Even after Javid's father spent a sizeable sum of money to ensure that the law would swing in his son's favor, the courts nevertheless gave him a five-month prison sentence.

Although his right hand healed and is no longer in a cast, Omid hoped that the next generations of young adults continue to fight for their rights and not fall to the disenchantment that smashed his dreams. He wished that he could one day live in an Iran where music in its all forms could be played, produced, and performed proudly and that no one lived in a state of fear.

Shirin Ebadi, the first Iranian and the first Muslim woman to win the Nobel Peace Prize, once said, "We must not enable anyone to impose his personal view regarding religion on others by force, oppression, or pressure."[4] I, like Mrs. Ebadi, can only hope that the Islamic Republic learns that force never constitutes rights and that civil obedience can only be reached through democracy and legitimate governance.

---

4   http://www.brainyquote.com/quotes/authors/s/shirin_ebadi.html.

Chapter 3.
Nahid: Prelude to Violence

D espite having a sizeable portion of its youth struggling with drug use, prostitution, crime, and an overall feeling of disenchantment arising from lack of expression, Iran is blessed with a large talented, disciplined, and highly educated population who have taken huge strides in trying to rebuild their nation and achieving honor in the name of their country. On a regional scale, Iranian students pursue higher levels of education more than other Middle Eastern nations—especially with regard to women, who make up more than 60 percent of the country's university students.[5] According to a UNESCO world survey, Iran has the second highest female-to-male enrollment ratio (at the primary level) on the planet.[6]

It is estimated that Iran's universities, institutions of technology, and colleges produce nearly 750,000 graduates on an annual basis.[7] Nevertheless, due to high levels of unemployment (35 percent), skyrocketing inflation, tense domestic social conditions, a propaganda-infested and progovernment educational system, and

---

5   http://www.payvand.com/news/03/nov/1133.html.

6   http://www.nationmaster.com/graph/edu_gir_to_boy_rat_pri_lev_enr -boys-ratio-primary-level-enrolment.

7   http://en.tpo.ir/UserFiles/File/Annual1383e.pdf.

an oppressive environment that restricts fundamental freedoms, a significant portion of Iranian students over the past twenty years believe that the state of life in Iran has limited and restricted their talents; many are in the process of immigrating to a Western location (if they have not already done so).

According to an International Monetary Fund survey in 2006, Iran ranked highest in "brain drain" among ninety nations.[8] It is estimated that more than 150,000 of the best young minds leave Iran on an annual basis, while an estimated 25 percent of all Iranians with postsecondary education now live abroad.[9]

For the most part, Iranian students over the past two decades have been the face of the opposition movements, criticizing the actions of the Islamic Republic. The demonstrations that followed the disputed presidential elections of 2009 were no different, as university students took to the streets to voice their outrage. Sadly, the regime reacted in the form of riot police, disciplinary forces, and *basij* militias, who savagely beat, arrested, and even fired on unarmed and innocent demonstrators, resulting in many deaths. Those who were arrested found themselves in Tehran's notorious Evin and Kahrizak prisons, where security forces used torture and rape on the arrested population in order to obtain false confessions or to curtail any further acts of civil disobedience. Sadly, these cruel actions led to numerous deaths.[10]

I spoke with many youth of Tehran about those days, and the story that sticks out in my mind the most concerns Nahid, a twenty-two-year-old woman from a wealthy neighborhood and a good family. Like so many, she dared to speak out against the injustices of the Islamic Republic in spite of the inherent risks. In February 2010, Nahid, who was studying civil engineering at Tehran's prestigious Amir Kabir University, found herself under arrest and in serious trouble for being a student activist. Her story has remained with me these years later, and truth be told,

---

8   http://news.bbc.co.uk/2/hi/middle_east/6240287.stm.

9   Ibid.

10   http://www.timesonline.co.uk/tol/news/world/middle_east /article6839335.ece.

it sometimes keeps me up at night as I hear her words play in my mind again and again.

—— \\\\ ——

It was a typical February evening in Tehran. The winter blues were certainly in their full effects, with the temperatures taking the usual dip as Tehran and the rest of Iran prepared for *Fajr*, the annual celebration commemorating the fall of the shah and the return of Khomeini to Iran along with the success of the 1979 revolution. However, the 2010 celebrations were marred by the disputed elections and its bloody aftermath that took place just a few months before.

The cold wind whipped across the darkened campus of Amir Kabir University. All the common areas, crowded with students during the day, were deserted in the late evening as the temperatures in Tehran plummeted. Lights burned in some of the dorms as some students studied for their next exams while others, like Nahid, were at home, hard at work trying to bypass the latest government Internet filter to access Facebook, which the great thinkers of the Islamic Republic of Iran considered a threat to their power and an insidiously evil influence on the minds of Iran's youth.

Nahid leaned back in her chair and stretched. She glanced away from her monitor toward the iconic blue and red picture of US President Barack Obama nestled among posters of bands like U2, Rage Against the Machine, and Lady Gaga and underground Iranian rock bands like Kiosk. Although Nahid was an activist, her room at home wasn't all that much different from those of other less active students who lived in the crowded dorms. In Iran, most students longed for the stimulation of the West in music, art, pop culture, and political freedom. Nahid was no different, except that she made her voice heard when others were too afraid to speak out. She clutched her cell phone between her left shoulder and ear, speaking to her friend Sarah while struggling to search the Internet for a filter breaker for her desktop computer.

"This is so frustrating!" Nahid said. "I haven't accessed Facebook in two days; the goddamn filter breaker has been hacked again." She tapped loudly on her keyboard while pushing her light brunette hair away from her face with her petite hand.

"I heard in class yesterday that the computer science students are coming up with a filter breaker that cannot be hacked," Sarah replied.

"That's what they said about this one," Nahid said as she tied her hair into a ponytail. "What's the point? They're just going to find a way to shut that down too. I can't stand it!"

Nahid pushed away her keyboard and partially rolled her chair away from her desk while her friend replied with silence.

"We can't fight them in cyber space anymore, Sarah! We need to get back to the streets like we did in the summer; just wait, this 22 Bahman [February 11, Islamic Republic of Iran's Victory Day] we're going to hit the streets like never before and throw them a party that they won't forget!" Nahid stood up from her chair and walked to the window of the three-story complex where she lived with her parents. She placed her right hand on the glass as the cold instantaneously wrapped around her wrist.

"Hey, be careful what you say over the phone," Sarah said, raising her voice. "Have you forgot that they may be listening to our conversation?"

"They can all go to hell!" Nahid said before removing her hand, which had made an impression on the window as the two girls shared a quick giggle.

"Well, I have to get back to my dreadful math midterm. You're so lucky you're not studying pure mathematics; it sucks so much!" Sarah complained in between yawns.

"Lucky? Try being one of only four girls in a room full of obnoxious and horny men hitting on you every minute of every lecture," Nahid responded, rolling her eyes while the two shared another quick laugh just before exchanging farewells.

Nahid returned to her desk and gazed at the green peace sign that hung above her computer. It reminded her of the past summer and the time she along with millions of other Iranians voiced their disapproval and discomfort with their regime. She thought about the sheer willingness and courage of young demonstrators around the same age as her, standing up to agents of the Islamic Republic along with their destructive arsenal. But before she could reminisce any further, Nahid's mother knocked on her door and entered her room with a plate of sliced red apples.

Her mother played a huge role in Nahid's life; she always motivated her daughter to push the envelope and challenge the status quo. In fact, it was her mother who persuaded Nahid to study civil engineering, a field dominated by male students, instead of pursuing the field of medicine, as her parents did. Ever since Nahid was little, her mother had inspired her to take an analytical approach toward her surrounding and especially the regime. Her mother had been an opponent of the regime ever since Nahid's grandfather was executed in the aftermath of the revolution for being a senior-ranking member of the shah's army. Hence, from a young age, Nahid was involved in politics through supplementary studies, blogs, and participation in political organizations at her university. She, like many others her age, volunteered for reformer candidate Mir Hossein Mousavi in the 2009 election campaign.

After entering the room, her mother placed the plate of fruit next to Nahid's keyboard and embraced her daughter.

"Are you feeling all right?" Nahid's mother asked. "You haven't been yourself lately." At first she ignored her mother and continued to surf the web.

"Are you still upset about that mullah stopping you and Sarah?" her mother followed up. She referred to an incident that took place a few days ago; while shopping for clothes, Nahid and Sarah were stopped on a side street by a cleric who was troubled by Nahid's attire, saying that her *manto* (overcoat) was too tight and exposed the shape of her bottom. Luckily the two were just given a warning, but they were both kept on the street and in the cold temperatures for nearly an hour and given a lecture by the cleric about the importance of being pious.

"I know living with these dreadful conditions can be difficult, but you're a strong woman, you come from a strong family.

Your grandmother and I have been your moral fiber and role models, and we want to see you smash through the oppressive and patriarchal boundaries that these bastards have created," she continued as she embraced her daughter closer while stroking Nahid's hair.

"I remember when I was graduating from high school ... thirty-seven years ago there were hardly any women doctors in Iran, and they lived in Tehran. It was then that your grandmother encouraged me to study medicine so that I would not only serve the people of my country but also be an example for the next generation of women, and that is why I encouraged you to study civil engineering, so that you could be a role model to the next generation of young girls and teach them the values of equality and women's rights." Nahid's mother continued with conviction in her voice before she sat on the edge of Nahid's bed. She had that warm smile on her face that Nahid had been accustomed to all these years. It was the kind of smile that gave her comfort and helped in shaping her confidence and teaching her right from wrong.

"It's not just the mullah that is bothering me, Mom. It's everything that they have done to this godforsaken place!" Nahid replied, once again pushing away her keyboard. Her mother hung her head as her petite daughter got up from her chair and approached her window, staring at the still fresh imprint of her hand on the glass with the dark street in its background. Silence fell in between mother and daughter.

"I'm tired of being honked at or hit on when I'm walking the streets, or waiting for the bus, or trying to hail a cab, or sitting quietly in the lecture hall before the lesson begins. I'm tired of being treated as an object, and yes, I'm also tired of having to worry every two seconds on the streets that I'm going to get stopped or arrested for my hair sticking out of my scarf or my butt sticking out from underneath my overcoat!" Nahid said while staring at the fading shape of her hand.

"It didn't used to be like this; back in the day, we used to wear miniskirts and walk in the streets without the slightest of hassles.

I mean, sure, there was the occasional honk or catcall, which was even flattering at times, but it didn't used to be like this; men were respectful of women in those days; people had boundaries and dignity. Heck, all of that went down the toilet when these ignorant mullahs took over and labeled us as objects," her mother recalled, staring at the ground as silence once again fell between the two.

"What am I saying?" she continued. "I mean, not all of our men are bad, there are many who come from great families, are educated, and have respect for women; have you not come across anyone like this at your school?" her mother asked.

"Are you asking if I like someone at school, Mom?" Nahid quickly replied while rolling her eyes in an effort to take away from the red blush that began to take shape on her cheeks.

"I'm just saying that there are good men out there as well and that it would be normal for someone your age to be friends with one who is respectful and educated, plus you don't have to hide it from me, your blushes already gave you away, missy," her mother responded with a wink and the same smile.

"Well, there is this guy, Reza, he's a senior in my program, but he doesn't know that I like him," Nahid answered with a smile as her face blushed like the apples sitting next to her computer, while her mother smiled in return and slowly nodded.

"I'm glad we can talk to each other like this," her mother said. "I want you to be happy, Nahid. I want you to experience what life has to offer as an empowered woman and do whatever you believe is right. I married your father and had a family soon after I graduated from medical school. I didn't get a chance to become a doctor, and I don't want you to go down the same road as I did. I want you to experience life for yourself before you decide to settle down; date, have friends and a career at the same time."

Nahid nodded, having already heard this speech from her mother on previous occasions.

"I don't even know if I could get a job after I graduate. I mean, I understand and appreciate you encouraging me to pursue my dreams, but let's be realistic, Mom; how many women civil engineers have you heard of working in Iran?" Nahid asked with her eyes wide open and her arms spread apart.

The room went silent again; Nahid could see that her mother didn't really have an answer for her as she sat on the corner of the bed, looking blindly at the floor again.

"I was thinking that maybe I should apply to foreign schools before I graduate and pursue the rest of my education outside of Iran; you know, just like you and Dad did," Nahid continued, breaking the silence as her mother quickly lifted her head up.

"Where did you have in mind?" her mother asked, once again focusing her eyes on her daughter.

"I was thinking Canada or the USA. I looked up a few schools there and they have excellent programs for civil engineering in Toronto, Texas, Boston, and New York, plus Sarah's sister lives in Toronto; she went over there six years ago on a study visa, and after getting her master's, she got a job and her employers sponsored her. She is now a Canadian citizen and married an Iranian boy there," Nahid answered, her skin taking on a red hue once again.

"I'll speak to your father, dear; perhaps it would be best if you left this hellhole and pursue a life somewhere that doesn't shackle the spirits of its people," her mother replied with the same warm smile as she stood up from the bed and hugged her daughter before walking toward the door.

The next morning, Nahid left her house and took a cab to the university, as usual. She used the commute to quickly wipe away the nail designs that she had put on her fingernails over the weekend. Nail design and coloring had been deemed immoral by the regime and prohibited by the dress codes set at universities and schools. Nahid had a previous run-in with the security at Amir Kabir University, who refused to let her enter unless her nails were spotless; she became used to the routine of wiping away the colors on her nails during her commute hours. Ironically, she would use the time on her commute back to apply colors to her nails. In fact, Nahid would often take an extra set of clothes in addition to her mandatory school outfit and change in the facilities of a restaurant not too far from the campus after school. Her school uniform consisted of black trousers, a long black overcoat, and a scarf that only exposed the face.

The entrance to Amir Kabir University was guarded by security officials working for the university's moral and guidance departments. These individuals had the sole purpose of ensuring that male and female students did not chat each other up or walk hand in hand while additionally reinforcing the state's Islamic dress codes.

After Nahid attended her first two lectures, she decided to head over to the school's cafeteria in order to meet up with Sarah and catch a quick bite. The cafeteria was divided in half by a plastic partition; one half was reserved for female students and the other for the males.

During the rule of President Khatami, Amir Kabir University was known to be a hotbed of political ideology, which erupted during the student riots of 1999. The university's cafeteria was considered the birthplace of political debates and political organizations. But ever since the recent demonstrations, students —especially male students—were warned that any political debates would be grounds for expulsion and even arrests.

After getting their meals, the two girls approached their usual table, but before they took their seats, Nahid and Sarah cautiously looked around their surroundings in order to make sure that there were no suspicious individuals who could overhear their conversations.

"I forgot to ask you last night, has there been any news on your cousin?" Nahid asked as the two girls set down their food plates and took their seats, having been ensured that their surrounding was safe.

"No, nothing yet; as far as we know, he's still held up in Evin," Sarah quietly answered as she stared at her plate and dug around her food with a spoon. Sarah's cousin had been arrested two months before this story for being an activist and being involved in organizing demonstrations.

"They haven't even told my auntie's family whether their son is dead or alive. It's been seven weeks now," Sarah said. Her bright green eyes seemed colorless to Nahid as she stared blindly at her plate.

"It must be so hard on your family," Nahid said as she placed her palm on top of Sarah's hand.

"You don't know the half of it; my poor uncle stands outside the gates of Evin every day with my cousin's picture, hoping that someone can recognize his son and give them an update, and my auntie, well, let's not even talk about her. The poor thing has severe depression. She lost thirty pounds and hasn't left her house in weeks," Sarah replied before pushing away her plate of food as tears began to form around the corners of her eyes.

"Look at the bright side, Sarah; at least you know he's alive, cause if he was dead they would have told your family already, along with some bullshit reason for his death like he fell on a blunt object and ruptured his skull or something," Nahid said with a warm smile. Sarah chuckled a little before wiping away her tears. Nahid looked at her friend with the same warm smile as the two ate a little from their meal plates.

"Any news from the math students about Mousavi or the upcoming demonstrations?" Nahid whispered, after she made sure again that no one was listening to their conversation.

"Nothing today; worst of all, no one knows when the new filter breaker will be up and running," Sarah answered, reaching for her cup of tea and blowing on the hot surface while Nahid shook her head.

"I guess the best thing we can do is just wait until more news comes through," Sarah said in between taking small sips of tea.

"I'm tired of waiting, Sarah; we need to create our own opposition, our own voice, a democratic and secular voice," Nahid whispered before looking over her shoulders again.

"It takes one person at a time, just like Reza has been saying; you know, the senior from my program. He is always involved in on-campus and off-campus politics. He thinks that opposition movements need to start small and genuine, a movement that belongs to the people and acts with the goal of removing these dictators and installing a democratic government," Nahid quietly continued while Sarah leaned over and listened as she raised one of her eyebrows.

"Speaking to cute senior students, are we now?" Sarah teased as Nahid partially turned away, her cheeks beginning to glow.

"It's not like that, Sarah; we're just friends! Plus he's really passionate about our country and has some great ideas on how it can be improved," Nahid answered, looking away as she quickly reached for her cup of tea and began drinking.

"Yeah right, I'm sure you're just friends," Sarah said, rolling her eyes and grinning.

"He's just a friend!" Nahid reemphasized, grinding her teeth.

"Hey, I'm not the one whose eyes glisten and cheeks blush every time someone mentions the guy's name," Sarah added as Nahid rolled her eyes, again looking away from her friend.

"Anyways, Reza and a few people from my program are getting together tonight at that small café uptown we went to a few weeks back; they want to discuss the 22 Bahman demonstrations. Perhaps you and your boyfriend would like to join us," Nahid said as the glow on her cheeks began to fade away.

"A group discussion?" Sarah replied with a big grin. "We haven't had one of those since the summer."

"Yeah, you're right, I think the last time we met was to organize banners just two weeks after the elections, just a couple of days before Shirin was arrested," Nahid replied; their smiles quickly turned to frowns while silence trickled onto their table.

Shirin was a mutual friend from the university; her story is a particularly sad one, as she was arrested during the initial days of the mass demonstrations that followed the 2009 elections. She was held in custody for nearly three weeks, and shortly after her release, she committed suicide.

A quiet girl that mostly kept to herself, Shirin was not involved in the university opposition movements, nor was she interested in politics. She only went to the demonstration through the persuasions of her older sister and her boyfriend. During the demonstration, their section was ambushed by large squads of riot police and *basij* militia members on motorcycles, which resulted in the arrests of Shirin and her boyfriend. They were taken to an unidentified location.

"Sweet," as her name was translated in English, and stunningly beautiful, Shirin was raped eight to nine times a day by government agents until she was released when it became clear to her interrogators that she was not a genuine rioter. In addition, her boyfriend's confession helped in her release, as he took all the blame and said that Shirin was at the demonstrations only because he manipulated and brainwashed her. Upon being released, Shirin returned to her family's residence and her worried parents. Just hours later, she slashed her wrists in the bathtub, where her parents found her body along with a suicide note that described the treatment that she had received.

"Poor Shirin; I heard that her father was hospitalized with severe depression. I miss her so much," Nahid said, breaking the silence as she wiped away the tears collecting around her eyes.

"I'll think about tonight; we'll probably come by. Text me the details when you get a chance," Sarah said as she hugged her friend before heading out toward her afternoon class.

Nahid's afternoon lectures felt like a painful blur, as she spent most of the time thinking about her late friend Shirin. Pictures of burly and forceful men taking advantage of Shirin began to pop into her head. She pictured her aggressors laughing, mocking, and hitting Shirin as blood ran down her battered face and legs. Screams and cries went off inside her head as she began to picture herself in Shirin's shoes. She cupped her face with her hands and stared into the darkness that poured in between her face and palms. The screams and cries began to get louder as she scratched her fingernails down her cheeks and the rest of her face. It wasn't easy imagining herself going through the horrific nightmare that pierced her friend. She didn't want anyone to share Shirin's fate, nor did she want any parent to go through what Shirin's parents experienced. The screams and cries stopped, and a single tear rolled down her face as Nahid clenched her hands into fists.

After her afternoon lectures, Nahid left the campus and, just like many other days, headed toward a nearby restaurant's lavatory in order to change into more fashionable attire. After putting on her makeup, she purchased a small sandwich from the restaurant and emerged onto the main street with the aim of taking a cab to the coffee shop to meet Reza and her friends.

Nahid raised her arm to hail a taxi. Almost immediately, a motorcyclist stopped in front of her, and she turned her head with her eyebrows raised. Before she could open her mouth, the motorcyclist grinned and said, "Excuse me, miss, have you ever screwed on a motorcycle while the engine was running?"

"Get lost, you dirty piece of shit!" Nahid shouted before swinging her purse toward the man, as he rode away, laughing.

Nahid quickly regained her composure and put her hand back up again, in the hopes of catching a taxi. Seeing her reaction toward the motorcyclist, the driver in a vehicle several meters behind the motorcyclist pulled up to Nahid and rolled down his passenger window; Nahid bent over in order to communicate her destination.

"How much?" the driver asked with a straight face, before Nahid could tell him about her destination.

"How much for what?" Nahid asked, her mouth wide open and her eyebrows raised well up and just underneath her head scarf.

"For a suck and fuck?" the man responded; Nahid gritted her teeth and turned away. Her feet pounded the pavement as she walked away from his vehicle.

"Hey, I'll make you a better offer than the guy on the motorcycle; you won't be disappointed!" the driver yelled as he slowly drove and caught up to Nahid.

"Why don't you go suck and fuck your mother, you piece of shit?" Nahid shouted, clenching her fist.

"What did you say, you fucking whore?" the driver shouted back as he slammed on the brakes.

"Leave me alone or else I'm going to call 110 [911] and give them your plate number," Nahid shouted as she reached for her cell phone in her purse, while the driver of the vehicle quickly sped away.

Having attracted the attention of the oncoming pedestrians, Nahid grew embarrassed and abandoned her plans for taking a taxi; instead she ran toward the bus stop. Soon after, the bus arrived and Nahid got into the back of the bus, which was designated for women. After collecting bus tickets from the male passengers, the bus driver approached the back of the bus to collect tickets from the women, who were lodged in the overcrowded and smaller part of the bus, divided from the men by a waist-high metal bar.

"Tickets, tickets! Make it quick, ladies, we got a long way to go!" the bus driver called, raising his voice in the crowded bus; Nahid worked her way through the columns of women in order to pay the driver.

"Can you please turn up the heat? It is freezing back here," an elderly female passenger said from the very back of the bus.

"It is what it is, lady, it's not going to get any hotter than this," the bus driver declared as he collected the last of the tickets.

"Well, at least let some of the ladies cross onto the men's side," the woman said. "We barely have enough space to breathe back here, while the men get to sit and cross their legs comfortably!"

The driver and some of the male passengers broke into laughter in response.

Chapter 4.
Nahid: The Betrayal

After a long and crammed bus ride, Nahid arrived at Tehran's busy Vanak Square and headed over to a café in a plaza just off the square. The cozy café was owned by one of Reza's longtime friends; most of the customers were university students, who enjoyed the café's debate-oriented atmosphere and hassle-free environment. Nahid arrived a bit late, and once she entered the café, she joined Reza, Sarah and her boyfriend, and another classmate, who were deep in debate.

Despite majoring in civil engineering, Reza had an extensive knowledge of politics, literature, and Western philosophy. He spoke about the democratic ideals of philosophers John Locke and Jean Jacques Rousseau while also making references to Iran's popular prime minister, Mohammad Mosaddeq, who was democratically elected in 1951 but overthrown in 1953 through a coup d'état orchestrated by the CIA, which resulted in the shah being restored to power. Reza had some genuine ideas about the future of Iran, and unlike many students, he had no desire to leave Iran for a Western location in the hopes of a better life. For him, Iran was an unfinished skyscraper built on shoddy infrastructure; he believed that it presented a challenge that could only be repaired by the youth of the nation.

Reza quoted Khomeini, who in the early days of the revolution stated that elections were sacred and that the votes of the nation would be respected under the Islamic Republic. He reminded his tablemates that 60 percent of the population of Iran was born after the revolution and either did not vote to have an Islamic Republic or were too young to vote. According to him, a call for a referendum was the only fair and logical action that could take into account the desires of this 60 percent majority, a notion that was agreed to by all who sat around the table.

Meanwhile, Sarah's boyfriend added that he strongly believed that even the majority of those who did vote for the Islamic Republic back in 1979 regretted their decision, and if given the chance, they would surely reverse their decision and vote for a democratic system that called for limited governance.

The five tablemates went on to discuss the events of the past summer and the atrocities that the regime had conducted since coming into power in 1979. But this was more than just a group of university students getting together to discuss the disenchantment that had swept across their county. It was more about a bunch of young people that drank hot beverages, smiled, told jokes, and even took some time to remember imprisoned and lost souls like Shirin and Sarah's cousin. In the midst of all this, Nahid took a second and wondered if life in Iran could ever resemble the confines of the small café: peaceful, unpretentious, and dedicated to furthering debate and intelligence.

Before the five parted ways, Reza told the group that he along with most of the seniors and graduate students from the civil engineering department were organizing a march toward Azadi (Freedom) Square on the anniversary of the revolution. He went on to inform them that unlike previous demonstrations, which were peaceful, this time he along with his fellow activists would be looking to get some retribution for their fallen brothers and sisters. The others agreed to take part in the march and meet outside of the main entrance of their university campus on the afternoon of the 22nd of Bahman.

As the others left the café, Reza called Nahid aside and told her how proud he was of her and other strong women who bravely stood up for their rights. Concealing her rosy cheeks in the dim lights located just outside of the café, Nahid expressed her appreciation for Reza's comments; with a glowing smile, she wished her companion a good night before setting out in the late evening.

With every step that she took toward the square on that cold winter night, the smile on her face became even more radiant. Every stride felt softer and lighter as her feet touched the cold payment. Reza was different; he was everything that Nahid wanted in a man. But it wasn't just his dark good looks; it was his attitude toward his country and people that really attracted her.

Despite the fact that the square was not that far from Nahid's house, she decided to take a taxi rather than walk in the plummeting February temperatures. This time, instead of automatically putting up her hand, Nahid decided to examine the oncoming vehicles and only signal if a car was an official licensed taxi.

The square was surprisingly quiet; several minutes went by without any licensed taxis in sight. Nahid started to blow into her palms, which had taken on a pinkish hue in the short span. Having two cups of tea at the café didn't help, as she stood on the corner with temperatures rapidly dropping.

Gazing at the oncoming traffic, Nahid didn't notice a vehicle that slowly approached her and parked just a few meters away. Seeing that Nahid did not notice his presence, the driver of the vehicle flashed his lights, and Nahid approached the vehicle in the hopes of getting a ride.

With the sour exchange from earlier in the day in the back of her mind, Nahid was cautious; the smile on her face quickly turned to an unblinking stare. The vehicle was an old and dented *Peykān* (an Iranian-produced vehicle), and although it looked more than capable of getting Nahid to her destination, its driver made Nahid feel uneasy; he sat in the shadows, his icy eyes the only feature available as Nahid could see them motionless and fixed on her. With every step that she took, she felt the cold breaking through her winter boots.

Just a few steps away from the driver's door, a squinting Nahid began to get a better picture of the driver's appearance. From what she could see, the driver was a rather robust figure with a dark beard; he appeared to be in his midforties. Nahid paused just a few steps away from the vehicle; the man's unblinking and dull eyes weren't what Nahid was used to in a taxi driver. She slowly turned around in the hopes of heading back toward the café. But before she could take more than three steps, the sound of the rusty car door slamming reached her ears.

"Hey lady, I think you should get in my car," the driver of the vehicle said loudly. "It's more comfortable than walking!" He had pulled his portly figure out of the car and stood just a few meters behind Nahid, who began to walk faster in the hopes that ignoring the man would cause him to return to his vehicle and leave her alone.

"You're not fooling anyone," he continued. "We both know why you're standing on the street corner, exposing your hair and that sad excuse of an overcoat wrapped tightly around your ass, not to mention being made up like a whore! Like I said, you're not fooling anyone, so just get in the car." The man began to close down the space between Nahid and himself. Her small feet moved faster as she momentarily turned her head and glanced at the dark figure, who was now within an arm's reach of her.

"Your parents don't discipline you for selling yourself for money, so the good arm of the law has to do it!" the man said, his flabby stomach moving side to side as he began to sprint after Nahid.

She breathed heavily while looking back at the man chasing her. The numbing cold restrained her legs as sweat began to run down her neck and back while her breath gasped into the dark freezing air. However, before she could scream for help, Reza appeared from the side street. The sight of him melted away the cold chains around Nahid as she ran toward him.

"Nahid, is everything all right?" Reza asked as a terrified Nahid fell into his arms.

"No, everything is not all right!" she cried. "That man was chasing me! Thank God I ran into you." Nahid panted as she gripped Reza's arms while pointing out the man chasing her.

"Just stay calm, everything is going to be all right," Reza said, smiling momentarily before turning his attention to the portly man not too far away from him.

"Hey, asshole!" Reza shouted. "Why are you chasing after this girl? She is old enough to be your daughter!" Reza clenched his fists and stepped in front of Nahid and faced the man.

"And who the fuck are you, her pimp?" the man shouted back.

"Watch your mouth, you piece of shit! This lady is my friend," Reza said, clenching his fists tighter and walking a few steps closer to the man, while a few onlookers on the sidewalk noticed the altercation and stopped.

"Her friend?" the man said. "Yeah, I bet you're her friend, you and every other man in this city!" The man puffed his chest and towered over the senior engineering student.

"Fuck you!" Reza shouted as he swung his fist toward the man, who ducked to the side and avoided the punch. The man then grabbed hold of Reza's arm, twisted it behind his back, and clutched Reza's neck with his other hand. The man quickly slammed a struggling Reza onto the hood of a parked car.

"Let me go, you piece of shit!" Reza shouted. A stream of blood ran down the side of his face while the number of concerned onlookers grew.

"Let him go!" Nahid screamed as she ran up to the car. Warm tears ran down her face while the man squeezed his arm tighter behind Reza's back, causing the youngster to shout in pain.

"Please, my son, let him go," an old man said. "The youth these days are rude and impolite; it's not right for a man of your stature to sink to their level." The old man approached within a few feet of the car while Reza grunted and wiggled to free his arm.

"Get back, old man!" the man shouted. "Everyone stay back!" The man tightened his grip on Reza and reached into his back pocket and pulled out his wallet. "See this, tough guy?" He slapped Reza in the face with his wallet before showing his identification card from *niroye entezami* (the disciplinary forces). Reza trembled and glared back at the documentation.

"You and your whore picked the wrong spot to sell pussy tonight!" the man shouted with a smug smirk as he reached for a pair of handcuffs and restrained Reza.

"Please sir, let him go!" Nahid screamed. "We're just friends, university classmates." Tears gushed down her face as she quickly clutched the man's left arm before he shook her off and slapped her face, sending her flying. Like Nahid, her tears dangled in the cold air before hitting the hard ground. Her ears ringing, she sat up and held the side of her face. She could see Reza cry as the burly man dragged him toward his car. When they got to the car, he picked up his wireless radio transmitter and spoke into it.

"This is brother Abdi from the plainclothes division. I need a car sent to Vanak Square immediately. I have arrested a hooker and her pimp and need some backup." The policeman then shoved Reza into the backseat.

"Please sir, you don't need to arrest us," Nahid sobbed as she sat on the cold ground.

"You're not going to get any mercy from me for prostituting yourself!" he said, raising his voice while walking toward Nahid as the crowd of whispering onlookers continued to grow.

"I'm not a prostitute, you piece of shit!" Nahid screamed at him while tears continued to run down her face. The policeman leaned over toward her and clutched her right arm.

"Shut your filthy mouth, whore! I'm taking you two in whether you like it or not!" He yanked her to her feet and pulled her close to his portly chest while the group of onlookers began to criticize the officer.

"Shut up! All of you shut up, or I'm going to take you all in as well for disturbing the peace!" the man shouted at the growing mob while tightening his grip on Nahid. The crowd began to slowly disperse.

Soon a green and white disciplinary forces vehicle appeared and took Nahid to a nearby precinct, and the plainclothes officer took Reza to the same facility. Nahid was taken into a small office, where her handcuffs were removed, and she was ordered to wait for a higher ranking officer.

The burning mark of the man's palm still fresh on her cheek, Nahid cupped her face in her palms and quietly wept for about a quarter of an hour until a man entered the small office. Hearing the door open, Nahid quickly brushed away her tears and lifted her head while pushing her hair underneath her scarf. The man approached the small desk, looked at Nahid, and sat down.

Nahid noticed that the man was not in a uniform. He was wearing a dark black suit with a black collared shirt underneath. Similar to the plainclothes officer who arrested them earlier, this man was also bulky and even had a darker beard along with short dark hair. His only distinction was a dark, thick unibrow; he was shorter and younger than the previous person.

"Name?" the man asked as he took out a small notebook from his jacket pocket.

"Hmm," Nahid mumbled, holding her scarf down and just above her eyebrows.

"Name! What is your name?" the man shouted as he smacked his palm on the table.

"My name is Nahid, Nahid Amiri," she quickly answered after nearly jumping out of her chair.

"What is your relationship with Reza Nasserian?" the man asked, staring deep into Nahid's eyes.

"Relationship? There is no relationship, sir, we go to the same university, that's all. I swear to God, we're just friends, we never had any relations outside of marriage!" Nahid tried to convince the man, as tears began to run down her face again.

"What is your relationship with Reza Nasserian?" the man asked again, clutching his pen in his right hand.

"I'm telling you the truth, there is no relationship! I'm a good girl," Nahid said, weeping.

"I don't give a shit if you were blowing him right in the middle of the street! I don't care about any of that! I don't work for the disciplinary police, and I'm not here to charge you for having relations outside of marriage!" The man raised his voice as a cold stream of sweat ran down the back of Nahid's neck. She stared at the back of her hands as she clutched her jeans. She prayed that her interrogator was not a member of the Islamic Republic's notorious intelligence agency.

"I work for the Department of Intelligence," he said. "Now I'm going to ask you one last time: what is your relationship with Reza Nasserian?" the man demanded. Nahid's hands began to tremble while she tightened her grip on her jeans. The sounds of screams and cries began to buzz inside her head as images of stripped and beaten women, strapped over a table as vulgar men raped them, flashed across her eyes. She thought about her friend Shirin and the pain that she and her family suffered.

"Reza and I go to the same university, and that is how I know him; we also hang out once in a while," Nahid answered after taking a long pause. She stared at at her hands as the tears stopped.

"Oh I see, you two just hang out; he sounds like a lovely guy, handsome too," the man said as he stood up from the chair and circled around the desk in order to face Nahid, who slowly nodded while avoiding looking into the man's eyes. He bowed his head closer to Nahid as she did the same and hid her face underneath her scarf. He paused for a moment and then, without any warning, he slapped Nahid across the face with his bulky hand, knocking her out of the chair and ripping her scarf off of her head.

"You fucking brat! You think you can bullshit me? I have a doctorate in sniffing out bullshit!" the man shouted down at a howling Nahid, who quavered and slowly sat up as she picked up the remains of her scarf, pressing it against the spot where she was hit.

"Get up! Get the fuck up! You think I'm done with you?" the man shouted as he grabbed Nahid by her shoulders and yanked her off the ground while shoving her back onto the chair.

"We know who Reza Nasserian is, we know that he is involved in opposition movements on campus, and we have been looking for him and his crew ever since one of his friends in custody gave him up two days ago. Just make it easier on yourself and tell me what they are planning for this 22nd of Bahman." He tugged Nahid by her shoulder as she held onto the bottom of her chair; her head wobbled as her ears continued to buzz.

"We wouldn't be having this conversation if your boyfriend had not taken the vow of silence," he continued. "He thinks he can hold back information from us; if only he knew what we're capable of."

He released Nahid's shoulders and leaned back against the desk while pausing momentarily.

"I can be very nasty if I want to, so don't be a martyr and just tell me what I need to know, and I promise that you can go free," the man continued while Nahid quietly wept with her hands cupped over her face again.

"It would be a shame to spoil a pretty flower such as yourself," the man said, leaning over with a smirk while running the back of his fingers against Nahid's hair; she quickly jerked her head away.

"I just love it when my catch squirms; it gives me more of a challenge," the man continued as he stood up, leered at Nahid, unbuckled his belt, and reached for his zipper.

The sound of the man's zipper being pulled down penetrated inside her mind. The images of rape flashed again in the darkness, only this time the victim wasn't some other innocent girl forced against her will. This time the images belonged to her as she pictured the burly man forcing himself on her while she shrieked in pain. She ran her fingernails down her face, scratching her skin as the man pulled down his pants.

"Stop!" she cried. "I'll tell you everything! Just don't touch me! Please! I swear! I'll tell you what you need to know." Nahid nearly jumped out of her seat, tears gushing out of her eyes as her aggressor flashed the same smug smile in return while pulling up his pants and zipping them.

"It's the entire senior department of civil engineering," she said. "They are planning a march toward Azadi Square on the 22nd of Bahman." Nahid could taste the sandwich she had eaten earlier in the day hurled in the back of her throat.

"Where are they meeting, and exactly how many of them are there?" the man asked.

"There are about sixty of them, and they are meeting at the front of Amir Kabir University," Nahid replied as she swallowed the foul taste while tears rolled down her face.

"What else? Are they armed?" the man continued.

"There are rumors on campus that handful of the seniors have small pistols, and I heard that their intentions are no longer peaceful," Nahid answered as she wrapped her arms over one another and around her sides before she dropped her head and bawled.

"Good," the man replied as he reached for his cell phone in his jacket and dialed a number. "I want the entire civil engineering senior students of Amir Kabir University along with the faculty members arrested first thing tomorrow," he ordered. "There are to be no exceptions! Is that clear?" He hung up and opened the door of the small office.

"I want you to transfer this girl to the woman's division of Kahrizak prison tonight, she is not to be in contact with anyone," he said. "I will take care of the other one myself. We're going to have a good time with him." A young officer entered the room and saluted as he took out a pair of handcuffs and approached Nahid.

"You promised me that I'd go free if I told you everything!" Nahid shouted. "I told you everything, you fucking monster, I told you *everything!*" Nahid wriggled her arms while the officer put the handcuffs on.

"You'll go free once you've been civilized and taught a lesson about obedience," the man replied with a smirk. He watched

49

Nahid being dragged out of the room while she stared blindly at him with her mouth wide open as tears streamed down her face.

———\\\———

According to Nahid, she spent two grueling months in Tehran's cruel Kahrizak detention center before being released, and while she didn't want to relive the harsh memories by giving details, she did confirm that the political prisoners and activists who were kept in that facility were in fact tortured and raped.

After her release, Nahid escaped from Iran and now lives in a Western country while trying to put her life back together and gain the confidence that she lost as a result of her prison term. She is still very much dedicated to the opposition movement and making sure that Iranians are liberated from the tyranny of the Islamic Republic. In our last conversation, her only desire was for the international community and human rights organizations to investigate the murders, tortures, and rapes that the regime has conducted in the past three decades.

As for Reza, neither Nahid nor anyone else I interviewed could verify his whereabouts. I share Nahid's desires for a free Iran and for human rights advocates to come to the aid of Iranians, especially those who have suffered from torture and rape at the hands of this regime. Make no mistake about it; the only reason that I'm writing this book is to highlight the struggles of innocent individuals like Nahid and Reza. I sincerely hope that one day the people of Iran can repay the likes of Nahid and Reza for the sacrifices that they have made and are making in liberating Iran.

Chapter 5.
Rasul: The Denigrated Woman

A long with many other calamities, Iran in the past few years has hit a marriage crisis, which has slowed the rate of marriages to a halt. The government's mismanagement of the economy, high inflation, unemployment rates, and soaring real estate prices have made it extremely difficult for couples to tie the knot.

In 2008, in order to increase the rate of marriages, Ahmadinejad's government introduced "semi-independent marriage," under which young people who cannot afford to marry and move into their own place may legally marry but continue to live apart in their parents' homes.[11] The highly controversial plan was soon shut down, as many women complained that the scheme offered men access to legal sex while offering women nothing by way of security and social respect.[12] Sadly, this was not the first time that the regime introduced draconian and bizarre marriage schemes. The highly controversial temporary marriage scheme,

---

11   http://www.timesonline.co.uk/tol/news/world/middle_east /article6839335.ece.

12   Ibid.

which is still in practice today, was introduced in 1992 under the Rafsanjani government.[13]

"*Sigheh*," as it is called in Farsi, is a fixed-term/temporary marriage popular in the Muslim world, mostly before the twentieth century. The process is similar to a marriage, except there is a date of expiration included in the marriage contract.[14] In addition, there are no minimum or maximum time lines set out for the existence of the marriage, hence a *sigheh* can last anywhere from one hour to ninety-nine years. During this period, couples are governed under the laws of marriage and are treated as husband and wife; the men are presumed to pay the women's *mahr* (or dowry).[15] Refer to the appendix for more information on Iran's marriage crisis and temporary marriages.

The following story was put together as a result of interviews with Iranian women, prostitutes, and men who in one way or another were involved in the world of temporary marriages. It is important to note that while these men who had a temporary wife (or more than one wife) agreed that their actions were disgraceful to women, they always relied on the excuse that their actions were legal and promoted by the state.

This story is about a forty-six-year-old man by the name of Rasul Tehrani. He had a successful jewelry store in Tehran's famous jewelry bazaar and had been married for twenty-six years; he also had had a *sigheh* for the past two years. His *sigheh* is a twenty-seven-year-old woman who divorced her husband after only a year of marriage (she caught him having an affair).

Before we begin, I would like to ask you not to judge all Iranian men as chauvinists who abuse women and treat them as objects. If you must judge and blame, then place the culpability on those who have served as educators and role models in ethical, social, and legal circumstances. Judge the regime along with the clerical ranks that for generations have downgraded women as second-class citizens while elevating the role of chauvinism.

---

13   http://news.bbc.co.uk/2/hi/6714885.stm.

14   http://www.al-islam.org/encyclopedia/chapter6a/1.html.

15   Ibid.

One afternoon in late September 2009, Rasul Tehrani—known around the bazaar and his neighborhood as *Hajji* Tehrani, the title given to a Muslim who has successfully completed the pilgramage to Mecca—was approaching the end of a sluggish day. Business had been bad lately, mostly because it was the holy month of Ramadan, which along with the traditional fasting and daily prayers has the tendency to bring Tehran's various businesses to a grinding halt. Not to mention that it was also the start of the new school year, which usually indicated tougher economic times as parents who have spent their money on summer vacations and back-to-school material for their kids prepared to tighten their belts and spend less on luxuries such as jewelry.

Staring out of his shop's window at the handful of customers walking Tehran's historical bazaar, Rasul began to ponder about closing down his store for the remainder of Ramadan, or at the very least for rest of the young week. He was fantasizing about taking Sepide, his *sigheh,* to his small villa located off the coast of the Caspian Sea. His nineteen-year-old son was out of his hair and off to his freshmen year at university in a different province, and he considered lying to his wife and saying that he was going to Dubai on business; he visualized Sepide alone with him in the cozy northern villa. His wife, Fatemeh, already had her suspicions about him taking on a *sigheh,* and whenever she confronted him and threatened to leave him, he would silence her by warning that she would be left homeless and poor since the divorce laws were in his favor.

He grinned, closed his eyes, and leaned over the glass display case featuring his finest jewelry. He thought about shutting up Fatemeh, who lately had been on his case for more money, his late arrivals, and his missing dinners altogether (along with smelling like another woman's perfume); he also fantasized about running around with a girl nearly half his age. The two thoughts began to swirl in his head and tingled down his spine. Drops of sweat appeared on his forehead as he opened up the two top buttons of his shirt and waved his collars back and forth. But before he could fantasize any more, two neighboring store owners walked in through the doors. Over the years, the three men had become good friends despite competing for customers and sales.

Greeting and welcoming the two, Rasul snapped at his assistant to take over for him while he directed his two neighbors into the backroom office of the store. Rasul's office was decorated with fine rugs, works of art, and the latest trends in furniture. Over the years, the three men often congregated in the office to discuss business, politics, and women.

Rasul displayed his new cappuccino maker and offered the men cups of the hot trendy beverage. The two rolled their eyes at one another and instead opted for the more traditional cup of tea. Even though it was Ramadan and wasn't anywhere near the break of fast, the three men reached for their cups with ease and began to take raisins from a bowl on the round table.

"I don't know about you two but I haven't made a single toman [Iranian currency; one US dollar equals approximately 1,100 toman (2010)] these past three days," said Bahram, the older of the three, as he reached for his teacup and began to blow away the steam.

"Who could make any money with all these religious holidays?" Akbar said. "Every day is either the death of this imam or the birth of that imam, not to mention the effects of the entire month of Ramadan." Akbar's store was located right across from Rasul's.

"The entire calendar has become one big day of mourning," Rasul added. "How can I sell diamonds and gold when there are no wedding ceremonies, no celebrations, and on top of that, every time that idiot [Ahmadinejad] talks, the price of gold goes up." Rasul took his seat while the other two men shook their heads.

"God bless the shah's soul; he gave us paradise, respect, and dignity, but we didn't appreciate him!" Bahram replied as he ran his hand over his head and pushed his milky white hair behind his ears before shaking his head.

"It's not even just the price of gold; every time this jackass speaks, he brings shame and dishonor to us," Akbar followed up before taking a sip from his cup.

"It's always the Jews, or Israel, or the Holocaust, or the nuclear bullshit with this idiot. He doesn't get it; we don't hate Jews, they are people of God too, unlike those coward Saudis, who hate us and are always plotting against us," Bahram added as he guzzled his hot beverage.

"The people can't keep a roof over their heads and food in their stomachs, and this idiot talks about nuclear power as if it is the number one priority," Akbar said.

"I said it before and I'll say it again," Bahram said, "these mullahs aren't here to serve us, they are here to serve their British masters." He stared at his empty cup, hinting at an age-old conspiracy that was shared among older Iranians, while the two younger men turned away from their older colleague and rolled their eyes at each other. A few seconds of silence followed as Rasul and Akbar finished their beverages; their host collected the cups and poured another round of tea for him and his table mates.

"Just look at what they did to the people over the summer; God only knows how many have been killed, imprisoned, tutored, and raped. They're not here to serve us," Bahram said, referring to the events that followed the presidential elections of 2009 before taking the freshly poured cup of tea.

"If you ask me, that geezer [Khamenei] and his minions would love nothing but for America and Israel to attack us just so they could extend their shelf life and fool us again into believing all the propaganda about the United States that they've been saying for all these years," Akbar said as he reached for some raisins while Rasul and Bahram nodded.

"It's just like the days when that bastard Sadam attacked us; all you heard was that the great Satan is helping our enemy, but did they once stop and talk about what happened with that whole Contra affair, or did they let anyone else here talk about it? No!" Bahram said as he again pushed his hair back.

The three shook their heads before slowly taking sips from their cups. Before anyone else said anything, Akbar's assistant rushed into the office and whispered into his boss's ear. Akbar immediately stood up from his chair, frowning. He proceeded to tell his assistant to keep the angry person causing a commotion in his store calm and to lie to the man that Akbar's mother has died recently and that he doesn't have the sum to pay him back yet. Grinding his teeth, Akbar nearly pushed his assistant out of the office, quickly waved good-bye to his friends, and headed toward the back door of Rasul's store before quietly leaving.

After Akbar's sudden departure, Bahram continued his criticisms of the regime and its effect on society. He described prerevolution Tehran as a society of respect and dignity where men honored their debts and treated women with pride. To no one's surprise, Bahram was a staunch supporter of the late Muhammad Reza Pahlavi and promoted the shah without fear in almost all platforms available to him. However, despite his passionate description of the quality of life before the Islamic Revolution of 1979, Rasul's reaction to his neighbor's homily was minimal; he stuck his hand underneath his chin and stared at Bahram silently while reaching for his tea.

Rasul wasn't a big fan of the shah. He wasn't too crazy about the mullahs either, but at the same time, he had prospered greatly under the recent rise of the real estate market in Tehran—the sale of his inherited property had made him a very rich man. With his newfound wealth, Rasul was now rich enough to relocate his family to North America; however, he refused to do so because he believed it was easier to make money in Iran. Plus, with his wife's recent behavior, moving to Canada or the United States almost inevitably ensured a separation, which would certainly result in a share of his wealth being granted to his wife under financial divorce settlements that were unprecedented in Iran.

The thought scared him as his fists underneath his chin and around the cup began to tighten. He had worked way too hard for his money and hated the idea of leaving her with a chunk of it. He bit down on his teeth and slowly began to grind them. It wasn't clear to him when he and the mother of his only son began to resent one another, but one thing was clear: he was in control and didn't want to give up an inch of his power.

He wanted to go back to thoughts of doing unspeakable things to Sepide, but every time he tried, the hostility between himself and his wife would pop back into his head. Having Bahram speak in the background also didn't help; before he could pursue his fantasies, he felt a vibration in his front pocket. It rattled his bones as he nearly stumbled, trying to remove his hand from underneath his chin while reaching for the sensual source of the vibrations.

It was his phone, which he pulled out while turning his body away from Bahram in efforts to conceal the phone's screen, which displayed Sepide's name.

"Hello, my dear, how are you today?" Rasul greeted as he flashed a big, toothy smile before fidgeting with the volume rocker of his phone as he stood up and walked away toward the other end of the office.

"Did you get it?" the familiar voice asked.

"It's Dariush," Rasul said to Bahram while still sporting the same smile; he hoped to fool his friend into thinking it was his son on the line.

"How are things in school, my dear?" Rasul quickly asked, bobbing his head and smiling.

"I don't have the time or patience to be your fucking son, Rasul, and I don't care who you're in the room with," Sepide said, raising her voice. "Now did you get it or not?"

"Can you believe that they didn't have the i-Phone," Rasul responded, "but they had a Samsung that the owner said was just as good as the i-Phone, dear." Rasul turned down his phone's volume while glancing back at Bahram and smiling.

"Samsung? I don't want a Samsung, Rasul!" she shouted.

Rasul smiled before turning his head away from Bahram and saying, "But the i-Phone costs one million, and I haven't sold anything in nearly a week!" Rasul cupped his palm between his mouth and the phone's receiver.

"Oh? I thought you said they didn't have it!" she snapped.

"No, it's just ...," Rasul tried to explain.

"I don't give a shit what it costs, Rasul!" Sepide shouted. "Either you buy me what I want or I'll pay a visit to your wife and tell her how much her cheap husband likes to come over to my apartment and screw me; I'm sure she'll be delighted to hear that!"

"Okay dear, I'll get it for you first thing tomorrow; just take it easy," Rasul answered quickly.

"That's better; now did you remember to come up with an excuse for your wife so we could get away together for a bit?" she asked.

"I will talk to your mother when I see her at home, Dariush," Rasul answered as he wiped away his forehead.

"I said stop talking to me like I'm your fucking son!" Sepide shouted as he chuckled, wiping his sweaty forehead before tilting his head toward Bahram, who continued to sit and quietly drink his tea.

"I can't stand being in this city during Ramadan; now are you going to talk to the bitch or not?" she asked.

"Yes, like I said, dear, I will speak to her tonight, okay? I have to go now, I'll call you soon." Rasul hung up the phone as he pushed down hard on the end button while squeezing the phone in his palm. He stared quietly at the blank screen of his phone for a few short seconds before returning to the table.

"I'm sorry about that; what can I say? Kids ... every day, they want something new," Rasul said.

"And how is young Dariush doing? You must be so proud of him," Bahram asked, staring deep into Rasul's eyes.

"Yes, I am very proud, he is the first person in my family to seek a higher education," Rasul replied, slightly turning his head and slowly rotating his eyes away from Bahram's. "Well, I should be closing down the store, the wife has invited some guests over for the break of fast tonight, and I better be home before they get there, or else," Rasul said.

"Yes, I should be leaving too; thank you for the tea, and be sure to send my greetings to the family," Bahram replied as he finished the remainder of his cup and left the office.

Rasul closed down the store just a few minutes after Bahram left and got into his Lexus SUV before heading out into Tehran's busy rush hour. Just as he began to drive, rain started to pour out of the sky, making visibility poor and turning the city's concrete jungle into a wet and sloppy blur. Trying his best to avoid the traffic, Rasul took the back streets and alleys as his vehicle splashed toward his residence uptown.

Not too far from his shop and on a narrow street, Rasul stopped at a red light and noticed a woman standing in the rain; she was wearing a tight and soaked raincoat. Impressed at the sight of Rasul's expensive vehicle, the woman squinted through his windshield and noticed him glancing toward her. She smiled and waved her arm at him as he slowly pulled up next to her and rolled down his window.

"Are you trying to catch a cab?" Rasul asked.

"I am, but no one except for you was kind enough to stop. I've been in this damn rain for ten minutes now," said the woman, who looked into the car and especially at the empty passenger seat.

"Perhaps I could give you a lift somewhere, " Rasul said. "I'd hate to see you catch a cold." Rasul nodded as the woman jumped into his vehicle.

"Oh, thank you so much, sir; you're a God send," she said. "I only wished that there were more gentlemen like you in this city." The woman unbuttoned her soaked raincoat, wiped the rain away from her scarf, and pulled down the passenger mirror to check on her makeup.

Rasul looked at her through the corner of his eye. She was in her midthirties and had dyed blonde hair, which stuck out of her scarf as she put on more lipstick. The woman then rolled back her coat and exposed a low-cut shirt, which was partially wet.

"So where are you headed to? " Rasul asked as he tried to catch a glimpse of the woman's cleavage.

"Wherever you want to go," she replied, smiling and rotating her upper body toward Rasul and slowly pushing her breasts together in the process.

"Wherever I want to go? What if I was going to drive off a cliff?" Rasul and the woman chuckled while he continued to sneak a peek at her chest.

"Well, I was wondering if I could take a few hours of your time tonight," the woman said as she gently moved her left hand over her breast before placing it on Rasul's lap while she winked at him.

He glanced at her hand over his lap before smiling back and nodding. This wasn't the first time he had picked up a prostitute.

"Thank God I found someone who is honest in this city and just wants to spend a few hours with me with no catch," he said as he glanced back at the woman with his grin transformed into a straight face.

"No catch?" she replied, laughing. "Surely a man of your expensive taste knows that the going rate is 50,000 tomans."

"Oh, believe me, lady, there is no one in this city who knows about the going rate better than me," he said, "but I'm afraid it is you who doesn't know." Rasul glanced back at the woman, who stared back at him with her neck tilted and eyebrows lifted.

"The going rate is 50,000 but the girl that charges 50,000 is eighteen years old, has her own place, and has a pimp who keeps a lookout for the authorities," Rasul said as the woman raised her eyebrows even higher. "The girl that charges 50,000 also offers a grass joint or a drink of whiskey before the sex and food and fruits after," he continued before pulling to the side of the road.

"So yeah, I know the going rate, believe me, and the cost of fucking someone in your age and condition is no more than 20,000," Rasul added as he leaned over the woman's lap and opened her door while the rain poured outside of the car.

"Okay, I'll do it for twenty! Please don't kick me out, I haven't had a client all week, and I need to feed my child!" she pleaded as she clutched onto his arm. He smirked and nodded as he closed the door and drove off.

The woman lived in an apartment in relatively poor south Tehran, near where Rasul had picked her up. Nevertheless, the location of her residence served Rasul's purpose, since no one living in that area would recognize him, especially his customers, other bazaaries, or the friends or family of his *sigheh* or Fatemeh.

The woman's apartment, a small studio, was surprisingly clean despite being located in a rundown building. Upon entering the apartment, Rasul noticed the woman's toddler sitting on a mattress laid out in the middle of the only room in the apartment, in front of a small television set, which looked to be the only furniture. The child stared quietly at him as his mother began to remove small plates and the child's milk bottle from around the mattress; she took them over to the kitchen. Rasul guessed the child was only about two or three years old as he continued to quietly stare at the strange man in their apartment.

Once she returned from the kitchen, the woman picked up her child and took him to the bathroom; from what Rasul guessed, he was placed in the empty tub before being told by his mother to stay in the bathroom no matter what happened outside.

With the bathroom door firmly closed, the woman then opened a small closet and took out a blanket and pillows; she placed the blanket over the mattress and put the pillow at the top, while Rasul took off his shoes and pants. The sex was brief as the woman kept the noise to a minimum, despite Rasul's aggressive attempts in trying to get her to moan. She also avoided looking at him despite his repeated demands for her to open her eyes. Once it was over, the woman sat on the edge of the mattress with the blanket wrapped around her waist and lower body; she stared at the bathroom door as Rasul began to put his pants on. With her dampened and now wrinkled shirt still on, she began to sob quietly with her back turned away from Rasul, who took a stash of bills out his jacket pocket and began to count it loudly before placing the agreed amount on the pillow.

He put on his shoes and opened the front door. Just as he stepped outside, the child in the tub began to scream and cry while her mother sat motionless as more tears rolled down her face.

The rain seemed to have stopped as he made his way in the traffic toward his uptown penthouse apartment. He arrived home around nine o'clock. He inserted his key into the lock but before he could open the door, his wife on the other side quickly yanked the door open.

"Where the hell have you been, Rasul?" Fatemeh asked as she stared down her husband.

"At the bloody store, woman, where else do you think I was?" he answered casually. He slowly walked around her, took off his shoes, and hung up his coat before heading for the living room.

"Bullshit!" she yelled. "I called the store, there was no one there to pick up, and I called your phone, which was off, so I called your assistant, who said you closed down the store around five!" Fatemeh nearly sprinted in front of him before he could enter the living room. "Where the fuck were you, Rasul?" she shouted while grabbing hold of her husband's shirt as he rolled his eyes and avoided looking at her.

"You were with your whore, weren't you?" she asked with her voice raised as he pressed his way past her and crossed into the living room while taking out his wallet and cell phone before sitting down in front of a big screen television.

"You were at her apartment, just like you were two nights ago!" she shouted while standing in front of him. He continued to avoid her and looked at his phone while clutching it tightly in his palm.

"That's right!" she said. "I know where the bitch lives. I followed you the other night. Did you buy her a unit in that apartment, or is Mr. Big Shot just paying her rent?" she shouted in her husband's face as tears began to slowly make their way down her cheeks.

Rasul continued to avoid looking at her.

"You've left me with nothing but shame in front of the neighbors. I can't even hold my head up in the neighborhood anymore. You think no one knows, but everyone knows about your twenty-seven-year-old whore!" She screamed at him as he jumped out of his seat and smashed his phone against the ground.

"You don't talk about her, you hear me?" Rasul shouted. "You just keep your fucking mouth shut before I toss you out on your ass!" Fatemeh took a step back while his phone lay in pieces on the ceramic tile.

"Thank God our son is away at school and doesn't live in this wretched shithole to see what a whore monger his father, the great Hajji Tehrani, has become!" she replied with a smirk on her face. She wiped away her tears but before she could say anything else, Rasul swung his open palm and smacked her in her face; she fell hard to the ground.

"I've been taking care of you for twenty-seven years now!" Rasul shouted. "If it wasn't for me, bitch, you would be hooking on the streets now just to get by!"

Rasul stood over her while she squirmed; blood slowly dripped from her nose.

"The apartment and the store belong to me," he continued. "They are both under my name, and if you ever follow me again or talk about my son like that again, I will throw you over the fucking balcony. Do you understand? "

Rasul bent down toward her while Fatemeh crawled her way out of the living room, moaning and leaving drops of blood and tears over the ceramic floors. He returned to his seat and turned on the television.

―――∞―――

Sadly, gender inequalities and spousal abuse takes place regardless of location and nationality. What is important is how the laws and ethics of any given society deal with these travesties. Besides laws and coercive measures that are set up to punish violence against women, developed states have also created educational tools to teach both men and women about the destructions of violence against women. There are also shelters for abused women, couples' counseling, and support groups established in order to provide better teachings in order to avoid unpleasant actions.

Based on my research on life in Tehran, I have yet to come across any of the above. The one area that was common among

Iranian women I interviewed was that there needs to be equality and greater protection for women in Iran. Regardless of their occupations or their place on the social hierarchy, every woman that I spoke to agreed that the Islamic Republic categorized women as inferior to men and as objects. This has not only created a depressive environment for women but also a self-fulfilling prophecy for a significant portion of females who have bought into the regime's stereotypes. With that said, the majority of women that contributed to this book have hopes that the next generation of young Iranian girls will not easily submit to the dictates of the regime and will fight for their rights. The 2009 demonstrations are a tribute to this, as young Iranian women stood shoulder to shoulder with their male counterparts in demanding democracy and fundamental human rights.

Chapter 6.
Parisa: Descent into Darkness

P rostitution has recently become a major problem, not only in Tehran but also in Iran's other major cities. In 2002, the Iranian newspaper *Entekhab* reported that the government had estimated there were "85,000 prostitutes in Tehran alone."[16] Other nonofficial reports from the same year indicated a much higher figure, in the area of 300,000.[17]

Under the Islamic Republic, prostitution became a zero tolerance taboo, and the punishment ranged anywhere from lashes to execution (for repeat offenders).[18] Ironically, in April 2008, Reza Zarei, the chief of police of the city of Tehran, was arrested in a brothel in the Iranian capital. Zarei, appointed chief of police after he promised to clean up the city from corruption, prostitution, and drugs, was found with six naked prostitutes.[19] I guess it must have been "Do as I say and not as I do" for the now dishonored chief.

---

16   http://www.slate.com/id/2189816/.

17   http://www.nytimes.com/2002/08/28/world/to-regulate-prostitution-iran-ponders-brothels.html.

18   http://www.slate.com/id/2189816/.

19   http://news.bbc.co.uk/2/hi/middle_east/7350165.stm.

Prostitution aside, in 2009, just a few months before the controversial presidential election, the US Department of State issued a report regarding human trafficking that placed Iran among "tier 3" countries, meaning that Iran's government does not fully comply with the minimum standards and makes no efforts to monitor and combat trafficking of persons.[20]

More alarming, child prostitution has risen 635 percent in Iran; many underaged girls are sold to neighboring Arab countries as sex slaves.[21] Rumors and even official reports are indicating that state officials themselves are behind child prostitution rings and sex trafficking of children and adults to the oil-rich Gulf states and even some European destinations.[22] For more information on prostitution in Iran, please refer to the appendix.

I spoke with seventy-two prostitutes during the course of my research, and one of the most compelling stories came from Parisa Sadeeqpour, who was twenty-two years old. Like many young women who end up in the sex trade, Parisa was disowned and shunned by her father after she fell in love with a neighbor and lost her virginity to him. She ran away from the remote Kermān Province and tried to make it in Tehran. That one act of misguided love with her neighbor condemned Parisa to a series of hardships that are difficult to imagine.

—— ·\\\\'— ——

The weather was surprisingly mild for a spring afternoon as Parisa sat on a bench near the entrance of Tehran's Park-e Lalle, where she and her lover, the boy from the house next to hers, planned to meet. She crossed her arms and rubbed her hands over them while periodically squinting her hazel eyes at the park entrance, hoping that among the many people entering the park, one of them would be her Mehdi.

---

20   http://www.state.gov/g/tip/rls/tiprpt/2009/123132.htm.

21   http://www.huffingtonpost.com/reporters-uncensored/irans-dark-secret-child-p_b_262222.html.

22   Ibid.

She looked at her juice box that she had purchased the day before at the bus terminal in Kermān before taking a sip. Memories of the days before began to play as she stared back at the shiny beverage box. The sound of her father smashing through the locked door of the small basement of her two-story house while she and Mehdi made love resonated in her head. It must have been her younger sister, she thought, who had told her father of the ten-month romance between the two eighteen-year-olds. Fuming mad, her father cursed and smacked Parisa in the face before nearly throwing his naked daughter out of the basement and into the small yard boxed in by tall walls. He then took on Mehdi, producing a barrage of punches and slaps onto the skinny boy that could be heard from the yard.

As her younger sister looked from the second-floor window, a teary-eyed Parisa desperately tried to cover her naked body as she ran back into the basement and began to plead with her father to leave Mehdi alone. Pushing his daughter away at first as he pinned down a bloody Mehdi, he then stood up, took Parisa by her petite shoulders, and shouted in tears that she was no longer his daughter and was to leave his house, or he would treat her in the same manner that he had Mehdi.

Crying while her hand draped over her breasts and her other hand covered her private area, Parisa ran into her bedroom, quickly got dressed, and briefly packed a few articles of clothes in her school bag before leaving her house. Her father stood in the yard by the opened doors as he stared down at the ground, avoiding his daughter, who sobbed as she helped carry the beaten and bloodied Mehdi out of the house.

After Mehdi was bandaged up in the only clinic in town, he told her that they should run away to Tehran and live in the big city, away from their parents and the eyes of the people of their small town. He promised her that he would get a job working for his cousin, who had a furniture shop in Tehran, and along with a bus ticket to Tehran, Mehdi gave her his cousin's phone number; he said he would allow them to temporarily stay with him. He then instructed her to go on ahead of him and ensured her that he would get on the next bus and meet her the following afternoon at the park in the center of Tehran as soon as he got hold of some money owed to him by his employer.

The afternoon was nearing its end as she kept glancing at her Disney-themed wristwatch and took the last remaining sip from the juice box. She bit down on the thin straw and squinted again at the large gates of the park. She called the number that Mehdi had given her, but the stranger who answered said that the person she was looking for did not live at that number. She glanced at her watch again; it was half past four as chilling winds blew against her side and over her black scarf tightly tied under her chin. Things would have been different had her mother still been alive, she thought. Her mother could have reasoned with her father, who hadn't been the same ever since their mother passed away from cancer three years ago and left him raising their four children.

"He's late, isn't he?" a strange girl asked from the park bench across the narrow way from her; Parisa raised her head while thoughts of the days before throbbed in her head.

"I'm sorry?" Parisa asked back as she finally noticed the girl sitting across from her.

"Your boyfriend ... he's late, right?" the stranger asked as she got up from her seat and sat down next to Parisa. Strands of her blonde dyed hair were visible under her head scarf as Parisa slowly shifted away from her and toward the edge of the park bench.

"Relax," the girl said, "I've been sitting here for the past half hour looking at you. You're in love, don't deny it." She giggled as Parisa looked away and back at the park gates.

"Listen, I don't want any trouble," Parisa replied. "I'm just sitting here, just trying to ... enjoy the park, that's all." Parisa looked over her shoulder again before fastening her head scarf.

The girl next to her broke into laughter.

"Trouble? Do I look like an undercover disciplinary officer to you?" she laughed as Parisa eyed the girl's pouting red lips; she guessed the girl to be around the same age as her.

"You're not from around here," she said while still giggling; Parisa shook her head in response. "I could tell; you're covered in black from head to toe, girl. No one dresses like that around here unless they're from outta town or a *hezbollahee* [regime supporter/religious zealot]." Parisa glanced at her attire and then at the clothes of her bench mate.

While living in her small town, she had heard that girls in Tehran wore tighter, colorful, and fashionable overcoats along with short scarves, unlike the traditional standards that covered only about half of their hair. She also noticed the girl's open-toe shoes, along with a pair of wrinkle-patterned jeans. Parisa could also smell her perfume and noticed her long pink nails, big lashes, and heavy makeup that went with her dyed hair.

"I mean, don't get me wrong, you just need ... more fashionable clothes, that's all. Heck, I wish I had big hazel eyes like yours and that body ... damn, girl, you kinda look like J-Lo ... you know, Jennifer Lopez," the girl added as she pointed toward Parisa's curvy figure. Parisa cracked a smile while she glanced down and imagined the Latino pop star, whose picture she had only seen twice before.

"There you go ... now isn't that a beautiful smile? Like I said, you've got to relax, girl, this is Tehran, boys and girls date and fall in love all the time."

The girl extended her hand toward Parisa and said, "My name Farima."

"I'm Parisa," she replied as she shook her hand and flashed a tiny grin.

"So where are you from, Parisa? It has to be south of here, cause you're far too tanned than most girls here." Farima reached into her leather purse and took out a pack of long and thin cigarettes before lighting one.

"I'm from a small town in Kermān," Parisa replied as she stared at the red lipstick print on the filter of the thin cigarette.

"So what brings you to Tehran?" Farima asked in between puffs.

"Well, it's kinda complicated," Parisa answered as she turned her head and glanced at the gates momentarily before staring at the dirt and dust beneath her tattered black shoes.

"You can tell me, I mean unless you don't wanna talk to me. I'm sorry if I'm taking your time," Farima said as she dropped her cigarette and twisted her foot over it.

"No, it's not like that. I've actually been dying to talk to someone my own age. It's just that I don't want you to judge me," Parisa replied as she continued to stare at the ground while Farima pulled herself even closer to Parisa and nodding in agreement that she would not judge her.

Parisa began by telling her bench mate about how she and Mehdi grew up together and spent their preteen years as playmates before their friendship blossomed into a romance which was subsequently shattered by her father. Parisa went on to describe how Mehdi and her made a promise to escape to Tehran and begin their new lives in the big city, where Mehdi would work in order to provide for them while Parisa went to school in the hopes of finally graduating from high school and enrolling in college. She also mentioned that the number that Mehdi had given her seemed to be a wrong number. With one eyebrow raised, Farima asked for the number and called it with her cell phone. Once again, the person who answered ensured Farima that the person she was looking for did not exist in the establishment that she had called. After getting off the phone, Farima persuaded Parisa to call Mehdi's house and inquire whether he had left or not. Farima also ensured her that she would bear the cost of the long distance; she just wanted to help out a person in need. Reluctant and unsure at first, Parisa took Farima's cell phone and called Mehdi's residence. Her jaw dropped and her eyes opened wide as Mehdi himself answered the phone.

He told Parisa that after suffering the beat-down at the hands of her father, he no longer wanted to have anything to do with her and while getting bandaged up in the town's clinic, he came up with the idea about them running away together to Tehran and gave her a bus ticket along with a fake number in order to get her out of his hair. He further added that despite her having strong feelings for him, she was nothing but a sexual experience to him and someone that he had already forgotten. Parisa cried and pleaded for him to come to Tehran and help her out, but he hung up the phone.

Nearly dropping the phone, Parisa wrapped her arms around her sides, leaned over, and cried. The wind struck against her cold cheeks as warm tears dripped down her face while Farima put her arm over Parisa. There was a piercing pain in her stomach as she wrapped her hands tighter around her sides while the sound of her basement door crashing open began to pound in her head again. Her stomach began to growl as the sentiments of being abandoned produced a bitter taste that washed up in the back of her throat. The empty juice box lay next to her feet, as her tears hit the dust and dirt of the park's gravely walkway. Farima offered her a napkin and wrapped her hand around the crying Parisa while repeatedly telling her that love was meaningless and that all men were slime and only good for giving women money.

Once Parisa stopped crying, Farima informed her that she lived with her aunt, who was only three years older than her, in an apartment not too far from the park. Farima invited Parisa to stay with her and her aunt until she figured out what she wanted to do. Reluctant at first, as the stereotypes of people from Tehran preying on small-town folk like her swirled around her mind, Parisa finally accepted the offer; the two left the park and headed toward Farima's apartment.

The two sat down to dinner as Farima described more about herself and her auntie; Parisa listened and gobbled the delivered fast food. Although Farima was only two months older than Parisa, she was the picture of independence for Parisa, who over the course of that evening learned that Farima was raised by her grandmother, who took care of Farima and her young auntie Nazanin. Farima's parents had died in a car accident when she was only five. Farima and Nazanin moved in together shortly after Farima's sixteenth birthday, just a few days after her grandmother passed away. The two young women were both high school dropouts and low on funds; after shuffling through various jobs that paid very little money, they decided to sell their bodies in order to sustain themselves.

Farima told Parisa that at first she would do sexual favors for boys living in her neighborhood, while her auntie hung around university campuses and approached students and faculty members. Over the span of the following year, Farima developed a more lucrative plan, which had both girls making money by meeting clients at parties and other social functions organized through a network of people familiar to Nazanin. She suggested that Parisa join her and her aunt. The idea at first frightened Parisa, and while Farima had opened her home to Parisa, she nevertheless was very clear that once Parisa had settled down, she was to earn a living and pitch in her share of rent and other expenses, regardless of how she made her money.

After a few days, Parisa called back home, but her father refused to speak to her, let alone grant her the right to return to her small town. Failing to land any substantial employment, Parisa decided to take a closer look at what exactly Farima and Nazanin did that made them a considerable sum of money, along with gifts of jewelry and expensive clothes. Accordingly, the two took Parisa under their wing and advanced her shiny cocktail dresses, designer wear, purses, and makeup; they even took her to a salon, where the natural hazel-eyed beauty was transformed into looking like the pop star that Farima and Nazanin constantly compared her to. Nevertheless, despite showing her the way, Farima never forced Parisa into doing anything that she didn't want to do. At first, she instructed Parisa to simply observe her and her aunt and learn the tricks of the trade and only take on the occupation if she desired.

Her first night out with Farima and Nazanin was memorable for Parisa, as the three girls attended the birthday party of one of Farima's regular clients. The birthday boy ran a lucrative automobile dealership owned by his father and had his very own apartment in an upscale neighborhood north of Tehran. The party was a mix of professional people wearing the latest trends, drinking alcohol, and dancing to the most popular music of the day.

Wobbling in her new pair of high heels, the curvy brunette in a skintight, short red dress followed the two blondes wearing similar revealing outfits into the crowded room. Farima was the first to hug and kiss the host, who was dancing in the middle of the dim living room; she introduced Nazanin along with Parisa. The three then walked over toward a set of chairs and took their seats while Farima and Nazanin pouted their lips and crossed their legs slowly as nearly every man in the flat began to leer at them.

It wasn't long until Farima and Nazanin, through a series of glances, lured two men to approach them; they sparked up conversations before joining others on the dance floor.

Parisa's heart began to race as she observed her friends taking the men by their hands and reeling them onto the dance floor. Discreetly trying to look down at the hips of their female companions in their tight dresses, the men quickly fraternized with the women as the four began to dance. The girls laughed, smiled, and gazed at their potential customers. Every now and then, they leaned forward just close enough for their breasts to touch the chests of the men as they whispered in the ears of their catch before slowly rolling the tips of their tongue and wetting their lips.

Parisa breathed deeply, gently stroking her neck as she witnessed the two bubbly blondes with the men who looked to be in their midthirties. Through whispers, the two men were informed of the nature of the girls' work, and they quickly reached into their pockets and pinned the contact information of the two into their phones. Nazanin set up a rendezvous at her client's place for later that night, while Farima told her dance partner to drop by their apartment the following evening. Shortly after, Parisa joined her friends as the three girls danced, laughed, and socialized in the center of the crowd before the night came to an end.

The next night, Farima instructed Parisa to stand outside of her door and listen as she negotiated the terms of the transaction. Parisa did more than just listen to her friend haggle over her price;

she stood with her ears glued to the door, biting her lip while her friend performed her services.

Over the next few days, before Parisa decided to take the plunge, Farima went over some ground rules. She was very passionate about these rules and believed they led to more money and clients and no hassles with Tehran's disciplinary forces, which periodically rounded up women working the streets. Accordingly, her first rule was that none of the three should ever work the street. Farima considered their trade a more deluxe form of entertainment rather than just mere street walking. She believed that the art of seduction was far more lucrative and ensured repeat clients instead of working the streets, which she saw as an act of desperation that put women at the mercy of abusive clients who almost always controlled negotiations over the price.

Subsequently, the price according to Farima was firm and not subject to negotiations. The girls charged 50,000 tomans for an hour and 100,000 for the night. Bringing a client back to their own apartment added an extra 15,000 to the initial price. Using condoms was a must, and while the girls were free to drink alcohol and smoke cigarettes, especially with their clients, Farima believed they should never use drugs.

Parisa's first time was with a man nearly three times her age. She and Farima attended a wedding party in a mansion in the city of Karaj, just south of Tehran. The person who invited the girls, a divorced man, was a frequent client of Nazanin and an uncle of the bride. Wearing a long sparkling black dress with a slit running up her legs, Parisa immediately drew his attention. After briefly engaging in conversation with the luscious brunette, he discreetly paid her nearly 90,000 tomans and convinced her to take a tour of the mansion with him; they engaged in intercourse upon arriving at the first bedroom.

While not quite as seductive as she had imagined the profession to be, Parisa's transition into her new role was slow at first; she only took two clients per week. However, with every client, she learned more and more, and nearly six months into her new life, Parisa managed to build a strong reputation as a high-end call girl advertised by her clients as the closest thing to Jennifer Lopez. Her self-confidence also began to grow, as she slowly erased everything about who she had been and where she was from. The seduction became an addiction for her, while the money was more of a bonus; all seemed to go well. That was until June 2008, nearly thirteen months after her move to Tehran.

Having spent the night with one of her regular clients, Parisa returned home with a hangover and was astonished to find Farima and Nazanin at each other's throats.

"What's going on?" Parisa asked as she pushed back her head scarf and slowly rubbed her temples with her forefingers.

"Nazanin's been doing drugs behind my back," Farima said. "I just found coke and a stash of these pills in her room." She opened her palm and showed her friend the pills.

"You don't get to say what I can or can't do," Nazanin said. "I'm the eldest, and for your information, we're all a bunch of whores living here! Do you get it? Whores, not nuns!"

"Rules are rules," Farima said. "No drugs means no drugs! Just look at yourself, Nazanin, you weigh less than you did when you were fourteen!"

"It's my fucking life and my fucking body," Nazanin said, "so why don't you and your small-town whore keep your rules to yourselves and mind your own fucking business!" Nazanin grabbed hold of Farima's hand and tried to take back the pills held tightly by her niece. Parisa held onto her forehead as she watched the pills fly out of Farima's hands and scatter all over the floor. The two pulled each other's hair and clawed at their faces, and then Farima punched Nazanin in her face, knocking her back against the living room wall.

"Yeah, we're all whores here," Farima said, "and you know what whores do? They get paid, and if you're going to spend your money and time fucking drug dealers instead of paying your share of expenses, then maybe you should just leave!" A tiny stream of blood began to run down from a cut on Nazanin's lower lip.

Nazanin packed her stuff and left the apartment the following morning. Over the past three months, she had developed a relationship with a drug dealer who used Nazanin for sex and, over time, turned her into one of his customers. That day was the last time the two girls saw Nazanin. Soon after leaving Farima and Parisa, Nazanin left the country and died of a heroin overdose in a brothel in Istanbul, Turkey. Shortly after Nazanin left, things began to fall apart further. Farima broke her most important rule, and in the summer of 2008, she got pregnant by one of her clients. Fortunately for her, the man that got her pregnant was wealthy and offered to marry her and raise their child as long as she quit the lifestyle that she was in.

Alone and all by herself, Parisa decided to move out and rent her own place in Tehran's posh and swanky Jordan Avenue. Although she had built up her own set of clients, Parisa stopped attending parties, and with Farima long gone, she decided to work the streets, taking only a handful of clients per week while increasing her rates to 65,000 per customer. Her territory was her neighborhood, which consisted of luxurious businesses and offices, consulates, and diplomatic bureaus, along with upper-class apartments. Similarly, her clients belonged to those establishments, and unlike what Farima had described, working on the streets, at least in her new surroundings, was hassle free, and given Parisa's stunning features, none of her clients ever haggled with her over her price.

Parisa walked the length of the street, attracting drivers who would usually pound on their brakes once they got a look at Parisa. They would chat her up about her costs before picking her up and driving to her place. This was her routine four evenings a week.

This was the case, until one fateful evening in September, when Parisa was arrested by a plainclothes member of Tehran's disciplinary forces. The weather was pleasant as she walked outside of her apartment in her tight capri jeans, a pair of short-heeled open-toed shoes, her favorite tight cream overcoat, and designer sunglasses, all topped off by a bright pink headscarf. She walked toward the main street, stood on the sidewalk, and observed the oncoming cars driving in the evening rush hour. It wasn't too long before a convertible BMW drove up in the lane close to her. She smiled and waved to the driver.

The man slowed down before pulling to the side of the street. Parisa bent over the car's window and asked the man for a ride. Snickering, the man responded and asked her if it was possible for him to take a ride instead, at which point Parisa lowered her sunglasses and winked at him. She opened the car's door, but before she could get in, two men grabbed her shoulders and yanked her back toward the sidewalk before showing Parisa their identification.

Her eyes nearly popped out of their sockets as she glared at the officer's identification; the other man slapped a pair of handcuffs on her. She was informed that the two undercover officers had been monitoring her routine for the past weeks and were waiting for the perfect opportunity to catch her in the act.

Parisa was taken to a disciplinary forces precinct, where the officers took her picture and fingerprints. They then took Parisa and several other young prostitutes to a long and narrow room that was furnished with several chairs, only a few feet away from a dark-colored desk which faced the chairs.

The officer sitting behind the desk ordered the young women to take their seats as he began to call their names. From what Parisa could see, there was a mix of young and middle-aged women; they sat silently with their heads down, while some of them wept quietly. Some were wearing the latest trends, while others were dressed in more ordinary attire.

Shortly after the officer recited their names, a mullah arrived at the office with a young armed soldier. He wore traditional cleric gear of white garments under a tanned body robe, with a white turban and thick glasses. The mullah swiftly moved in between the women and the dark desk; he closely observed the women, who had grown even quieter as soon as he arrived. Parisa stared at the floor and dug her nails into her palms. With his thick glasses sitting on his nose, the short and portly mullah began to stare at her.

"Were all of them brought in today?" the mullah asked the officer as he slowly stroked his dark beard.

"Yes, *Haj Agha* [the title usually given to clerics and men who complete the pilgramage to Mecca]," the officer answered.

"My, my ... they seem to be getting younger every day," the mullah said, staring at the women.

"Yes, *Haj Agha*; this one over here is only sixteen years old," the officer replied as he pointed to a teary-eyed girl sitting to Parisa's left.

"My God! Sixteen! Have you no shame, girl? Have you no fear of God's wrath?" the mullah shouted as he took a few steps and leaned over the girl, who began to howl and cry while the scent of rose water and body odor generating from the mullah hit Parisa's nostrils.

"Are there any repeat offenders?" the mullah further asked after he walked back toward the desk while still eyeballing the women. The officer shuffled through a set of files.

"Just one, her name is Sanam Yavarry. This is her third time this year, *Haj Agha*," the officer reported.

"Third time?" the mullah shouted again as he yanked the file from the officer and smacked the crying woman over the head with it.

"Please, *Haj Agha*! No one will hire me, and I have a four-year-old child to feed," the woman cried as she got down on her knees.

"Shut up, you whore! Don't you dare talk about your child!" he shouted. "Your child should be cursing you with every breath that he takes, just like how God and the angels are cursing you right now, all of you!" The mullah leaned down and shouted in the woman's face, who continued to cry as most of the other women started to join in.

"Have your men transport her to the women's prison after administering the ninety lashes; her prison sentence is for one month; also make sure that she has her child with her in prison; maybe that will teach her to stop living a life of sin and temptation," the mullah ordered. The officer behind the desk approached the door and called two other officers into the room while the woman screamed and clung to the mullah's legs, begging him for mercy. Nearly kicking her, the mullah shoved the howling woman away as the two officers dragged her out of the room before closing the door behind them. Parisa kept staring at the floor as the woman continued to scream outside of the door. The cries began to get louder in the room as Parisa tightened her fist, nearly piercing the skin of her palm with her long nails while tears began to run down over her makeup and her face.

"What's her name?" the mullah asked, referring to Parisa.

"Parisa, Parisa Sadeeqpour," the officer replied as Parisa bit down hard on her teeth. Her eyes stared at the floor as she heard the sound of her basement door shattering.

"This is her first time," the officer said, "and according to her national ID card, she is from Lale Zaar Kermān."

"You're a long way from home, girl," the mullah said. "Does your father know what you're doing here?" The mullah squinted as he stared at Parisa, who slowly lifted her head.

"No, *Haj Agha*," she said, "my father doesn't speak to me anymore." Parisa spoke quietly as the mullah raised his eyebrows in reaction.

"Very well," he said. "Then perhaps we should send you to jail too, that is, after you have had your thirty lashes, seeing that it is your first time."

"Please, *Haj Agha*! Please don't send me to jail, have mercy. I'll do anything! I'll go back to my town! I'll give up prostituting!" Parisa shrieked as she fell to the ground while the mullah raised one of his eyebrows and smirked.

"We're going to do God's work and return you to your father," the mullah said, "but that is after administering thirty lashes." The mullah signaled to the armed soldier, who hauled the sobbing girl out of the room.

The soldier escorted Parisa outside of the precinct and put her into the backseat of an old military SUV. The mullah followed slightly behind them and got into a sedan, keeping an eye on Parisa the entire time. To her surprise, the soldier didn't use handcuffs on her and drove to a four-story building not too far from the precinct. Parisa was not familiar with the area but knew it was an upper middle-class neighborhood in which mostly families lived. The soldier parked the car and ordered the confused Parisa to get out. He led her up the stairs and into the last unit on the fourth floor of the apartment building.

"You should take a shower before he arrives," the soldier said shortly after they entered the slightly furnished unit.

"Before who arrives?" Parisa asked.

"The mullah from the precinct," the soldier answered as Parisa's eyes grew wide. With the air in her lungs restrained, she stood motionless as the sound of the basement door being smashed in played in her head over and over again.

"I know that it must be hard for you to understand," he said, "but you don't have much time. He likes his girls clean, so take a shower and put on some clothes. There is a closet in the other room." The soldier pointed to the only bedroom in the apartment.

"You mean … that sick dirty fuck is going to rape me?" Parisa asked, raising her voice as tears ran down her face.

"Hey, keep your voice down," he said as Parisa began to breathe heavily.

"If you don't do as he says, then it'll be all over for you. He'll make your life a living hell; I've seen it before. Just do as he wants and hopefully it'll all be over soon," the soldier said. "Just don't do anything stupid. He's not the kind of person you want to screw with. Do as he says, and if you're lucky, it will be just this once and he'll let you go. Look, I'll be right outside the door if you need anything."

"If it's any consolation, you're not the first one," the soldier added before stepping outside of the unit and waiting behind the door.

Breathing heavily, Parisa moved quickly through the unit. She saw a balcony and hoped there was an emergency staircase; she looked for another way out, only to arrive at the miserable realization that there was none. Her cell phone and purse, along with all her credentials, had been taken from her upon arrest. She opened up the kitchen window and stared down at the distance between her and the ground. She wanted to scream but the images of a thick rubbery whip smacking against her naked and bloody body set off alarms in her mind; she collapsed to her knees and placed her hands over her head.

With the smell of rose water and the mullah's body odor still stinging her nostrils, Parisa ran into the bathroom and vomited into the sink. She turned on the taps and washed her face before staring at her reflection through the mirror. Although she was a prostitute, she had never taken on an undesirable client like the mullah. She stared at her reflection as water began to fill the sink. She prayed that her encounter with the mullah would indeed be just this once like the soldier told her.

Having showered, Parisa wrapped a towel around herself and went into the bedroom. She opened the closet and discovered a few pieces of cheap yet clean lingerie that she put on, and then she lay down on the bed and waited for the mullah to arrive. He soon entered the apartment and slowly took off his clothes. Parisa looked the other way while the taste of vomit rose in her throat.

While Parisa did not share much of the details about her first time with the mullah, she recalled that after having sex, she rushed to the bathroom and vomited again.

One thing that was clear was that the mullah had taken a shine to Parisa, and despite her payers that he would grant her forgiveness after the raunchy encounter, the mullah demanded that she take part in a temporary marriage (*sigheh*) for the period of one year, during which Parisa was to come back to the apartment upon the mullah's request; she was also forbidden from working as a prostitute. The mullah in return granted Parisa ten million tomans (roughly US$10,000) along with paying her rent and expenses, while he ensured that she would not receive any jail time or lashes for her prostitution charges. For her own protection, Parisa did not disclose much information about the mullah; she would only say that he was an important clerical figure in Tehran, he was in his late forties, and he had a wife and three children.

Nearly every time that she went over to the apartment, the mullah would warn her that if she ever mentioned their indiscretions to anyone, her fate would be much worse than prison and lashings. In addition, the mullah held onto Parisa's passport, her national ID card, and her other identification, promising to return them at the end of the year.

He also kept an eye on Parisa during this entire time, through having different armed soldiers randomly park at the front of her apartment building. She also suspected that he had her cell phone monitored and listened in on her phone calls.

Time passed slowly and painfully as Parisa found herself a sex slave to the mullah. She grew to hate him, and about nine months into her forced temporary marriage, her hate magnified as the mullah began calling her four or five times a day; he also insisted that she ask for his permission before leaving her apartment to do even trivial things like grocery shopping. Parisa began to feel extremely depressed; she often went to the balcony of her apartment and contemplated jumping off her third-story balcony. Her entire life seemed to evolve around spending time in the two apartments.

Her life, however, went from bad to worse when Parisa found out that she was pregnant. The mullah refused to use contraception, and he at first denied that the child was his, but he soon accepted it once Parisa threatened to reach out to his family. Despite the fact that abortion is illegal in Iran and punished through harsh prison terms, the mullah had Parisa taken to a shady doctor who performed the makeshift procedure.

Parisa did not object to the abortion and welcomed the procedure, even going as far as telling the mullah that the last thing she wanted to do was give birth to his offspring. Nevertheless, the pregnancy and abortion only added to Parisa's depression, which often found her getting into loud physical confrontations with the mullah, who she had scratched a few times, while he always retaliated by knocking her to the floor before forcing himself on her. While she had picked up a casual smoking habit from Farima during her first few months in Tehran, Parisa found herself smoking up to two packs a day. Even more dangerous, Parisa began to slash and cut her arm using a kitchen knife, which terrified the mullah. He finally had enough and revoked the marriage contact, two months shorter than the initial terms.

To further distance himself, the mullah informed Parisa that a relative of his owned a corporation in Dubai and was looking to hire a few secretaries for his offices there. He ensured Parisa that she would have a job at the corporation, at least temporarily, and returned her passport and identification. He also obtained a tourist visa for her along with a plane ticket to the United Arab Emirates.

Chapter 7.
Parisa: The Escape

The prospect of starting fresh in a new city with a job that didn't require her to sell her body delighted Parisa. A few days before leaving Tehran, she purchased a new wardrobe, which consisted of office suits, collared shirts, and sensible shoes. While she was getting on the plane in Tehran, Parisa felt like she was in a fairy tale that was approaching its happy ending. She had never been on a plane before in her life and chatted up the lady next to her about the wonderful job she was about to start while constantly displaying a radiant smile. Once her plane landed and she collected her suitcase, Parisa headed to the women's lavatory and inspected her makeup and outfit; she was wearing a black three-button suit and black silk pants with a pair of shiny black stilettos. She then headed over to the area designated for passenger pickup, just as the mullah had instructed her.

Smiling the entire time, she looked through the crowd and soon noticed a man holding up a sign with her name written on it. The mullah had told her that she would be working for a man by the name of Jamal. Parisa approached the man with the sign.

"Hello, I'm Parisa," she said. It's such a pleasure to meet you, Mr. Jamal." Parisa extended her hand toward the man while smiling.

"Okay, just follow me," the man replied, ignoring Parisa's hand as he turned around and strode quickly ahead of her. Parisa looked on with her mouth open as her hand laid in midair before she quickly grabbed hold of her suitcase and rolled after the man, wobbling in her heels as she tried to catch up to him.

From what she could tell, based on the man's accent, he was from Tehran, and judging by his scruffy beard and hair, along with his T-shirt, Parisa immediately assumed that he was a driver for the corporation and certainly not her employer.

The man waited outside of the terminal as Parisa caught up with him. He walked slowly up to Parisa and two other women standing on the sidewalk.

"Passports!" the man demanded as he flapped his right hand toward the three women. Parisa glanced at his hand before looking at the other two women with her eyebrows raised.

"Passports!" he repeated. "Give me passport!" the man said, raising his voice and speaking in broken English, as the women immediately reached into their purses and handed their passports to the skinny, scruffy man. As soon as he collected the passports, he walked the three women to the parking area and ordered them to get into a big SUV before taking his seat next to the driver of the vehicle.

Unlike the Iranian man, the driver of the vehicle looked to Parisa to be of eastern European origin, as did the other two blonde girls, who sat quietly next to Parisa while wearing the same type of outfit.

As the SUV drove away from the airport, Parisa stared at the desert sands; she felt despair crawl up her body and wrap around her neck. She berated herself heavily as she began to envision the worst: the nightmare of becoming a sex slave yet again. The worst part was that she had trusted the mullah, who she pictured to be laughing at her expense as he probably preyed on another poor girl. She cursed him and imagined stalking up on him with a knife while he lay naked in bed, unsuspecting. Her arms swung wildly as his blood oozed out and ran down the knife and her arm while staining her sneering face. She imagined him screaming and begging her for mercy, but instead she would deliver the final coup de grâce and end her misery. But she wasn't there, in fact she was nowhere, and the familiar feelings she had sitting on the park bench just a few years ago swept over her.

The drive was not long, and shortly after leaving the airport, the SUV arrived at a hotel just off the main highway. The driver and the Iranian man ordered the girls to get out of the vehicle, and the group entered the hotel, which was ten stories high. While it did not bear the more famous hotel trademarks and stars, it was nevertheless more than modest and offered rooms to mostly South Asian businessmen and guests who preferred to stay closer to the airport.

The two men led the women past the hotel bar and up an elevator to the seventh floor, where each girl was given her own room. Still praying that she had not suffered the worst, Parisa followed the Iranian man into her room.

"This is your room," the man said. "You must only bring back clients to this room; the price is one hundred American dollars for an hour. If you need clothes or anything else, just let me know and I'll get them for you. You are not to leave this hotel. Do you understand?" He raised his voice as Parisa dug her nails into her palm while a single tear ran down her face.

"But I was told that I'd be working at an office!" Parisa insisted as she wiped away the tear.

"I don't give a shit what you were told," he said, "I paid that fat bastard $10,000 and I'm not letting you go until I make a profit on my investment!"

Parisa put her head down and began to sob.

"So don't think about keeping a penny from me until your debt has been paid," he continued, "and if you think I'm fucking around, just try to disobey me, bitch." The man reached into his pocket and pulled out a knife. Parisa stared at it as the sound of a blade snapping open pierced up her spine.

"I will cut you up and sell every last bit of your organs!" he continued as he gently slapped Parisa on the cheek with the thick side of the blade, while she quivered and slowly dropped her head, weeping quietly.

"And don't even think about running to the cops, bitch. They will just deport your ass back to Iran, where my associate will be waiting for you. He will make sure that your debt is paid, and don't forget, I've got your passport." He took out her passport from his back pocket and waved it in the air.

"Now take a shower and put on some sexy clothes and makeup. Your job is to chat up the men in the hotel bar and do everything in your power to bring them back here. Do you understand?"

Parisa quietly nodded while her tears covered her face. Locking the hotel door behind her, Parisa sat on the edge of the bed and broke down as tears gushed out of her eyes in a thick stream. It seemed that she had swapped one hell for another.

After coming to the realization that her best chance of returning to Iran was to pay off the money she owed the pimp, Parisa put on short and revealing clothes and headed to the hotel's bar. Ironically, in a country where adultery is a serious offense and couples face jail time for public displays of affection such as kissing, Dubai seemed to have turned a complete blind eye toward prostitution, as it is estimated that Dubai alone had nearly 30,000 imported prostitutes.[23]

Like the other thousands of sex workers in Dubai, Parisa's clients were mainly Pakistani, Indian, and other South Asian businessmen. Given the high number of tourists, Parisa found herself taking on as many as five clients per night, and while she made the pimp a lot of money, Parisa nevertheless cried herself to sleep every night, and as the days and weeks passed, her despair only deepened.

The thoughts of escape were pointless as she observed the men belonging to the outfit stationed at the front lobby day and night, where they kept an eye on who was entering and leaving the hotel. Her only true hope was to make the amount owed to the pimp and return back to Tehran. Parisa even kept a ledger and documented

---

23   http://www.guardian.co.uk/world/2010/may/16/dubai-sex-tourism -prostitution.

the number of clients she took and the amount of money she gave to the pimp each night. By her estimation, she would have paid the sum (along with interest) in nearly one year and could return to Iran by the end of 2010, nearly fifteen months after her arrival.

Her only inspiration and companionship during this difficult time was another Iranian prostitute by the name of Shiva, who also worked in the same hotel. The two women became friends, and when she felt that she could trust Parisa, Shiva told her compatriot her story. Shiva was twenty-five years old, she was from Tehran, and she had been working in Dubai as a prostitute for over three years. Similar to Parisa, Shiva was also a victim of sex trafficking; she had been promised a job as a personal caretaker to an elderly woman in Dubai by a man in Tehran, who claimed to be a job recruiter.

Once Shiva arrived in Dubai, she found out that the recruiter had sold her to the outfit for around the same price that Parisa was purchased. Although she put up a fight upon realizing her doom, her resistance was met with brute force; she was raped and beaten the entire first week by the same man that threatened Parisa with a knife. Shiva decided to stay in Dubai and work, even after paying her debt. She felt ashamed of herself and didn't know how she could face her family back in Iran.

She did, however, send back home whatever small amount of money the pimp would let her keep. Wearing a warm smile on her face, Shiva often joked and reminded Parisa that people like them go through hell in this lifetime just so they can go to heaven in the next. Her room was a few doors down from Parisa's, and the girls would often spend time comforting each other during their off hours. Shiva even taught Parisa a bit of English that she could use in speaking with clients.

After a few months of working at the hotel and through Shiva's influence, the pimp even let Parisa go outside of the hotel, to nightclubs and other attractions, in order to bring back more clients. One night, six months after arriving in Dubai, Shiva visited Parisa's room and the two began to talk.

"The son of a bitch didn't even give me my $20 for today; slow day, my ass. I took on two clients today for God's sake!" Shiva said, sitting on the edge of Parisa's bed as she took off her heels and rubbed her feet.

"At least the bastard gives you money here and there," Parisa replied while sitting in front of a mirror as she removed her makeup.

"How much more do you have to work to pay off the rest of the money?" Shiva asked as she looked at her friend.

"I don't know, maybe another year," Parisa replied.

"You should do what I do," Shiva said. "Every time you have more than three clients, just pay the pimp for the first three. Those assholes are so wound up about making sure we don't escape that they lose count of a client here and there. Trust me on this one, these bastards take our hard-earned money plus they get paid by the hotel for bringing them customers. It's only fair that we take a little off the top," Shiva added.

"The hotel pays them too?" Parisa asked, raising her eyebrows.

"Of course the hotel pays them, this whole country is built on blowjobs and happy endings," Shiva answered.

"You can get a ticket for spitting on the sidewalk here, but it is perfectly moral for an Arab sheikh to walk around with a flock of girls who are all in their teens," Shiva said; she shook her head and lay on the bed while her feet curled over the edge.

Parisa continued to remain silent.

"Just look around us, here in this hotel: Chinese, Thai, and Georgian girls, and the more expensive hotels, Russian, Polish, and Ukrainian girls; all sex workers. You think that they all got up one morning and decided that they wanted to be whores and service a bunch of Indian, Pakistani, Arab, and assholes from other countries just because they get a kick out of it?"

Shiva stared at the ceiling of the room as she continued.

"No, Parisa, we're not here because we like being whores. All of us are here either because we were tricked or because we're desperate and need to send quick money back to our homes. If you want my advice, scam as much money as you can from these bastards and leave this fucking place and never look back." Shiva continued to stare at the ceiling as Parisa turned around on her seat and glanced at her reflection through the mirror.

There were no guarantees that the pimp would let her leave even when she had paid back her debt. Shiva's advice made all the sense in the world to her. All she had to do was take enough money to buy herself a plane ticket back to Tehran plus a little more to last her for a few weeks while she got back on her feet.

Over the span of the next few months, Parisa began to save up unnoticeable sums of money that she received from her clients; Shiva hid the cash for Parisa in her room. She had managed to pay back nearly all of her debt and saved up around $2,500. One day, after asking the pimp's permission to go shopping, Parisa finally escaped. She took a cab to the airport, where she met Shiva, who had arrived by herself so as not to arouse the suspicions of the pimp. She had brought with her the money that she was hiding for Parisa, along with her own passport.

"I can't believe you're leaving," Shiva said as the two girls hugged.

"You don't have to stay here. Leave with me, Shiva," Parisa said.

"There is nothing there for me in Iran," Shiva replied. "Those fucking mullahs are worse than the Arabs; at least here I can be a whore while dressing like one too." The two friends laughed and smiled in between the tears that continued to wash down their faces.

"I'm going to miss you, Shiva. I couldn't have made it without your help," Parisa said as the two gazed at each other while still embracing.

"You get out of here and never come back, you hear me? You get out of this life while you can, promise me?" Shiva pulled Parisa toward herself and hugged her while Parisa nodded in tears.

Saying her farewells, Parisa headed to the ticket kiosk, where the attendant inspected her passport before finally allowing her to purchase a ticket and board the plane. She had a window seat next to an elderly Iranian man, who had noticed her teary and red eyes.

"Is everything all right, my girl?" the elderly man asked.

"Yes, thank you for asking. I am just happy that I'm headed back home," Parisa answered while she wiped away her eyes using the sleeves of her overcoat, which she had put on along with her head scarf, due to Iranair's mandatory clothing protocols.

"I don't even know why our people bother to come to this scorching rock in the middle of nowhere," the man said. If it wasn't for my son and grandchild, I wouldn't bother to set foot here or spend my money." He offered Parisa a tissue. "Forgive me, my dear," he continued. "I don't want to be prying, but I take it that you came here for work?"

"I got ... I mean, I was supposed to get a job as a secretary working for some corporation, but I guess you can say that it didn't turn out the way I wanted it to," Parisa responded as she took the tissue and wiped her eyes and cheeks.

"Well, I'm not sure what you have planned back in Tehran, but if you're still looking for a job, my daughter is a lawyer in Tehran, and she is looking for a secretary. Mind you, it's only modest pay and nothing fancy, but it's honest work, and I believe you will find her to be more than fair," the elderly man said.

"Take your time, dear, and think about it," he said. "You can let me know once we get to Tehran, or better yet, I can give you her business card and you can call her yourself." He reached into his pocket and handed a business card to Parisa.

"Thank you so much," she said. "I don't know what to say. I guess there are still good people living in Iran," Parisa replied as she stared at the business card.

"Our people have always been good; it's this damn regime that has tainted our morals," the elderly man whispered.

After the plane landed in Tehran, Parisa made her way to Farima and her husband's apartment, where she stayed until she could find her own place to live. She also looked up the daughter of the kind elderly man on the plane. The lawyer gave her the job, and Parisa went to work for a modest salary. But the cost of living and the rampant inflation in Tehran left her with next to nothing in spite of working a second job at a boutique. Although she hates the idea of returning to work as a prostitute, Parisa told me that she might have to just to earn enough money to live on.

She wished that in the future, and under a much reformed society, life could be easier, where fathers and daughters could communicate and place greater trust in one another and that sex education is provided to teenagers all over the country. She further hoped that in the future, shelters and social services are provided for girls who run away from their homes or have been mentally or physically abused. Lastly, Parisa hoped that people like the mullah who abused her and other government officials are brought to justice for the crimes that they have committed against the people of Iran.

Chapter 8.
Siavash: The Troubling Secret

~~~ᗡᗡᗡ~~~

In September 2007, while attending a meeting of the United Nations General Assembly, Iran's President Mahmoud Ahmadinejad decided to add a new number to his repertoire of insane controversy. Appearing as a guest speaker at New York's Columbia University, Ahmadinejad stated that there were no homosexuals in Iran.[24] Later, however, his spokesman indicated that his comments were misunderstood.[25] According to the spokesman, what Ahmadinejad meant to say was that compared to American society, Iran didn't have many homosexuals.[26] Of course, compared to the North American society, there are lots of things Iran, under the Islamic Republic, lacks. Two of most notable absences are fundamental freedoms and basic human rights. As of 2011, there are six states in America that grant same-sex marriage licenses,[27] and in Canada, same-sex marriages were legalized in 2005 nationwide with the introduction of the Civil Marriages

---

24 http://www.cnn.com/2007/US/09/24/us.iran/.

25 http://www.foxnews.com/story/0,2933,301043,00.html.

26 Ibid.

27 http://www.freedomtomarry.org/states/.

Act.[28] In addition, Section 15 of the Canadian Charter of Rights and Freedoms provides protection against discrimination based on the grounds of sexual orientation.[29]

In Iran, on the other hand, homosexuality is not only forbidden, it is punished by imprisonment, corporal punishment, and even execution under the Islamic penal system.[30] Ironically, it has been widely reported that the state, along with its officials, has been using sodomy and rape as tools of punishment against activists and demonstrators for years. This form of punishment was said to have been used especially against activists who were jailed in the aftermath of the highly controversial presidential election, which was followed by mass demonstrations. Additionally, in June 2011, an article in the *Guardian* indicated that the Islamic Republic had gone as far as to distribute condoms to criminals in jails, encouraging them to systematically rape the activists who were imprisoned.[31] Sadly, just a few days before finishing the first draft of this book, there was a report from Iran's state-run news agency that three men were executed for engaging in sodomy and acts that are against the Sharia laws of the country.[32] Refer to the appendix for more information on homosexuality in Iran.

While researching this topic, I was only able to interview four gay men living in Tehran. Although my sources indicated that there are a fair amount of homosexuals living in Tehran, the lack of interviewees was attributed to the terrors of coming out and subsequently becoming a target of the regime. In addition, the four men that I interviewed for this book all indicated that homosexuals in Iran face a systemic shame that has confined

28   http://www.nytimes.com/2005/06/29/world/americas/29iht-web.0629canada.html.

29   http://laws-lois.justice.gc.ca/eng/charter/.

30   http://www.independent.co.uk/news/world/middle-east/brutal-land-where-homosexuality-is-punishable-by-death-792057.html.

31   http://www.huffingtonpost.com/2011/06/24/iran-distributing-condoms-criminals-rape-activists-jail-_n_883949.html.

32   http://www.huffingtonpost.com/2011/09/06/gay-men-hanged_n_951162.html.

them from ever discussing their sexuality. As a result of this, most homosexuals try to blend in with what society considers the norm or live a life of complete solitude.

Out of the four men, two of them are married to women, while the other two men live with their parents, keeping their homosexuality a secret while at the same time struggling to deal with the constant pressures of their parents, who are trying to persuade them to marry.

This story is about Siavash Omrani, who is twenty-six years old and a graduate student at Azad University in Tehran. Like all males in Iran, Siavash attended all-boys' schools until university, where he endured years of sexual and gender confusion and hoped that his feelings toward the same sex would eventually disappear. More importantly, for his own sake, Siavash hoped such feelings would soon disappear due to the religious orthodoxy of his family and his father in particular, who was a decorated war hero. Mr. Omrani also served as deputy to one of the ministers of the Iranian Parliament. In addition to being a Hajji (a title usually given to holy men who complete the Haj), Siavash's father was also a regular contributor to the neighborhood mosque, which he attended on a daily basis. His mother also placed a great deal of importance on religion, as she often hosted special prayer ceremonies and fundraisers at their residence. Nevertheless, Siavash was always frightened by the orthodoxy of his father and despised having to do his mandatory military training. Unfortunately for him, his education was coming to an end, and his father had given him an ultimatum that once he had received his master's degree, he had no other option but to join the army and then start a family.

Desperately seeking the approval of his family and out of the fear of bringing shame to them (or even worse, having his family disown him), during Siavash's freshmen year, he attempted to pursue women romantically. He often invited female classmates to coffee shops and restaurants, and even though he managed to establish a relationship with one (to whom he later lost his virginity), no matter how hard Siavash tried to establish the relationship, he could never find himself attracted to a woman.

Along with nightly prayers for waking up one day and being "cured" of the feelings and desires he had for other men, Siavash began facing an identity crisis, which resulted in manic depression and thoughts of suicide. By the time he reached the third year of his undergraduate studies, his mental state had deteriorated, and he suffered a breakdown, causing severe weight loss and anxiety attacks. He sought professional help and began visiting a psychologist. After a few sessions, the psychologist determined that Siavash was indeed homosexual; knowing about the status and position of his father, the psychologist refused to continue treating Siavash. He was extremely sympathetic to Siavash but was concerned about the punitive measures of the state against homosexuality, especially given the sensitive nature of his father's line of work. But before discharging Siavash, he reassured him that he was not the only person to experience such feelings and recommended that Siavash should try to seek the company of men who were in the same situation as he was. Soon after that, Siavash began seeing a fellow computer science student by the name of Behnam.

—⟶ᴍᴠ⟵—

They had just finished making love, and Siavash got out of bed and put on his jeans and a white T-shirt along with his glasses. For a long moment, he gazed at Behnam, who glanced back at him with a smile as he rested his head underneath his arm. Contentment filled Siavash as he walked onto the balcony of Behnam's apartment with a cup of homemade wine. He looked out at the city sprawling before him, a mix of low-rise and tall apartments, all clashing in a strange yet beautiful melody of steel and concrete. In a little while, the call to prayers would reverberate off the facades of nearby buildings, but for the time being, only the white noise of a busy city reached him: the hum of traffic, the wail of a distant siren, and the rumble of pigeons on a nearby rooftop. It was times like these, when he should have been cherishing his temporary happiness, that the fear crept into his thoughts, fear about what would happen if his family found out he was gay, fear of the police, fear of prison, and worst of all, fear of the wrath of his father.

His arms leaning over the side of the balcony, Siavash began slowly sipping the red wine. With the harsh realities that most gay men experienced in Iran floating and crashing in the back of his mind, Siavash, with every sip of his sweet beverage, began to reminisce about how he had ever managed to play down his anxieties and ended up with someone like Behnam, someone who came from a totally different background than he did.

It was only about fifteen months ago that the two began to talk in the university halls right outside their lecture room. While fully noticing Behnam through periodic glances, the nerdier Siavash began to take a shine toward the rugged sports enthusiast throughout their lectures. Nevertheless, it was Behnam who broke the ice and approached Siavash first. Swallowing the last sip of the wine, Siavash recalled the day they met.

Standing next to the lecture door and waiting for the class before his to end, Siavash noticed Behnam approaching out of the corner of his eye. Behnam was the kind of person who wasn't easy to miss, as his broad shoulders stood out among most males, while girls giggled and whispered to one another nearly every time he walked by.

Behnam casually walked up to Siavash and stood next to him; his left arm rubbed against Siavash's. Cold sweat trickled down the lower part of his back and his forehead; Siavash promptly removed his glasses and wiped his brow with his sleeve.

"I like your glasses," Behnam said as he tilted his head toward Siavash.

"I'm sorry, are you talking to me?" Siavash responded, his heart pumping in his chest as he quickly restored his black shiny glasses on his face and turned to Behnam.

"Well, you're the only person standing next to me," Behnam replied; he smiled while Siavash swallowed a ball of saliva.

"Oh, right; yeah, thanks, I got them not too long ago," Siavash responded with an awkward smile. He turned toward the classroom door while wiping his forehead again.

"You're Siavash, right? My name is Behnam; I've seen you around the campus. I think we have programming together," Behnam said as he leaned over and offered his hand.

"Yeah, I think we do have programming together, and C++," Siavash replied as he turned around and shook Behnam's hand with a big smile.

"The buzz around the class is that you're doing pretty well in C++. Do you mind if we study together one of these days? I've been having a bit of trouble understanding the last couple of lectures."

"Uhhhh, yeah, definitely. I would love to help you out," Siavash answered before gulping down his saliva again while staring blindly in midair.

Behnam invited Siavash to his flat just two nights later. Thinking about being alone with Behnam in his room made his heart nearly jump out of his chest. He didn't want to put on any displays that would indicate that he was remotely interested in Behnam, and so Siavash focused on his studies and came up with a lesson plan that would take up almost the entire time he intended to study with Behnam.

Behnam's apartment was located in a high-rise in an affluent north Tehran neighborhood. Behnam and his older sister had shared the flat together until she got married and moved to the United Kingdom with her husband. His parents had the flat right next to Behnam's, but they were away from Iran for most of the year. His father ran a successful import and export business from Germany, giving Behnam enough finances to go to school and live his life on his own.

The events of that night began to roll over Siavash's eyes as he continued to stand on the balcony. He had stared at the elevator numbers in Behnam's lobby as he waited for the lift to arrive. His palms began to sweat as he moved his study binder from one hand to the other. Although it was spring and the temperatures were on the rise in Tehran, Siavash had been perspiring more than usual; his armpits underneath his light windbreaker were soaked. He got into the elevator and pressed the number of Behnam's floor. He kept looking for a reason for being there; after all, his finals were only a few weeks away, and he should have been home studying on his own instead of helping Behnam catch up. The words of the psychologist he saw just a few months ago began to circulate in his head. *But what if Behnam wasn't gay?* He thought. Then surely he would be ruined in front of Behnam and the rest of the computer science department. What would happen if the word got out to his father? He would certainly make a bloody mess out of him before disowning his son.

He punched the Stop button of the elevator with the side of his fist and began to breathe heavily before removing his glasses and staring at himself in the glossy mirrors of the elevator. He was there to help a fellow student and nothing more, Siavash kept telling himself. He pushed the button again and continued going up in the elevator. Arriving at Behnam's apartment, Siavash kept the greetings to a minimum; Behnam offered beverages and snacks, but Siavash refused and instead focused on getting through with their study session.

The two headed to Behnam's room and sat next to each other at a large flat desk. The space between them was scant; Siavash could feel Behnam's arm and shoulder rub against his, and he leaned away to avoid the contact. But once they started to get deep into their studies, Siavash involuntarily drifted closer toward his handsome host, who stared brightly into Siavash's eyes as he explained their study material. With his head just a few inches away from Siavash's shoulder, Behnam leaned over, and Siavash stopped talking and stared at his face as his host gazed at Siavash and then kissed him.

With Behnam's lips on his, while his heart pounded in his chest, Siavash closed his eyes and kissed him back before pushing him away and storming out of the apartment. The next day in class, Siavash sat as far as he could from Behnam and avoided looking over at him, despite Behnam trying to make eye contact. He also held out Siavash's binder, which he had left behind as he stomped his way out of the apartment.

Once the lecture came to an end, Behnam quickly walked over to Siavash. He held onto his arm as Siavash began to walk out of the class. Turning around with his fist clutched tightly, Siavash yanked his arm out of Behnam's hand and stared him down.

"I'm sorry about last night," Behnam said. "I just want to apologize; you think maybe I can buy you a cup of coffee?" He took a step back while Siavash loosened his fist and nodded slowly.

Siavash walked ahead of Behnam, and as the two arrived at the small on campus café, he took a seat opposite of Behnam, rather than the one that was next to him.

"You left this at my house last night," Behnam said as he handed the binder to Siavash, who took the binder back while he continued to avoid looking into Behnam's eyes.

"About last night, I'm sorry; I just thought that you might understand," Behnam said as Siavash continued to look away. "I thought you might know what's it like, with Moms, Dads, and everything else this place has to offer."

Siavash slowly lifted up his head and glanced at Behnam.

"You don't have to pretend to be hard," Behnam said. "Sometimes we all need to let someone in, someone who can help us understand ourselves better." He slowly reached over the table and placed his palm on Siavash's fist, which slowly opened up. Behnam smiled as he looked at Siavash, his eyes heavy with tears.

Perhaps Behnam was the person the psychologist advised about; nevertheless, Siavash didn't lay his guard down and at first entered into a friendship that didn't feature any physical romance. Instead, the boys discussed the hardships they had faced with regard to their sexuality and the secrets they kept from their families.

Although Behnam's parents seemed to be far more liberal and open-minded compared to Siavash's parents, his father always envisioned that Behnam would follow his footsteps and take over his business. Even though his parents already had grandchildren from Behnam's sister, both his mother and father placed their only son higher on the shelf and had already begun seeking suitors for him to marry once his school came to an end. Ironically, this was nearly the same story that had dogged Siavash ever since he started university. His mother always asked Siavash for his opinion about various women who she thought would make a great daughter-in-law, while his father pressured him into leaving school early and joining him in a government position.

Spending time with Behnam became therapeutic for Siavash, who found himself lying to his parents in order to spend more time with him. Every day with Behnam was a revelation and a new experience for Siavash, as the two eventually expressed their feelings toward each other physically.

"You still worry about telling your parents about us," Behnam said as he walked over to the balcony and stood next to Siavash.

"It's not that; I'm just worried that I might lose you," Siavash answered as he faced Behnam.

"You're not going to lose me, Siavash. I'm just going to Germany for the rest of the month. You know my dad, he's giving me a hard time every day about not going there and learning about the business," Behnam replied as he put his arm around Siavash's waist. "I'll be back by the end of July, mid-August at the max, and by then, we both would have told our parents."

"But what if they don't accept us for who we are?" Siavash asked.

"Then fuck them," Behnam replied. "If they don't accept us, we'll leave and walk away from them forever!" Siavash gently bit his lower lip while turning his attention toward Behnam. "Look, I've got immigration status in Germany. I can sponsor you as my partner, and if our parents don't accept us, then you and I can escape this prison and live where we're not treated like criminals." Siavash slowly nodded.

Over the span of the next six weeks, Siavash tried to convince himself to come out and reveal his sexuality to his parents. On a few occasions, he managed to summon enough courage to face his mother, but the visualized reaction of his father would shut down his plans. Since Behnam had opened his eyes to a world he would have never dared to enter by himself, Siavash decided to wait for his return and use his encounter with his parents as motivation in telling his own parents.

On the day of Behnam's arrival, Siavash called his cell phone several times, but each time he called, a young lady would answer, informing Siavash that Behnam was not home. This pattern went on for the next three days, as a worried Siavash continued to call, e-mail, and text Behnam; he even messaged him on Facebook. Finally, on the fourth day, Behnam sent Siavash a text, telling him to meet him in the small park a few blocks away from his apartment. Upon receiving the text, Siavash immediately left his house and took a taxi toward Behnam's neighborhood.

He arrived at the park just past three in the afternoon; the merciless summer sun beat down on the top of his head. He walked quickly past the gates as his belly began to quiver. All he could hope for was that his friend was fine and that nothing had happened to him. The sun hitting his eyes, Siavash squinted and located Behnam just after walking past the first few empty benches. The park seemed deserted, and to Siavash's surprise, Behnam was smoking a cigarette as he sat casually on the bench.

"When did you start smoking?" Siavash asked, his arms spread apart as he walked up to Behnam, who glanced away.

"You need to stop calling me, Siavash," Behnam replied as he casually continued to blow smoke out of his lungs; he still had not looked at Siavash.

"What? What do you mean I need to stop calling you?" Siavash said. "I've been sick to my stomach worried about you for the past four days!" Siavash said, his arms still spread apart and his mouth wide open.

"I mean you need to forget about me!" Behnam stared at Siavash before flicking away his cigarette.

"What the fuck is wrong with you? How can I forget about us?" Siavash asked as he raised his voice, his mouth still wide open.

"There is no us anymore, Siavash; there never was! It was just a stupid mistake, you hear me? A stupid mistake!" Behnam shouted.

Siavash stared at him before screaming and swinging his fist toward Behnam's face.

After he punched Behnam in the face, the two began to tussle by the benches in the nearly empty park. Being the brawnier of the two, Behnam quickly countered, striking Siavash in the head as he fell onto the hot pavement, with his glasses knocked off his face.

"I met someone in Germany, an Iranian girl," he said. "She is a friend of my family and I love her. We're engaged and are planning to get married by the end of the summer and then moving away to Germany."

Behnam tried to catch his breath while Siavash lay on his back. The hot sun pounded down on him as he held tightly onto the spot that Behnam had punched.

"If you call me again or try to approach her, I will contact your father and let him know that his son is a fucking queer and breaking the law by sodomizing university students. Do you understand?" Behnam said, standing over Siavash, who struggled to sit up while quietly sobbing.

"Just go home, Siavash. Forget about me, about us," Behnam said as he took one last look at Siavash and walked away. Siavash sat on the hot ground, sobbing.

Siavash spend the rest of July 2008 in a waking coma, as all the feelings he experienced before he met Behnam returned and even magnified. Never having suffered heartbreak, especially in such a devastating fashion, Siavash spent hours in his room, staring at his own reflection in the mirror while he contemplated swallowing a bottle of aspirin. He looked again at every e-mail, Facebook message, provocative text, and secret photo that they shared; Siavash desperately wanted to know why Behnam did what he did. He finally realized that perhaps Behnam and he weren't all that different, and despite having open-minded parents, Behnam had done what Siavash needed to do: meet a girl and get married. But how could it be that easy, Siavash kept asking himself. How could someone go through the kind of romance and affection that they both had toward each other and subsequently fall in love with someone in such a short span of time?

Along with giving him advice that he should seek individuals who shared the same sexuality and were having difficulties explaining themselves to their parents, the psychologist also recommended that Siavash stay true to himself as much as he could. Doing what Behnam did made sense to Siavash; however, it was difficult for him to stomach it. After spending fifteen months with Behnam, one thing that Siavash was sure of was that he was in fact gay; by marrying a woman, he would not only fail to be true to himself but also potentially destroy the life of an innocent woman, who would enter into marriage with dreams and expectations of love and devotion from her husband.

Chapter 9.
Siavash: The Mistake

———❦———

By the first week of August 2008, Siavash decided to try and move on with his life. Searching through chat sites, Facebook, and other social media networks, Siavash began to look for a companion he could make friends with, someone who could be trusted enough for him to communicate with before taking the next step. He reminisced about the first few months of his relationship with Behnam, the way the two used to talk, smile, and discuss events and people that interested them. But it would be hard to find a person like Behnam, who was open with his sexuality (at least Siavash thought) and made the first move. Not to mention that Siavash was altogether a shy person when it came to meeting new people, regardless of their sexual orientation.

Using a fake name, Siavash came across a likely person on a chat site. The man went by the name of Kamron and claimed to be in the closet with regard to his homosexuality and suffered from orthodox parents who were pressuring him into marriage. Kamron ensured Siavash (who used the name "Shahin") that he just wanted to meet and talk to someone who could relate to his struggles and understand him. He was suspicious at first, but after chatting a couple of times, Siavash set up a meeting with Kamron at Tehran's Melat Park. Kamron requested a photo of Shahin, but still not trusting the stranger, Siavash refused and instead described what he was going to wear to the park.

The meeting was set for a weeknight, which meant that the park would have fewer observers and thus be more discreet. The night before the meeting, Siavash couldn't sleep. Nervous and excited at the same time, he hoped that Kamron would be approachable and honest about himself. Although he wanted to take it slow at first, Siavash even began to fantasize about how Kamron looked; he crafted a figure in his head based on the minimal descriptions that he was given.

As Siavash walked quickly through the park, he felt the sweat bead along his spine and under his arms. His heart beat faster. He had heard rumors from Behnam that gay men in Tehran often met at night in the park, but at the same time, he had been warned by his former lover of traps deployed by undercover disciplinary police, who posed as gay men in order to make arrests. He removed his glasses and wiped his brow. He squinted around at the few faces walking the park and thought that if he were found out, his parents would be devastated. With that in the back of his mind, Siavash took a seat on a bench. The lingering memories of the first time he was attracted to another male flashed before his eyes.

It was during a lunch break in his first year in high school. The popular kids were playing soccer in the school yard while he, as usual, sat on the sidelines, watching them play. Not surprising, Siavash wasn't the most popular guy, nor was he the most athletic, but there was a tall and handsome boy in another class who was popular and athletic. Siavash didn't know his name but he sure wanted to be his friend. He wanted to know what it was like to be that popular, that athletic, and that handsome. The attention that the popular boy received from the other boys interested him, and soon Siavash found himself having a series of new and frightening feelings about the popular boy. He found himself having sexual dreams about his schoolmate, only to wake up gasping for air and in a pool of his sweat. After this, he would often sit up in his bed and quietly pray, pleading to God to keep such dreams from ever entering his mind. Even when he became classmates with the popular boy in the next years, Siavash would try and ignore him despite the boy's attempts in engaging in conversation with Siavash and offering his friendship.

While staring at the rays of the sunset over a large tree, for the first time in his life, Siavash realized that he had spent most of his life trying to be who he was not. He had fallen into depression, and if he had learned anything from his time with Behnam, it was that he felt the happiest when he was the most comfortable and honest with himself. As the sun faded away, Siavash noticed someone sitting at the edge of his bench.

"I believe you're looking for me, friend," the man next to him said with a smile on his face.

"I beg your pardon?" Siavash said, his palms sweaty as he began to squint at the man while recalling the description he had been given.

"I'm Kamron," he said. "Aren't you Shahin from the chat site?" The man was strongly built, as he had described himself over the Internet; he had a long, thin face but Siavash noticed that he wasn't sporting a goatee as he had said. Instead, he had a thick but short dark beard.

"Yes, I am. I mean, how are you doing? I didn't notice you there," Siavash replied, as he rubbed his palms over his lap.

"I'm sorry I am late," Siavash said. "I'm sure you're no stranger to uptown traffic. I recall you mentioning that you live around here?"

Siavash extended his hand to the man on the end of the bench.

"Why don't we do what we really came here for and save the chitchat for afterwards?" the man said, smiling and winking at Siavash while rubbing his fingers against Siavash's palm as he shook his hand.

"Um, I'm sorry," Siavash said. "I don't quite understand. What do you mean by what we really came here for?" He quickly removed his hand while raising one of his eyebrows.

"I tell you what," he said, "why don't you come look me up once you've figured out why you're here? I'll be in the last toilet stall of the men's room around the corner." He stood up and headed toward the washrooms.

Siavash stared as he casually walked away while more sweat streamed down his neck and back. His heart pounded louder and harder with every step that the stranger took.

He wasn't sure what the man meant by the last toilet stall. Could it be that he wanted to talk somewhere quieter, or was he hinting at a place where they could have sex? Siavash rubbed his damp palm over his forehead. The thought of having sex with strange men in park lavatories scared him. He wanted to make a genuine connection with someone and wasn't there for the thrills of a forbidden and dangerous sensation. But maybe the man did want to talk in a quieter place. What was it that Kamron wanted, he wondered. Even if he just wanted to talk somewhere more private, selecting the park washrooms wasn't really the most ideal spot for having a conversation about being gay. Perhaps he should stop at the lavatory and inform Kamron of his discomfort and suggest that the two find a cozy café near the park to talk.

With that in mind, Siavash tore himself away from the bench and slowly walked toward the park washrooms. With every step that he took, a million thoughts went through his mind. His temples pounded as his shirt was soaked from sponging his perspiration; he feared the man could be a member of Tehran's disciplinary police or the *basij* (the religious militia). Flashes of being dragged away in tears in front of a group of people while his father stood by, avoiding the cries of his bloodied son, went through his mind as he stood just outside of the washroom.

He stared at the generic male sign displayed outside of the washroom. With his palms dried, Siavash swung open the door and peeked inside. The stranger was leaning against the last stall and gazing at the main door. Siavash walked in after conducting a makeshift inspection of the empty facility.

"Kamron, is it?" he said. "I think you might have the wrong idea about me."

"Huh? The wrong idea?" the man asked, raising his voice and clenching his fists before taking a step toward Siavash, who simultaneously took a step back.

"Yeah, I think you do. I'm not here for what you seem to have in mind," Siavash began to explain, but before he could finish his sentence, the man suddenly punched him, sending his glasses flying and knocking him to the ground.

Dazed, Siavash held on to the side of his jaw as a jolt ran along the punched area, all the way up to his temple. He reached for his glasses as the man quickly grabbed a handful of his hair and nearly yanked him off the ground before smashing his head into the sink; blood gushed out of the corner of Siavash's eyebrow as he fell to the ground. He struggled to get up and forced his way up on his hands and knees; he noticed blood dripping down next to his hands. The man began to kick Siavash, who moaned after each kick.

"I have the wrong idea about you? You're a fucking faggot, a queer, a disease to our way of life!" the man shouted in between delivering kicks.

"You thought I was going to let you fuck me? I'm going to make you wish you were born a woman, you piece of shit!" he continued, as Siavash shouted for help. An elderly man walked through the main door of the park washroom.

He said, "What the hell are you doing, you're killing him!"

"This doesn't concern you, old man!" Siavash's aggressor said. "Just mind your own business and get the fuck out!"

"Please sir, help me!" Siavash cried. "This maniac is going to kill me!" He lifted up his head and looked at the elderly man as blood covered half of his face.

"You let this kid go, or else I'm going to call the police!" the elderly man warned, waving his finger in the air while clenching his other hand into a fist.

"I said this doesn't concern you," Kamron said, adding, "I am a member of the *basij* and I'm making an arrest right here, so get out of my way or I'm going to take you down too!"

Just then, another man walked into the washroom.

"What's going on in here?" the other man asked, staring at the bleeding Siavash over the shoulders of the elderly man.

"This thug is beating up this poor kid, claiming to be a *basiji*," the elderly man replied.

"Then show us your identification!" the man shouted. "Members of the *basij* have ID cards."

"I said get out of my way or else I'm arresting you two along with this faggot!" Siavash's attacker shouted.

"Please, you have to help me," Siavash repeated. "I just came in to use the restroom when this maniac attacked me for no reason." The new younger man emerged from behind the elderly man and stood a few feet away from Siavash and his attacker.

"I'm not letting you walk out of here with this kid unless you show me your identification!" the man said, holding out one of his hands while Siavash's attacker stared at him, motionless.

"Hey, pops," the man said, "come over here and get this kid away from this asshole. If he tries anything, me and my friends outside are going to break every bone in his body!" The elderly man walked up to Siavash and helped him to his feet as Kamron backed away and leaned against the concrete wall of the facilities.

The elderly man's arm wrapped around his waist, Siavash put on his glasses and stumbled out of the washroom. The elderly man offered to take him to the hospital, but Siavash refused; he held tightly onto the area that was bleeding and ran out of the park gates; he signaled for a taxi to take him to a nearby clinic. On the way, with pain running through his swollen jaw, he took his hand off his eyebrow, which had stopped bleeding. He then wiped away his tears and struggled to take his cell phone out of his pocket. He ran down the numbers on his phone and looked at two particular names on his contact list: his father and Behnam. He flipped his phone closed and stared out the cab's window. He felt like he was in a nightmare that he could never wake up from.

Over the course of the next hour, while getting stitches placed on his left eyebrow, Siavash looked back at the events that had occurred that night. He thought that if it wasn't for the two men who came to his rescue, he would have surely by now been held up in a precinct somewhere or at least beaten nearly to death at the hands of his brutal attacker. With his glasses off, he thought about how his parents would have reacted had he been arrested. The images of his father smashing their telephone and shouting profanities and his mother quietly sobbing after hearing that he had been arrested swirled around his mind. *Could they ever understand their son and why he had gone to the park?* he asked himself. Could they ever support his decision to live as a gay man, free from the pressures of a heterosexual relationship?

He thought about Behnam again; he wondered if he was still in Tehran, or had he left Iran for Germany? He pictured Behnam and a beautiful girl in a wedding dress, who stood by his side as they danced in a ballroom as Behnam's parents looked on with smiles and tears. They looked happy, Siavash imagined, while his damp eyes stared blinding into empty space. The word "queer," along with spinning red light and sirens, rang in his head. He left the clinic and headed home.

He waited outside of his house and entered quietly after the lights of his parents' bedroom went out. Siavash got up the next morning to a world of pain. His head and face felt twenty kilos heavier, his jaw was swollen, and his eyes were puffy and red after he cried himself to sleep. He quietly went downstairs after showering while desperately trying to improve his appearance. Facing the stove as she prepared lunch, his mother called his name loudly as he entered the kitchen.

"I'm here, Mom," he said, quietly taking a seat at the table with his back to his mother.

"Well, good morning, young man," she said. "We were hoping that you would have joined us at dinner last night."

"I'm sorry," he said. "I got home late. I was helping a friend set up her new computer." He casually placed his hand over his forehead to cover his stitches.

"And when are we finally going to meet this nameless female friend of yours, Siavash?" his mother asked, as she continued facing the stove.

"Her name is ... Nazanin," he answered after taking a short pause.

"That's such a pretty name," she said. "Perhaps we could invite Nazanin and her family over for dinner one of these days, or if you think you're interested, then maybe your father, myself, and you can go over there and meet her parents, maybe even make an offer for their daughter's hand in marriage," His mother poured a cup of tea and walked to the table as Siavash quietly shook his head and rolled his eyes. As she sat down, she finally saw his bruised and battered face.

"Oh my God!" she cried. "What happened to your face, Siavash? Akbar! Get in here now, something has happened to your son!" She took her son's face in her hands while stroking his swollen jaw and bandaged eyebrow. His first reaction was to yank his face away from his mother's tight grip, but instead he chose to remain in her embrace as his father approached the kitchen.

"What in God's name is going on, woman?" he said. "Why are you screaming?"

"Look what they did to my child!" she replied as she stood out of the way while his father noticed the bruises and marks on his son's face.

"What ... happened to you?" he asked. "Who did this to you, Siavash?" He raised his voice, clenching his fists while his thick eyebrows rose up into his forehead.

Siavash slowly turned away his head and stared at the empty seat on the opposite edge of the table. A stream of tears ran down his face. The nightmarish events of the previous evening flashed before his eyes. He wanted to tell his parents everything. And not just about the night before, but about Behnam, about the popular boy at his high school, and about everything else that he had been hiding from them all this time. He wanted to scream that he was gay, that he was dying inside all this time and didn't want to hide it anymore. He wanted to be embraced by his parents for who he was. But he knew he could not.

"Well, are you gonna talk or sit there crying like a queer?" his father said, raising his voice while his fists remained clenched.

Siavash flinched as his father mentioned the word "queer"; quickly brushing away his tears, he turned to face his father.

"I ... we ... I mean, my friend Nazanin and I wanted to grab a bite to eat after I helped set up her computer," Siavash lied, "so we went out to a burger joint near her house. After we ate, we ran into these thugs outside, who started to harass Nazanin ... so I got into a fight with them." Siavash glanced back and forth from his father and then back to the empty edge of the table.

"You had dinner with a woman who was not *mahram* [a legal relationship within Sharia laws] to you? Have you no respect for your religion, boy?" his father asked.

Siavash continued to look away from his father and stared at the edge of the table.

"At least you stepped up like a man and not a queer," his father continued. "There might be some hope for you after all." His father patted Siavash on the shoulder. "Now, why don't you tell me what they looked like? My good friend is the chief at the 32 Division, and he owes me a favor." Siavash's father sat down at the table while his mother poured two cups of tea for her husband and son.

"It's not important, Dad," he said. "They were just a bunch of lowlife thugs; there is no reason to get your friend involved." Siavash glanced at his father before turning his attention toward the steaming cup of tea sitting in front of him.

"All right then, but I want you to be careful from now on," his father said as he reached for his tea and began sipping from the cup. "Uh, I almost forgot, speaking of the chief, he has invited us for dinner this Friday. His daughter Azadeh is back from England after graduating from dentist school, and he thinks it is time for her to settle down, so we decided that it would be a good idea for her and Siavash to meet each other." He glanced toward his wife and then to Siavash, who clenched his fist and grinded his teeth, staring at his steaming cup of tea.

"That's wonderful news, Akbar," his mother said. "I can't wait to meet the chief, his wife, and of course Azadeh. She sounds like such a lovely girl, Siavash. I'm sure you and she will fall head over heels for each other. What do you think?" his mother asked.

"I keep telling you two to stop pushing me into marriage," he said. "I'm still in school; I'm not ready for marriage."

"Don't you dare raise your voice to your mother," his father said. "I've had enough of you using school as an excuse! How many times do I have to tell you that you don't need that stupid degree when I can get you a high-paying position? Plus, this is a great girl from a very good family, so don't embarrass your mother and I. Do you understand, Siavash?" Siavash turned his head away and slowly nodded.

"Then it's settled," he said. "I will let the chief know that we will be at his house this weekend. You better hope that the left side of your face clears up by then, or else I'm going to do the same to the right side." His father wagged his finger at Siavash before finishing his tea and walking away from the table.

Siavash continued to sit quietly and stared again at the empty edge of the table. Images of Behnam dancing slowly with his bride flashed before his eyes again. He was holding her gently while his cheek rested on her forehead. She seemed so glamorous in her gown, even though Siavash had no idea what she really looked like. He closed his eyes and pictured himself wearing a tuxedo and dancing slowly with a faceless woman in a wedding dress while his parents smiled and looked on. His mother had tears sparkling in her eyes; she held onto a stack of money that she was planning on tossing over the head of the happy couple once the song came to an end. Everyone looked happy in his fantasy, everyone except for him, who felt like he was holding onto a mannequin. How could he marry a woman that he could never love, never feel close to, or never be true to?

During that week, Siavash kept to himself and tried to avoid as much conversation with his parents as possible. He thought about running away and seeking asylum in Europe or North America. He even went for a consultation with an immigration lawyer who had an office in Tehran and Toronto. But after learning about the difficulties that he would face in becoming a refugee, along with the legal complexities, Siavash decided to give up and tried to convince himself to focus on making a good impression at the dinner, at least for his parents' sake. Deep down inside, he wanted to be like Behnam and wished that he could wake up one day and fall in love with a woman and have the life that his parents and everyone else seemed to want for him.

He put on the black suit that Behnam had picked out for him when they were both graduating from their undergraduate studies. The swelling on his jaw had gone down, and his faced looked normal, except for a small bandage over his left eyebrow. His father had picked out a bouquet of roses and instructed Siavash to present them to Azadeh upon arriving at the chief's house.

At the chief's house, his father walked up the stairs as his mother followed slightly behind. Siavash squeezed his palm tightly on the plastic wrapping on the bouquet as the thorns of the roses penetrated through the plastic and nearly through his skin. He grinded his teeth and wondered if this was how Behnam felt when he met his fiancée. Perhaps it was only difficult at first; maybe he would undergo the transformation that Behnam seemed to have experienced.

His father knocked on the door of the second-story apartment unit; the police chief opened the door with a big smile on his face while his wife stood behind him with nearly the same expression. The men quickly hugged and patted each other on the back, as the women smiled and greeted each other with kisses on the cheek. Azadeh stood quietly behind her mother, and Siavash handed her the flowers. For someone who had spent time overseas and was educated, Azadeh seemed rather quiet and bashful to Siavash.

As they were taking their seats in the living room, Azadeh brought the flowers, which she had put into a tall crystal vase, and set them down in the middle of a table. She then sat across from Siavash, glanced at the red and white roses, and smiled at him. For the rest of the night, she didn't say much to him, but every time he would look at her, she would smile in return. Her smile made him feel warm, and despite her bashfulness, Azadeh appeared kind and gentle. He didn't want to break her heart and hurt her. Staring at the crystal vase, Siavash pictured the two of them dancing at their wedding, holding her to his chest; he felt her warm smile coat over his body. This was something that he had only felt when he was with Behnam.

The dinner resembled more of an arranged marriage, as both fathers made jokes about who would pay the cost of the wedding and who would cheap out on the food, while the women talked about the wedding dress and how beautiful the ceremony would be. Based on Azadeh's responses, Siavash felt that she was already on the same page as his parents and her parents. She smiled at the jokes and even voiced her opinion about the ceremony and what kind of dress she liked. All jokes aside, both parents decided that it was best for their children to spend some time together before anything was set in stone. They set up an engagement, which under Iran's Sharia law would allow the two to spend time together before getting married.

They exchanged phone numbers and e-mails, and they even became friends on Facebook. Siavash promised himself that he would spend as much time as he could in getting to know Azadeh, who became more confident and outgoing as the two began to see each other during the rest of the summer. Nevertheless, the closer he became to Azadeh, the more afraid he became of breaking her heart and ruining her hopes of marriage and love.

He thought a lot about Behnam during that summer and wanted to reach out to him, at least to ask for advice. He wanted to know how Behnam managed to put aside his feelings for him and fall for a woman he had only known for a short period of time. But every time he began typing an e-mail to Behnam, the sour events of the last time they met crept into the back of his mind, and he would find himself deleting the e-mail. Even worse, he kept picturing the savage beating he got the last time he tried to make a connection with someone who he thought was in the same circumstances as him. He realized that being gay in Iran meant a life of secrecy and disappointments, filled with dramas of family rejection, phobia, and violence. It wasn't something that he wanted, but at the same time, he didn't want to disappoint Azadeh.

While Siavash had dated a girl before, in his freshmen year, his understanding of the opposite sex was limited, and in order to make a better connection with Azadeh, he decided to seek advice about women from an unlikely source: his father. He encouraged Siavash to attend the mosque with him for lessons on marriage, ethics, and family values; he also recommended attending free lectures at the university given by a popular cleric who had his own television show. His father spoke highly of the cleric and painted him as an expert in matters of family and marriage; his father even relied on him for advice from time to time. Siavash found the environment of the mosque intimidating, and after numerous requests from his father, he finally decided to attend one of the TV mullah's lectures.

The lectures were held on Fridays at a lecture hall in the University of Tehran; they were usually broadcast by the state-owned media networks. One particular Friday, a week before the end of the summer holidays, Siavash attended a lecture in the hopes of gaining a better understanding of the new role he was struggling to adopt: the role of a husband.

Siavash arrived at the nearly full lecture a bit late and took a seat in the last row of the hall. Settling down quietly, he noticed the mullah standing in the center of the stage, writing on a chalk board; the crowd hung onto his every word.

"The Quran along with the Hadith of Gabriel outlines the five pillars of our religion," he was saying. "They are, one: *shahada* (creed), two: *salat* (daily prayers), three: *zakat* (almsgiving), four: *sawm* (fasting during Ramadan), and five: *hajj* (pilgrimage to Mecca)." The mullah wrote each item on the chalkboard while the men in the crowd took notes.

"These are the pillars that we must follow, married or unmarried, man or woman, it doesn't make a difference; these five come first and must be followed in order to live a life of purity and righteousness!" the mullah said loudly after turning away from the board and addressing the crowd.

"These days," he continued, "the son comes home and tells his parents that he is in love; the daughter comes home and she says that she is in love too, but what does this word 'love' really mean?" The mullah returned to the chalk board and wrote the word "love" on the opposite side of the five pillars. Siavash was intrigued, hoping that the mullah would shed light on the subject he needed help with.

"Let me be clear when I say that this word 'love' is not your friend. No. On the contrary, this is a word created by the West to corrupt our youth and to pull blinders over your eyes and deceive you all from your duties to the pillar and to God." The mullah tapped the word "love" with the chalk while facing the crowd. His mouth agape in suprise, Siavash began to roll his eyes. Surely he thought the mullah would at least hint toward the emotional duties that a man had to his wife.

"Even when you're married, you have to understand that you're a servant of the Lord, and it is your duty to fight temptation and deceptions that aim to stray you from the pillars and your faith," the mullah followed up as Siavash grinded his teeth.

"The West has created these deceptions to rid us of our faith and to bring us down to a life of sin, a life of sleaze. I tell people this all the time; an invasion does not necessarily need tanks and bombs. All that is needed is a moral invasion to take us off the course that God, the Prophet, and our dear departed leader [Khomeini] and our present leader [Khamenei] have struggled to pave for us," the mullah said as he walked away from the board and sat behind a desk that had side-by-side pictures of Khomeini and Khamenei.

Siavash slowly shook his head and clenched his fist while also noticing the enthusiasm of the crowd.

"True love and devotion is to be shown only to God," he said. "These men and women walking around these days, telling each other, 'I love you,' are only fooling themselves. They are implanted with the West's ways and are thus putting themselves and their own selfish needs ahead of God and their faith." The mullah raised his voice as Siavash tightened the grip around his fists. He took off his glasses and rubbed his eyes before placing his hand over his forehead while closing his eyes.

Perhaps this was the reason behind his father behaving so coldly toward his mother, he thought. But how could anyone remotely buy into what the mullah was persuading? How could love between two individuals be a disease, regardless of their sexual preference? He was disgusted with his father and even with his mother, who seemed not to be engaging her husband either. He believed in God and respected his religion of Islam, but why should he or anyone abandon their emotions and human nature? He was angry and wanted to walk up to the mullah and ask him what was selfish about two people loving one another. He was angry with Behnam and pictured himself going up to his former lover and punching him in the face, only to come to the realization that he was punching a mirrored reflection of Behnam, whose now shattered remains lay by his feet. He opened his eyes and discovered the mullah talking about satellite television and the evil effects it had on the youth, but before the mullah could say anymore, Siavash got up and stormed out of the lecture hall.

He was angry at himself, angry that he had agreed to meet Azadeh. Maybe it was wrong for him to give up on being who he really was and what really made him happy. Walking in the streets around the university, Siavash thought about what really made him happy. Behnam's face yet again flashed before his eyes as his fists automatically tightened. He thought about Azadeh, and although the two had not engaged in any physical acts of romance, nevertheless the time he had spent with her was pleasant. As he pictured Azadeh and her warm smile, his fists relaxed and a nearly forgotten grin returned to lips. The mullah didn't inspire him in any shape or form, but for the first time, Siavash seemed to have figured out what he wanted, and that was not to hurt her. He reached for his cell phone and called her, asking her to join him in a coffee shop not too far from her house.

They both arrived relatively at the same time, and Siavash pulled aside a chair for Azadeh to sit on before taking his own seat. After ordering beverages, Azadeh, concerned about why her fiancé had asked her to join him in such a blunt fashion, began the conversation.

"So what did you want to talk about?" she asked, gazing at Siavash, who took out his phone and fidgeted with a few buttons.

"Just wanted to see you sweetie and ... chat, that's all," Siavash replied while still looking at his phone. The waiter brought them cold beverages with straws hanging from them.

"Are you sure everything is all right?" she asked. "I noticed that you've been a bit down lately."

Siavash returned his phone to his pocket and began slurping his drink all the while avoiding his fiancée's eyes.

"Yeah, sweetie, everything is fine," he said. "It's just that ... I care a lot about you and I'm sort of new to this whole relationship thing. To be honest, I don't want to disappoint you."

Azadeh smiled, reached across the table, and took his hand.

"You're not going to disappoint me, Siavash. I care about you too, and just like you, I'm new to this as well." She gazed into his eyes with the same warm smile he had seen the night they met. He paused just for a second before dropping his head and continuing to slurp his cold beverage. "All that I can ask from you is to be honest with me, as I'll be honest with you."

Siavash looked away before slowly removing his hand.

"I'm not like my parents," she added. "You can tell me anything, and I swear that I wouldn't judge you." Azadeh tried to catch a glimpse of his eyes.

"It's just ... I don't know how to tell you," Siavash began, "but ..." Before he could finish his sentence, his phone vibrated in his pocket. It was a text message from Behnam, Siavash noticed, as he excused himself from the table and headed to the washroom in the café.

He took a deep breath and stared at Behnam's name on the screen before opening his phone and reading the message. The message read that Behnam had just gotten married; he wanted to inform Siavash and expressed his apologies for their last encounter. He also wished Siavash all the best. He closed his phone and removed his glasses before splashing water on his face. Water dripping from his face, Siavash stared at his reflection in the mirror over the small sink. He paused and moved his head closer to the mirror while staring deeply at his eyes, which he did not seem to recognize anymore. The cut on the corner of his eyebrow was still visible; he closed his eyes and pictured holding Azadeh under the dim lights of a ballroom as they slowly danced as man and wife. He felt happy as her warm smile melted over his body and heart. He looked back at his eyes once more, but still did not recognize them. Staring at his own reflection, Siavash felt that there was something missing from the way he looked back at himself. He dried his face and returned quietly back to his seat and his concerned fiancée.

"Is everything okay?" Azadeh asked as he sat down.

"Oh yeah, yeah," he said, "That was one of the guys from school who just got married today."

"That's wonderful; what's his name?" Azadeh asked with a big grin on her face. Siavash looked down at his half-empty glass.

"His name is ... Kaveh," Siavash answered as he slowly swirled his straw in the glass. "Listen, I know we set a date for spring for our wedding, but I was wondering if maybe we could move it up to the fall." Siavash continued to spin the straw in his glass as Azadeh smiled and nodded.

Siavash recalled the events of the past two years of his life: meeting Behnam and being introduced to a whole new world while having it come to an abrupt end, meanwhile running through the unexpected and shocking event at the park, followed by meeting Azadeh. All these events had a tremendous effect on his life. However, he recalled that nothing in his lifetime was such life defining as the events of that particular Friday.

—·ΧΩ·—

The last time Siavash and I spoke, he jokingly told me that he finally understood what Ahmadinejad meant when he said that there are no homosexuals in Iran. It is not that there literally are no homosexuals in Iran, but that whoever is a homosexual and did not opt out for the controversial sex change operation devised by the regime is either married and miserable or single and miserable.

Siavash has been married for nearly two years; he and his wife are preparing for their first child. His greatest fear is disappointing Azadeh and his unborn child. Siavash believes that destroying his own life and being dishonest with himself is one thing, but ruining the life and hopes of his wife, who is pregnant and in the dark about her husband's sexuality, terrifies him the most. He has indicated that even though he still finds himself attracted to men, his only option remains in suppressing those feelings and convincing himself that he is in love with his wife.

Siavash has further indicated that the stress of being someone he is not has caused him to fall back into deep depression and develop ulcers. Of course, he has kept that from his wife as well; he takes medication in order to battle both the depression and the pains in his stomach. His only hope is that once his child is born, Siavash will transfer more into the family figure and husband that he has been praying for since his engagement. Lastly, as Siavash is preparing to welcome his child to this world, he has indicated that he wants to be the kind of father whose child feels comfortable discussing issues of sexuality. He wants to be a father who can be supportive, regardless of his child's sexuality, and hopes that parents in Iran can start to acknowledge that being gay or lesbian is a reality and not some sort of disease that engulfs unlucky families. His last words were for parents to bridge a genuine connection with their children where real issues are discussed. All he can do is to make a promise to himself that he will not follow in his father's footsteps in raising his child.

As I mentioned at the beginning of this chapter, writing and researching about homosexuals living in Tehran proved to be the most difficult task in putting this book together. The chief reason is that gays and lesbians living in Iran not only face persecution from the regime, they also face persecution from society at large, including in most cases their families. I truly hope the best for people like Siavash and wish that one day they could live comfortably with themselves.

Chapter 10.
Mohammad: The Approaching Storm

U nemployment and underemployment have recently become the primary concern of Iranians, especially those who live in urban areas. The official state's unemployment numbers released in 2010 projected a jobless rate around 15 percent.[33] However, many in Iran believe the number to be much higher, near an astonishing 35 percent. Over the past decade, government-created jobs accommodate at best only about half of the population entering the work force.[34] This frightening trend has led to an exodus of skill and talent, leaving the country on the verge of a shortage of skilled labor. For those employed, on the other hand, life has not necessarily been easy either. With inflation at around 20 to 50 percent, even those who are employed find it difficult to make ends meet.[35] Today about 20 percent of the population of

33   https://www.cia.gov/library/publications/the-world-factbook/geos/ir.html.

34   Ramin Jahanbegloo. "The deadlock in Iran: pressures from below," *Journal of Democracy*, 2003.

35   Ibid.

Iran lives below the poverty line, while an astonishing 55 percent of urban dwellers live in and around it.[36]

In Iran and especially in Tehran, many of those who are employed today find their daily salaries are not adequate for the expenses of life; as a result, most people work two or more jobs. Some of these odd jobs involve black market activities, which are deemed illegal by the state. The end result of high inflation and staggering unemployment has been the thinning out of what used to be a vibrant middle class.

Sad to say, out of 420 individuals that I interviewed in the course of writing this book, only 100 had full-time jobs, and out of that number, 47 were working side jobs (most drove their personal vehicles as a taxi once their day jobs came to an end).

Among those struggling to keep a roof over their heads and food on the table is Mohammad, a thirty-one-year-old married man with twin one-year-old boys. He is employed by the state's television and radio network. Mohammad's group was responsible for broadcasting sporting events on Iran's channel 3, which mostly included games from Iran's premier soccer league. However, for the past two years, after the end of his shift, Mohammad has been using his personal vehicle as a makeshift taxi; he picks up and transports passengers for a few hours, especially during Tehran's busy rush hour. In addition to that, on some nights and weekends, Mohammad sets up satellite dishes and delivers pirated music CDs and Hollywood DVDs. (This is banned in Iran, as the regime considers Western music and movies anti-Islamic and fears their cultural influence could undermine Iran's revolutionary zeal.)[37] Mohammad's brother Hamid works alongside Mohammad, distributing the pirated CDs and DVDs. Hamid is an electrical technician and works at a cell-phone boutique shop owned by his father-in-law, selling mobile devices and repairing old cell phones.

---

36 http://www.pbs.org/wgbh/pages/frontline/tehranbureau/2011/04/comment-urban-poverty-in-iran-a-sea-or-a-mirage.html.

37 http://www.nytimes.com/2009/03/02/world/middleeast/02visit.html.

It was a Friday afternoon in early October 2009; Mohammad ignored the sound coming from a small television set and instead stared out the window of his mother's small apartment, watching the yellow and orange leaves dance in the air before falling into a small water garden in the backyard. His widowed mother lived in a humble, lower middle class part of Tehran and struggled to survive by living on her dead husband's insignificant pension.

Fridays are considered the weekend in Iran, but this was the first day that Mohammad had had off in nearly six months. Ever since his twin boys where born fifteen months ago, he had been working nonstop, seven days a week and nearly fourteen hours a day.

Sitting on the living room rug, Mohammad rested on the big cushions that lay against the wall. His mother and wife began placing small pastries and Turkish coffee on a plastic cloth. His toddlers were sound asleep in the bedroom. Mohammad leaned his head back on the top of the cushion and closed his eyes. He placed his hand over his face and began to rub his eyes with his thumb and index finger before running his hand through his thinning hair. A gentle breeze came through the open window. His mother walked over from the kitchen and closed the window. She paused next to the window, tilted her head toward Mohammad, and looked at him closely.

"What's the matter, Mohammad?" his mother asked. "You haven't even touched your Turkish coffee yet. You've been awfully quiet today." Mohammad turned his eyes away from the small water garden and toward his mother.

"It's nothing, Mom, I'm just a little tired," he answered as he rubbed his eyes again while moving his feet so she wouldn't notice the large holes at the bottom on his socks.

"Tired? Your sons are not even two!" she said. "You are a long way from knowing what tired really feels like!" She chuckled as she leaned on a cushion across from him while Mohammad's wife, Mona, walked over from the kitchen and rested against the cushion next to her husband.

"At least finish your coffee so I can read your fortune, Mohammad; he and his father used to love it when I made Turkish coffee just so I could read their cups and tell them their fortunes," Mohammad's mother told Mona. Mohammad sluggishly reached for the small cup in front of him.

Not taking any of the pastries, he swigged back the bitter, hot beverage before turning his cup upside down on the saucer. He looked out the window again and noticed that the leaves that were floating on the water just a minute ago were now submerged and swimming below a tiny sheet of water. An old Persian metaphor, that drowning can take place under one foot of water just as easily as under ten feet, swirled in his head as he again closed his eyes and rested his head back on top of the thick cushion. After a few minutes, his mother reached for his upside-down cup and began to interpret the shapes that appeared.

"Hummmm, there is quite a bit going on in your cup, Mohammad." His mother paused as she studied the cup closely while Mohammad lifted up his head and looked over at her.

"It looks like a tsunami is heading in your direction," she said as she squinted; he walked over and sat next to his mother and peeked at his cup.

"You're going through a rough road, son; the next few months will be tough on you and your family, but it will be over soon," she continued, looking closer at the cup and pointing toward the various shapes as Mohammad began to see her interpretations.

"See this, it looks like a man sitting on a mule is climbing a steep mountain while pulling a heavy load, with the storm right behind him, but he's almost made it to the top of the mountain!" She smiled and turned the cup so he could see; Mohammad cracked a smile as well.

"I hope you're right, Mom. Life hasn't been easy lately," Mohammad replied as he looked toward the window again while his smile quickly disappeared.

"I know, dear. Perhaps it's time that I sold this sardine can and gave you and your brother your inheritance; life has become so difficult in this goddamn city these days," his mother said.

Mohammad quickly turned around.

"No, Mom! We're doing fine and so is Hamid. God, we should be helping you out. I still don't know how you can manage to get by in these hard times on the nickel and dimes from Dad's pension."

Mohammad stood up and walked over to his seat while his wife left the living room and headed to the bedroom, where their boys were sleeping.

"Plus, you're not going to get much for this place, and even then, where are you going to live once you sell it?" Mohammad asked.

"Thank God Hamid's in-laws bought them a place of their own. At least they don't have to worry about paying rent and looking for a cheaper place to move to every year, like we just did."

Mohammad's mother slowly nodded her head while looking at the plate in the middle of the white plastic cloth.

"You should stop worrying about us and Hamid and just concentrate on staying healthy. We'll be all right, Mom," Mohammad said as his mother slowly lifted up her head and smiled at her son.

Mona soon returned from the bedroom with his sons, now awake. Mohammad signaled for them to leave, and his mother reluctantly wished them farewell before smothering her grandchildren with kisses and giving her daughter-in-law a pot full of the leftover rice and chicken she had prepared for their lunch.

With the sound of the call to prayer echoing from a nearby mosque, the family of four got into Mohammad's small, dented Renault hatchback. Before they left his mother's street, Mona shrieked at him as to why he didn't he didn't accept his mother's offer to sell her house and give half of the proceeds to them. His infant twins were falling in and out of sleep in the cozy backseat, as she reminded him about their expenses and the fact that they have spent nearly no time together since Mohammad has been working around the clock.

Wrapping his hand tightly around the steering wheel, Mohammad rolled his eyes at Mona several times while swallowing hard. Ignoring her husband, Mona continued in the same shrill voice to make her point about him asking his mother to sell her apartment. Grinding his teeth while glancing at his wife and then back at the road, Mohammad pulled his car over to the side of the quiet street. He looked back at his napping twins before facing his wife. His left hand gripped tightly around the wheel, Mohammad whispered in a deep harsh voice that he would never ask his mother to sell her house. His wife looked quietly at her husband before slowly nodding as he further told her that no matter what, he will manage to pull through for them and that she should be optimistic and thankful for being blessed with two healthy boys.

The next day at work, Mohammad and his two colleagues got an unexpected visit from the division supervisor, who caused an immediate stir every time he came down to the control room. His plaid polyester coat reeking of rose water, the dark-bearded supervisor walked into the center of the room and glared at the three workers, including Mohammad.

"Good morning, sir," Mohammad said. "We were not expecting you this early; would you care for some tea?" Mohammad and the other two men stood up from their seats. They knew that the man didn't like any of them; he always appeared to be on the verge of firing someone.

"Why we don't fire the lot of you, I don't know," the supervisor said as he stopped in the middle of the control room and launched into a tirade they had all heard before.

"My boss and the Ministry of Culture and Islamic Guidance are on my ass again because you idiots continue to remain completely oblivious to the memos I send." He raised his voice as Mohammad stood quietly while grinding his teeth.

"I clearly instructed you last week to tune out the chants of protestors who come to the games; you are to replace them with generic crowd noises from previous soccer games. I also told you idiots to broadcast the games in black and white if there are large sections of the crowd wearing green."

As the supervisor shouted at the workers, dust from his jacket flew into the air and under the bright lights of the control room.

"I don't want to have these green-wearing hooligans chanting nonsense on my station. Do you understand?" he continued, pointing his finger at Mohammad.

"Yes sir, I promise that it will not happen again, sir," Mohammad quickly answered, as sweat bubbled up under his thinning hair.

"It better not happen again! Or else I will find someone who can follow my instructions and get them right!" The supervisor raised his voice before storming out of the control room.

"Fucking *hezbollahee* [common term used to describe regime supporters]!" Mohammad's colleague Majid whispered, just a few seconds after their supervisor left.

"Ssh! Don't say stuff like that, Majid!" Mohammad whispered back. "Don't you know the walls here have eyes and ears?" Mohammad rolled his eyes at Majid, just before they both glared at Ahmad, the other person in the room, who quickly began to switch buttons on the control panels in front of him.

"I don't give a shit if he or anyone else hears me!" Majid responded, shaking his head. "Those bastards stole our votes! Our dignity! Raped and murdered our people and you're expecting me to smile and nod like a fucking retard and assist those sons of bitches in adding to the misery of our people?" Majid glared at Mohammad, who sighed loudly in response while shaking his head and looking blindly at the floor.

"I know what you're talking about, Majid, and believe me, I'm frustrated about it too. I'm not expecting you to do what makes you feel uncomfortable, but I'm expecting you to think about your wife and daughter, your rent, and your bills," Mohammad answered. "I don't want you to get fired, Majid, or even worse, to end up in jail as an agitator, a supporter of the opposition; you'll end up on the streets." Majid clenched his fists and bit his lip before nodding his head.

Mohammad sighed, as he ran his slender fingers through his thinning black hair, and told his subordinates to doctor the tape of the game they were to run that night, excising the chants of protesters and editing out footage of all spectators who wore green. The rest of the day passed quickly, and Mohammad was glad to get out of there. Walking to his car, Mohammad heard someone call his name; he turned around and saw Majid sprinting toward him. A smile on his face, Majid hugged Mohammad and apologized for losing his cool in the control room.

Majid explained that he had been under stress ever since he and his family had to move in with his parents after his landlord raised his rent. Choked up, Majid also informed Mohammad that his financial crisis had affected his marriage; his wife had threatened to divorce him and move away with their three-year-old daughter. Placing his hand on Majid's shoulder, Mohammad asked his colleague if there was anything he could do help. A thin layer of tears building up over his eyes, Majid hung his head and asked Mohammad if he could lend him a sum of one million tomans, which he promised he would pay back within two months.

Mohammad felt sorry for his colleague. At least he had a car he could use to make money on the side, not to mention the black-market operation he ran with his brother. Looking at Majid, Mohammad was reminded of the leaves he was watching the other day. While he was still floating on the water, avoiding drowning, Majid on the other hand seemed to already be submerged. Mohammad agreed to loan Majid the money by the next day, even though it was most of his savings. The two parted ways as Mohammad got into his car and set out for his evening taxi route.

Pulling out of the uptown parking complex of the media center, Mohammad began to do some quick math in his head. He figured out that if he worked at his three jobs for the entire rest of the month, he would be able to pay the rent and have some left over for their expenses. That way he could lend Majid the money without worrying. Worst case scenario, he would ask his brother for a little help if his expenses got out of hand. At least his brother didn't have to worry about rent, he thought. He couldn't help but feel envy over Hamid, who with the money he saved from not paying rent bought luxuries and toys like a big screen TV, state-of-the-art stereo system, and brand new rugs; he also drove a brand new Peugeot. But most of all, Mohammad was jealous that his brother's wife didn't hassle him about the state of their finances.

Before he could compare his life to that of his brother, Mohammad arrived at a busy square, where a group of people stood by the side of the street and shouted their destinations as oncoming drivers like him slowed down and picked up passengers in accordance with where they were headed. Mohammad was driving toward the center of Tehran, and after listening carefully to the calls of the passengers, he let three people into his car.

Over the past two decades, it had become common for vehicle owners to pick up passengers, charging rates somewhat below official taxis. This method had proven to be useful to passengers as well, who find it cheaper to take shared cab rides rather than taking more costly personal taxis.

Usually before each passenger got into a personalized taxi, the driver and the passenger negotiated the price of the fare. Mohammad, who had gotten ripped off a few times, made sure to establish the fare with the old man, young lady, and young man who got into his car. The lady sat next to Mohammad, while the men sat in the backseat. Mohammad headed south toward the center of the city, hoping to pick up at least one more passenger headed toward his destination.

Driving through the frustrating, slow, and busy Tehran traffic, Mohammad noticed a shiny Mercedes pull up next to him as he waited for the traffic to move. The driver looked to be in his midtwenties; he had a black designer shirt on and wore sunglasses while laughing on his phone. Mohammad also noticed the woman sitting quietly next to him. Her scarf was draped loosely over her blonde hair, while bandages were wrapped around her chin and nose; Mohammad assumed that she probably had some cosmetic surgery done. The young man looked carefree, laughing on his phone and not caring about the annoying traffic or the hazardous smog that lay in a haze just outside of his window.

Mohammad wondered where he was going and what his plans were. One thing that was for sure, he wasn't driving toward the center square with three passengers or contemplating making the dreadful run to deliver pirated DVDs after the rush hour cooled down. But before he knew it, the traffic moved, and the young man in his backseat, who Mohammad noticed had been leering at the woman sitting beside him, brought his head between the two front seats and managed to gain her attention.

"You know," he said, "you're too fine to be walking the streets by yourself, beautiful."

The young lady twisted her head away from him in disgust.

"Excuse me?" she yelled. "Who the hell do you think you are talking to, you thug!" She raised her voice as Mohammad kept one eye on them and one eye on the road.

"Watch your mouth when you're talking to me, bitch!" the young man shouted back, nearly climbing over the front seat. Mohammad tried but failed to grab the man by the wrist while trying to concentrate on the road and the situation that was brewing in his car.

"That's no way to talk to a lady!" the man sitting behind Mohammad said. "Don't you have any manners, punk?"

"Mind your own fucking business, old geezer!" the young man snapped as he turned around and faced the old man in the backseat. Mohammad pulled to the side of the street and slammed on his brakes.

"Just pay your fares and get the hell out of my car!" he yelled. "All of you! Come on!" He yanked the hand brake as the woman quickly opened her purse and handed him a few bills before jumping out of the car and disappearing into the masses walking on the dense sidewalk. The old man followed suit, as Mohammad waited for the rude passenger in the back to do the same.

"You're supposed to drive me to center square, asshole!" the young man replied as Mohammad extended his arm toward him, flapping his palms and waiting for payment.

"You should have thought about that before you started harassing my customers," Mohammad said, "and plus, the center square is only a dozen blocks away, so give me my money and get the fuck out of my car."

The young man looked at Mohammad and his extended arm before grinning and opening the back door, walking away without paying.

"Hey, asshole! You didn't pay!" Mohammad shouted as he got out and stood in between the door and the car as other drivers honked and drove by in the busy traffic.

"Consider yourself lucky that I didn't give you a broken nose, asshole!" the young man yelled back as he faded into the pedestrian traffic.

"Piece of shit!" Mohammad shouted as he sat back in his car before slamming the door shut.

He rubbed his eyes again before running his fingers through his hair. He noticed more hairs had fallen out as he stared at the strands sitting on his fingers and palm. Mohammad spent the next few hours picking up passengers and driving them to different locations through the suffocating traffic. Just before nine, he was close to his apartment; Mohammad decided to stop home for a quick dinner before heading out with Hamid on their distribution route. But before returning, he stopped to get gas for his car.

Since 2007, gasoline has been rationed in Iran in order to make up for shortfalls in the country's archaic refining industry.[38] Fearing harsher United Nations sanctions, Ahmadinejad's government issued gas cards for each vehicle; drivers can now pump up to eighty liters of gas at the price of 100 tomans per liter (the price from 2008). In the event that an individual goes over the eighty-liter limit, the price then is set at 400 tomans per liter. Many in Iran believe that the rationing of gas has been the main culprit in amplifying what is already an astonishing and rampant inflation rate. Taxi drivers have felt the direct impact as now a significant portion of their income is spent on gasoline. General

---

38 http://www.nytimes.com/2007/06/29/world/middleeast/29iran.html.

vehicle owners, in addition, have suffered greatly as long lines and waiting times at the gas stations have significantly increased and added further delay and thus aggravation to their daily lives.

That day was no exception, as Mohammad approached the long line of cars stretching out of the station and down the street. The entrance line was clogged by so many cars that it had caused a temporary traffic jam going back for nearly two blocks. Without much of a choice, Mohammad shook his head, rolled his eyes, and proceeded to the back of the line.

Nearly a quarter of an hour later, Mohammad approached the entrance of the gas station and pulled up to the next available pump. As he handed his gas card to the pump's attendant, his phone rang. It was his brother Hamid, who was on his way to Mohammad's house. He told Mohammad that he had rounded up the list of their orders and was ready to make their regular Saturday rounds. Mohammad and Hamid had around 150 clients and tried to meet their requests by making weekly deliveries; they took orders from 20 to 25 clients a night. While they were willing to expand to other areas of town, their clientele for the most part consisted of people they could trust through word of mouth and, for financial reasons, people who lived not too far from them.

Hamid was the one who located movies and music CDs, while Mohammad looked for clients through his connections both from his daily work and his taxi shifts; they both divided the profits in half. For the most part, it was an amicable partnership.

Returning the gas nozzle back to the pump, the gas station attendant walked around the car and toward Mohammad's window in order to collect the money.

"That'll be 8,500 tomans sir," the attendant said, handing Mohammad back his gas card.

"What? 8,500?" Mohammad asked as he popped his head out of the window and glared at the attendant.

"Yes sir, you had five liters remaining on your card; the remaining twenty liters are charged at the regular 400 tomans per liter," the attendant replied. Mohammad placed his palm over his eyes and rubbed them while he shook his head. After a momentary pause, he reached into his coat pocket and paid the attendant.

He soon arrived at his apartment and slipped his shoes off before heading into the kitchen. He opened the fridge door and took out the cold leftovers his mother gave them the day before. Setting the black pot on the kitchen counter, he began to dig into the stale rice while squeezing his spoon through the cold chicken breasts. Mona came into the kitchen with a smile.

"Where have you been, Mohammad?" she asked, still smiling, as Mohammad bent over the kitchen counter while shoveling the leftovers into his mouth.

"I was with my mysterious … God, where do you think I was, Mona?" he asked with his mouth full.

"No, I'm not grumbling, sweetie. It's just that Ramin [one of his sons] took his first steps today!" she replied with a big grin; Mohammad dropped his spoon into the pot, raised his head, and looked at his wife with a big grin.

"Oh, that's … that's fantastic," Mohammad replied as he hugged and kissed his wife.

"You can tell that Ramin is a bit faster than Uptin [Mohammad's other son], but Uptin is cuter," Mona said as Mohammad returned to the pot of leftovers.

"There're both cute," Mohammad replied. "You just watch, lady, you're gonna be fighting girls off with a stick when they grow up."

"So are we going to have you for tonight?" his wife asked while placing her hands over his shoulders and slowly rubbing them.

"No, I can't. Hamid is going to be here any minute now," he replied, wiping his mouth with his jacket sleeve before taking a bottle of water from the fridge and gulping it down just as the doorbell rang.

"Okay, but before you go I need 80,000 tomans," she said as Mohammad walked over to his shoes.

"80,000? What do you need 80,000 for? I just gave you 100,000 last week," Mohammad replied.

"Oh you know, the girls and I are to going to the beauty spa; what do you think that I need it for? I have to buy groceries and diapers for the kids ... again!" she replied as he ran his hand through his hair and scratched his head before giving his wife a couple of travelers' checks.

He might have not done much of the family shopping, but he knew how expensive groceries and everyday items had become. Just the other day, Mona had told him that she paid 18,000 for a kilo of beef, while it cost her 13,000 for a whole chicken and 22,000 for a bag of rice. At the rate things were going, he wouldn't be able to take another day off for at least four months.

Slowly walking down the stairs, Mohammad began to do more math in his head. His monthly salary was 900,000 tomans (approximately US$900), while he made an additional 250,000 through picking up passengers and selling DVDs. His expenses the month before, including rent, groceries, utilities, and gas and the medical bills for his twin boys, came to a total of just 1.2 million tomans. Plus there was the million he promised to loan his friend Majid, which he was worried to tell his wife about; he hoped that Majid would pay him back before she realized that the money was missing from his account.

Just before stepping outside of the main entrance of the four-story apartment building, Mohammad paused; he leaned against the wall to the left of the door and held out his palm while looking up. He prayed to God to help him keep a roof over his family and food on their table. He prayed that he would never ask anyone for a loan, especially his mother. The last thing Mohammad wanted to do was to burden his poor mother, who recently faced the tragedy of losing her husband, Mohammad's father.

A little later, Mohammad and Hamid headed out into the dark hours of the night and began their nightly distribution route. Grinning right off the bat, Mohammad informed Hamid that one of his twin boys took his first steps today; although he was overjoyed, he nevertheless wished that he could have been there in person. Hamid, whose wife was pregnant with their first child, smiled and placed his palm on his brother's shoulder and reassured him that his sacrifices would pay off one day when his boys were in university, thanks to their parents' sacrifices. Nodding his head, Mohammad gazed at his brother and smiled just as they were about to arrive at the first drop point of the night, an apartment complex that housed a number of their clients.

Mohammad hadn't been with Hamid the previous Saturday, and just before getting out of the car, Hamid warned him that last week he ran into a resident of the complex that sported a dark beard and looked to be a *hezbollahee*. He had stopped Hamid and questioned him about his presence in the apartment complex. Hamid had lied and told the man that he was there to visit his sick auntie, refusing to say which unit his made-up auntie lived in.

Grinding his teeth, Mohammad listened as Hamid further said that the man threatened to call the disciplinary forces if he saw Hamid there again. There were far too many clients in the complex that Mohammad couldn't afford to lose. He rubbed his eyes with his thumb and index finger. He glanced at Hamid and then at the large black plastic bag filled with CDs and DVDs. He slowly nodded his head as they both got out of Hamid's car and carried the bag through the gates of the complex.

The two casually stood next to the building's buzzer as Mohammad rang the number of one of his clients while Hamid kept a lookout. They entered the building, went to the only elevator located at the end of a narrow lobby, and pressed the button. The elevator shortly arrived, and after the doors opened, Hamid hid the black bag behind his back and took a few short steps away from Mohammad.

Noticing his brother's wide-open eyes and mouth, Mohammad looked over and gazed upon a man in the tiny elevator, who had noticed the two and was staring Hamid down. The man was short and portly and had on a gray polyester coat along with black trousers. He had a dark beard and held a circle of prayer beads in his right hand. He sort of reminded Mohammad of his supervisor. Witnessing his brother's unblinking reaction, Mohammad guessed that this was the man Hamid had just warned him about.

"Well, well, look who we have here," the bearded man said. "Let me guess; you came back to visit your sick auntie again?" He stood in front of the elevator door, which subsequently closed, while Mohammad clenched his fists.

"I see you brought another visitor with you this time and ... medication for your poor old auntie?" the man said, pointing to the black plastic bag hidden behind Hamid's back. "You think I am a fool? You think I don't know what you are doing here with that smut in your hands?"

The man took a step closer to them while Mohammad tightened his fists and grinded his teeth.

"I have children living in this building, you punks!" he said. "I ought to call 110 [911] right now and have you two arrested for corrupting the youth of this country!" Before he could actually act on his threat, Mohammad snapped and nearly leaped the short distance between him and the man, grabbing the bearded man by the collar and slamming him against the closed doors of the elevator.

"Corrupting the youth?" he said. "I have to work like a dog all day just so my family can survive while bastards like you have been siphoning the blood of the people for the past thirty fucking years, and you have the audacity to say that I'm the cause of corruption in this country!"

Mohammad gripped the man by his collar as he gasped for air and struggled to free himself. Hamid dropped the plastic bag, and the DVDs and CDs spilled onto the floor as he tried to pull his brother away from the bearded man.

"But guess what, asshole?" he continued. "Your shelf life is near expiration; the people have woken up, and they have had enough of you vampires," Mohammad shouted at the man as Hamid managed to pull him away from the man, who fell to his knees while trying to catch his breath.

"Let's get out of here before he calls the police!" Hamid said, as he pulled his brother away from the man before quickly picking up the spilled contents of the black plastic bag. Shortly after, the two ran to Hamid's car and drove away.

"What in God's name is wrong with you?" Hamid asked as he stomped his foot on the gas. Mohammad held his hands over his face and covered both of his eyes.

"What if that guy was someone important, Mohammad? He can make our lives a living hell!" Hamid raised his voice as he glanced back at the pile of DVDs and CDs in the backseat of his car.

"My life is already hell, Hamid," Mohammad sighed, removing his hands from his face and staring outside at the dark buildings.

"We'll have to call those clients and tell them that the deliveries will be made on another night," Hamid said. "Fuck, you realize we might have just lost twenty-five customers?" Mohammad blindly stared out the car's window.

Chapter 11.
Mohammad: The Tragedy

———⟊⟊⟊———

The awning of the bank hanging over his head, Mohammad limped through the entrance soon after the doors opened. His feet aching and sore, he slowly walked toward the short line. Waiting for his turn, a house fly landed on his collar; he began to swat it away only to have the insect land back on the same spot. Mohammad approached the teller, withdrew the money he had promised Majid, and rushed back to work.

Arriving a few minutes late to work, Mohammad quickly walked through the lobby to the elevators before noticing a number of disciplinary forces conversing in the lobby. Immediately dropping his head and turning away from the men in uniform, Mohammad jabbed the elevator button a few times and quickly got in it. He leaned against the elevator wall and recalled his brother's warning about the man they ran into last night.

He began to think about the building where they had seen the man, wondering whether a high-ranking person could live there. The complex was newly built, and the cars parked in the streets were modest by Tehran's rich standards (although they were worth more than his and his brother's cars put together). To think about it, his clients living in the complex all had luxurious furniture along with the state-of-the-art electronic entertainment systems. Cold sweat began to run down the back of his neck as he gulped down his spit. He quickly wiped his hair with his hands while catching a glimpse of the others in the elevator. Mohammad quickly exited the elevator and headed to his work station.

With the thought of losing his job and ending up in jail for pirating immoral and illegal material swirling in his mind, Mohammad dropped his head and quietly approached the hall next to his office. He peeked from the corner of the hall and saw Majid, with his hands cuffed behind his back, being escorted by officers out of their office, while his supervisor in the same dusty polyester coat stood at the entrance of the control room with his arms crossed. Men from other departments gathered outside of their office doors and watched the scene.

"Get this thug out of my sight," Mohammad's supervisor said as a teary-eyed Majid was led away. Holding his briefcase tightly, Mohammad quickly rushed through the crowds and over to his supervisor.

"What is going on here?" Mohammad asked, as the men in uniform escorted Majid out of his sight.

"It doesn't concern you!" his supervisor replied, not even looking at Mohammad.

"But he's my assistant," Mohammad said, "I have a right to know what he has done!"

"He is an antigovernment hooligan and a complete disrespect to this institution and our holy leader," the supervisor replied, raising his voice while still not looking at Mohammad as his arms remained crossed. "At least I'm glad that we still have loyal and trustworthy employees here like brother Ahmad, who brought his treachery to my attention and is thus deservedly being promoted for his loyalty," the supervisor added. Mohammad's grip around his briefcase became tighter once he realized that their colleague had been behind Majid's arrest.

"You all should learn from Ahmad," the supervisor said loudly. "Let his loyalty and unconditional obedience serve as an example!" Ahmad walked through the glass doors of the control room, smiled, and partially bowed his head to the supervisor while standing next to the man who just promoted him.

"Starting tomorrow, Ahmad will be my new assistant; now everyone congratulate him and get back to your posts!" the supervisor said, shaking Ahmad's hand and walking away. The crowd of people returned back to their offices without even acknowledging Ahmad.

Frozen to his spot, Mohammad stared at Ahmad, who at first didn't acknowledge his presence. Mohammad had been working at his post for the past four years and was hoping to land the position that was just handed on a silver platter to Ahmad, who had only been hired nine months before. He grinded his teeth and stared at Ahmad, who smirked at his former officemate and began walking past Mohammad down the deserted hallway.

"Why did you sell Majid out? He was your colleague!" Mohammad said as he paced past Ahmad and stood in front of him while tightening his grip around his briefcase.

"You would have done the same, so drop the act and don't pretend like you're a fucking saint," Ahmad replied.

"He has a three-year-old child and a wife; how could you do it, you piece of shit?" Mohammad grabbed Ahmad's collar with his free hand.

"Get your fucking hands off me!" Ahmad replied, yanking Mohammad's grip from his collar. "I'm your superior now, and if you don't want to end up like that fucking idiot, then I suggest you start kissing my ass!" Ahmad quickly added, staring Mohammad down before walking away.

The rest of the day was even more unbearable. Mohammad was summoned by his supervisor and informed that he was being demoted to an assistant with less pay for not reporting Majid's antigovernment slurs.

After receiving the unpleasant news of his demotion along with his supervisor's tongue lashing, Mohammad marched to his office and sat behind his desk while powering up his calculator. Based on his calculations, the demotion in his wages meant that he and his family would have to move to an even smaller apartment, and his wife would have to cut back on buying groceries and perhaps look for a job while his mother looked after the kids. Thinking of his mother, he imagined asking her to sell her apartment and slammed his fist on his desk.

He paused and stared at the number displayed on the thin screen of his calculator. The bitter taste of demotion in his mouth, Mohammad slowly got up from his chair and looked around the empty office. His eyes locked onto a picture sitting on Majid's former desk. It was a photo of Majid's three-year-old daughter; the little girl was sitting on plush green grass while holding a bright daisy in her hands and smiling. He put the picture down as images of Majid being taken away flashed before his eyes. Tears layered over his eyes as the images of yellow and orange leaves submerging in the water garden of his mother's yard began to run in the back of his mind. Poor Majid, he kept saying, while his tears dropped onto Majid's desk.

His day went painfully slow. He sat in his office and tried his best to avoid everyone, especially Ahmad and his supervisor. During his lunch break, he went to the bank and deposited the amount he withdrew for Majid, instead of eating among his colleagues. He even made sure to leave later than usual, after the two men were gone. Trudging down the hall and toward his car, Mohammad got behind the wheel and glanced at the descending autumn sun. He put the key in the ignition but didn't start his car; instead, he lowered his head and rested it on the steering wheel. His eyes closed, all he could think about was the number displayed on his calculator. It wasn't long before the picture of Majid's daughter took over his thoughts as he began to think about his own boys, picturing them giggling and running around their small apartment. Perhaps Majid being arrested was a blessing in disguise, as he no longer had to lend him the amount that was nearly half of his entire savings.

With his boys in mind, he started the car, and although he didn't have the strength or the motivation to make his usual taxi rounds, he nevertheless pulled out of the parking structure and looked for passengers seeking a ride.

It wasn't long before he noticed an elderly woman standing on the edge of the sidewalk, waving to the oncoming cars. Rolling down his window, he pulled up next to her.

"Where are you headed to, lady?" Mohammad asked.

"Enghelab Square," she said, "but I want an exclusive ride, not shared with other passengers."

"That's fine, but it will cost 7, 000," Mohammad said. She nodded and got into the backseat. Mohammad began driving toward south central Tehran. He eased out into the busy traffic, and a car in front of him cut him off.

"What a terrible driver," the elderly woman said.

Mohammad shook his head and sighed. "Nothing unusual about that. I take it you're not from the city?" he asked, glancing at her through his rearview mirror.

"Why do you ask?" she said. "Is it that obvious that I don't live in Tehran?" She tucked her gray hair beneath her black head scarf.

"Here, when people get behind the wheel of a car, things such as mirrors, signals, speed limits, staying in the lane, and giving pedestrians the right-of-way is meaningless; cutting people off is normal, so you might as well get used to it," Mohammad replied.

"It wasn't like this when I used to live here," she said. "Everything in this city is just so chaotic now." The old lady looked out the window at the traffic and shook her head.

"If you don't mind me asking, how long have you been away?" Mohammad asked, glancing through his rearview mirror.

"It's been more than thirty years now," she said. "I moved to America about six months after the revolution. I wouldn't have come back if it wasn't for my sister passing away."

"Do you have any children?" Mohammad asked.

"Two boys and a girl," she replied.

"You made the best sacrifice for your kids," he said. "I wish I had the resources to get my wife and kids away from here." The woman looked at him and nodded.

"It's a jungle out here; actually much worse than a jungle," he said. "At least the jungle has its own laws; here people live like a virus! Siblings betray one another and their parents, and coworkers sell each other out so they can get a promotion. Forgive my language, but it is like living in a pool of human excrement."

Mohammad shook his head before slamming his fist against the horn and shouting at another car that had just cut him off.

"Leaving Iran is the best decision," he continued, "not just for people with families but for everyone. I'm thirty-one years old and the only good thing that I recall happening here during my entire lifetime was the events of the weeks after the last elections. Those days, if you saw someone in need of help, someone running away from those savages, or even someone who was wounded, you would immediately give them shelter, take them to the hospital, or drive them to safety, knowing that at least you were doing something to help out your countrymen.

"But now things are back to the way they used to be," he said. "Heck, things are worse than before with all this inflation, unemployment, propaganda, censorship, arrests; we're so busy trying to survive that we don't even take a second to think about the person next to us." Mohammad stared blindly into the gray traffic while the woman looked back at him quietly and slowly nodded her head.

The rest of the car ride was quiet; the elderly woman only spoke to ask about Mohammad's twins, their names and their ages. Upon arriving at the square, the woman gave Mohammad 10,000 tomans instead of the 7,000 they agreed upon. She told him to keep his spirits up and, at least for the sake of his children and better opportunities, try to leave Iran for a place that offered a greater quality of life. For the first time during the day, Mohammad smiled; he thanked the old lady before continuing his route.

Several hours later, Mohammad stopped by a sandwich shop to eat. While gulping down a sub along with a cold beverage, he called his brother to get an update on their nightly drop-offs. Hamid informed him that most of the clients they skipped the night before were irate and threatened to go to their competitors unless their orders were delivered that night. Hamid suggested that they stop selling to that particular complex all together and avoid the hassles of running into people like the bearded man.

Mohammad explained that he had lost a significant percentage of his salary through his demotion and told his brother that he would make the rounds to that particular complex all by himself, keeping the proceedings for himself as well. Reluctant at first, Hamid agreed. Mohammad swigged his drink, threw away the small remainder of his sandwich, and headed to Hamid's in order to pick up the orders from the night before and those for that night.

On his way to his first delivery, Mohammad called Mona. He had planned to break the news of his demotion but instead told her that he'd be coming home late that night, after making his rounds. He asked her to put the twins on the phone and listened to their voices while picturing them. After telling his wife how much he loved her, Mohammad hung up the phone. With tears in his eyes, he pictured Majid's little girl as he wiped them away.

He arrived at the complex from the night before and parked his car, sitting behind the wheel for several minutes. His heart pounding in his chest and the images of Majid's daughter fading away, Mohammad quickly grabbed the black plastic bag in the backseat and paced toward the gates of the complex.

After being buzzed in, Mohammad avoided the elevator and instead ran up the stairs. He quickly went door-to-door, making his deliveries while collecting his fees and telling his clients to e-mail him their list from now on. Running his hand through his sweaty hair, Mohammad quickly ran down the stairs to the lobby. His heart still pounding, he peeked through the lobby door to see if anyone was in the building. With no one in sight, he quietly walked through the lobby and exited the building.

As he headed toward his car, he noticed a green and white car belonging to Tehran's disciplinary forces parked close to the complex. Sweat soaking through his shirt and running from his armpits to his sides, he glanced down and reached for his keys as he approached his car. His heart nearly stood still and he dropped his keys when he saw the bearded man from the night before, leaning against his car in the shadows. His arms crossed, the man smirked at Mohammad as two uniformed officers emerged from behind the vehicles parked next to his car.

"Whose shelf life is over now, punk?" the bearded man asked loudly, while one of the officers twisted Mohammad's arms behind his back and cuffed him.

"Make sure you search his car too; I'm sure you'll find more contraband in there," the man said to the other officer, who proceeded to search his car, producing another plastic bag intended for his other clients.

As he sat in the backseat of the disciplinary forces' car, Mohammad didn't think about losing his job and the difficulties of making ends meet; instead, all he could think about was the blurry shapes that his mother had pointed out to him as she read his Turkish coffee cup, just two days ago. It seemed that he finally understood what his fortune meant, and it wasn't exactly what his mother had proclaimed. He realized that he wasn't the person riding the mule that was pulling the heavy load up the steep mountain.

Mohammad—and everyone else like him—was the mule that was being mercilessly ridden and abused on a cruel path by the regime. But despite all of that, the tidal wave was on its way and looked to knock the figure off the mule. Picturing the images of regime leaders crashing off a cliff and drowning in the heavy waters brought a smile to Mohammad's face. He thought about the events following the 2009 elections, events that surely brewed the coming storm.

---⚸---

Mohammad was arrested and held for a period of three days under the charges of distributing material that was un-Islamic and illegal, in addition to charges of assault. It turned out that the bearded man was in fact an important high-ranking government bureaucrat, who made sure that Mohammad lost his job as part of his punishment. Mohammad was additionally given a probationary sentence of ten months and had his bail set at two million tomans, which was nearly all of his family savings.

Being unable to land a government job—or any jobs for that matter—in the public industry due to his charges and poor reputation, Mohammad is now working alongside his brother at the cellular boutique owned by Hamid's father-in-law. He and his wife and kids moved into his mother's apartment, which is in the process of being sold in order for the proceeds to help Mohammad rent a bigger apartment and pay for their expenses. His mother, meanwhile, has agreed to move into their new place and take care of the twins, while his wife has taken a job as a sales assistant in a woman's clothing store.

Mohammad continues to drive his car as a taxi, and despite his probation, he and Hamid still deliver pirated DVDs and CDs at night, along with installing satellite dishes. Their expenses remain nearly the same despite Mohammad's now significantly reduced income. As for Majid, Mohammad's former colleague was released after spending forty days in jail. His wife and child left him while he was unemployed, and he similarly lives with his parents.

In the last conversation that we had, Mohammad indicated that he is incredibly frustrated at his current status in society, and although he admits that his knowledge of politics is limited, he plans to be as vocal as possible when the next demonstration is held. Mohammad strongly believes that the individuals who are running his country have very little knowledge about the actual affairs of the state. Despite being in charge of one of the most oil-rich nations on the planet, the regime has turned its back on the masses and is busy stuffing its pockets with the proceeds of oil instead of investing much needed funds in areas of employment, social security, and health care.

Chapter 12.
Nasrin: Courtroom Injustice

Shirin Ebadi, the first Iranian and first Muslim woman to win the Nobel Peace Prize, once said, "The condition of women in Islamic societies as a whole is also far from desirable. However, we should acknowledge that there are differences. In certain countries, the conditions are much better and in others much worse."[39] When discussing life in Iran, it is only appropriate that we reflect on the status of women. Although I have focused on themes such as temporary marriages and prostitution, I agree with Ebadi that the position of women in Iran is certainly not desirable.

A true pioneer among Iranians and a constant voice in efforts for democracy, human rights, and especially women's rights, Ebadi has been in exile since 2009, due to her support of Iran's opposition movement.[40] According to Reuters, in November 2009, the regime took away Ebadi's Nobel medal and her award diploma, making her the first person to ever have their Peace Prize confiscated by national authorities.[41]

---

39   http://www.brainyquote.com/quotes/authors/s/shirin_ebadi.html.

40   http://www.thedailybeast.com/newsweek/2010/01/08/shirin-ebadi-the
-activist-in-exile.html.

41   http://www.reuters.com/article/2009/11/26/idUSGEE5AP1X5.

Every woman I spoke to in the course of writing this book expressed strong dislike for the status of women in Iran. All felt that the regime, through its policies and rhetoric, had relegated women to the status of second-class citizens. One particular woman with this viewpoint was Nasrin Etemadi, a forty-seven-year-old housewife and mother of two boys. In 1999, Nasrin was forced into taking a retirement package from the Ministry of Agriculture just so that she and her husband could collectively pay their rent and other expenses. Ironically, Hooshang Etemadi, her husband, who also worked in the same ministry, was promoted to a highly paid senior position two years after Nasrin's retirement; with his wages, Hooshang was able to purchase an apartment for the family to live in. The older of the two sons, Poorya, is attending graduate school, while the younger son, Payam, is about to enter university. Please refer to the appendix for more information and a historical take on women in Iran.

The evening sound of kids playing soccer in the alley behind her second-story apartment joined the warm July breeze coming through the kitchen window. Nasrin was preparing a tray of freshly brewed tea along with a dish of creamy pastries brought by her guests, her husband's coworker and his wife, Nasrin's good friend.

She looked out of the window at the kids playing in the evening sun, through black metal bars that were fixed to the building outside of all of her second-story windows. The checkered impression of the bars fell over her upper body in the form of a shadow, as Nasrin stood back and stared at the black bars. The memories of the day that her husband had them installed rolled back in her mind. Her husband had ignored her request to talk about the issue, while barking orders at the men installing the bars; he only told his wife that the metal bars were for their security since he had noticed a suspicious man outside their building, staring at their windows. That was just a few weeks after they had moved into their apartment. This was the last time that Nasrin recalled being happy while living with her husband.

Things at home between she and her husband had not been great lately, but then again judging by the shouts and screeches coming from the other apartments, Nasrin wasn't the only disgruntled spouse. Nevertheless, unlike her neighbors, Nasrin's problems with her husband didn't generate from infidelity; on the contrary, she trusted Hooshang, even though she did follow him a few times to make sure that he wasn't cheating on her. Her problems began in 2002, nearly eight years ago, a few months after her husband bought them their apartment.

Before moving in, the two struggled and worked hard to pay their bills along with putting together enough money to send their first son to university, but they were happy and lived together as a family. Even when Nasrin was forced into taking a retirement package from her employer, she did it knowing that she was making a sacrifice for her family; slowly, they were climbing their way out of hardship. That was before Hooshang was promoted, and after just one year, he managed to put together enough money to buy their second-story, three-bedroom apartment.

Since then, the two often argued about money and expenses, and in nearly every argument, Hooshang would dangle the idea that he owned the family home and was in absolute control. With her dowry set over twenty-six years ago at only eight gold coins, Nasrin would fold and walk away from every argument. Divorce would only break her sons' hearts, not to mention leave her with a handful of gold coins, worthless given the rampant inflation rates in 2010 Tehran.

In addition to their arguments about money and the ownership of the apartment, Hooshang refused to support Nasrin or her father, who was having disputes with Ali Moradi, his tenant, even when he was on his death bed. After the two were married, Hooshang expected his father-in-law to grant them a helping hand and buy them a place of their own; when that didn't happen, he made sure to bar his in-laws from ever coming over, especially after buying the apartment.

Nasrin's father recently passed away, and Hooshang refused to help out his wife in her battles against her two brothers and Moradi, who was refusing to pay the contracted amount of rent and was engaged in a rigid court battle with the estate of Nasrin's father. Deep down inside, Nasrin felt that Hooshang never supported her, especially since her father passed away, on the grounds that he didn't want her to gain the financial independence that she desired. Financial independence would end his control over her and grant her peace of mind should she ever want to move on with her life.

Nasrin sighed, the thick bars blocking the exquisite rays of the declining sun and much of the scenery of the neighborhood; she gently picked up the tray of steaming tea cups along with the plate of creamy pastries and headed toward the living room, where her guests were waiting.

"Did you tell your boys the joke you told me yesterday at work?" Hooshang's colleague, Masoud asked as Nasrin slowly walked into the living room, balancing the tray of tea cups along with the plate of pastries in her hands. Her husband chuckled, while Nasrin, being familiar with her husband's sense of humor, frowned at her husband.

"You guys are gonna love this one," Hooshang said to Poorya and Payam, still chuckling while ignoring his wife's glare. "At eighteen, a woman is like a soccer ball—she has twenty-two men chasing after her; at twenty-four, a woman is more like a basketball— she has ten men chasing after her; at thirty-two, she becomes more like a tennis ball, and only two men are chasing after her; finally, at forty-two, she becomes like a cannon ball, where instead, all the men run away from her." Hooshang and Masoud laughed while Nasrin's sons sat quietly in their chairs, glancing at their mother before hanging their heads. Masoud's wife, Sarah, rolled her eyes at Nasrin as she took a cup of tea and a piece of pastry from the tray.

Nasrin tried to avoid the eyes of the woman she had become friends with over the years. She quickly turned to her husband and nearly shoved the tray of hot beverages and snacks in his face while continuing to glare at him. His laughter coming to a stop, Hooshang slowly removed one of the cups from the tray while staring down his wife, who quickly moved the tray and walked away from her husband.

"Did you get it, Poorya? A cannon ball! That's how destructive they become after the age of forty!" Hooshang repeated, watching his wife walk away from him while his elder son smiled awkwardly and then stared back at the floor.

"So how is your mother doing, dear?" Sarah asked as Nasrin set the tray on the table and sat down next to the woman.

"She's better; it's been six months now that Dad passed away, and she's starting to accept it," Nasrin replied, partially sighing as she reached for her cup.

"Hooshang has been telling me that there have been problems with the inheritance and the division of your dad's estate," Masoud said. Nasrin slowly nodded while sipping her tea.

"It's not just the division, we've also been having problems with the tenant who has been renting out my dad's old store and the office unit located behind the store. I've been in and out of the courts ever since Dad died, trying to get a ruling against the tenant for not paying the contracted amount of rent," Nasrin replied. shaking her head while breathing deeply.

"Problems with the division? I don't understand, didn't your father have a will?" Sarah asked, raising one of her eyebrows.

"No," she explained, "Dad was in the process of making one, which ironically would have favored me, but he fell ill and passed on before he ever got the chance to do so, and because of that, my two younger siblings are entitled to almost twice what I would have inherited, just for being men." Nasrin rolled her eyes and shook her head again while the room went silent momentarily.

"Only here will you find the oldest child of the family, and the one who has been nursing her elderly parents for years, getting less inheritance than her two younger brothers, who reside overseas and live without a care for their parents," Nasrin added, breaking the silence as the woman sitting next to her shook her head.

"This is what it comes down to, this is what we're teaching our children, that a man has twice as much value as a woman," Nasrin continued before finishing her cup and setting it down on the table in a hurry.

The sound of the china clattering against the wooden table swirled in the living room as the awkward silence once again took over. Her boys continued to stare at the floor, and Nasrin could see, out of the corner of her eyes, Hooshang's annoyed facial expression.

"Don't blame the way things are here, blame your father for dying without making a will and taking care of his only daughter," Hooshang said with a straight face, as the women in the room jerked their faces toward him with their eyes stretched wide open.

"Your wife does make a good point, Hooshang," Masoud said, after his wife glared at him. "The law is a bit too archaic here and certainly not in the favor of women."

"Like I said, there is nothing wrong with the laws in this country; they are based on universal laws, which simply preach that men are superior to women and thus deserve more!" Hooshang replied. Nasrin stared at him, squinting her eyes while quietly grinding her teeth. Even their sons lifted up their heads and looked at their father as Nasrin felt the discomfort of her sons, sitting on the edge of their seats.

"Universal laws? Since when did pathetic rituals of places like Afghanistan and Saudi Arabia become universal laws?" Nasrin asked, nearly raising her voice as she continued to glare at her husband, her teeth grinding back and forth in her mouth.

"Of course it is a universal law!" he replied. "Just look at significance men have in the professional sector. The best surgeons in the world are men! The best engineers in the world are men! The best judges, chefs, architects, lawyers, artists, CEOs ... all men!" Hooshang added, glancing toward the quiet and still faces in the room, who now all looked back him.

"Can I get anyone anything? Maybe top off your teas," Nasrin suggested, quickly entering the conversation as she pointed to the half-empty cups of her guests, who glanced away from Hooshang and back at her.

"Airline companies trust their planes to be flown by men while the women serve the passengers food and beverages, just like in the real world. You women should be on your hands and knees thanking God that Iranian men don't treat their women like the men in Saudi Arabia and Afghanistan treat their wives," he continued as his wife dug her fingernails into her arms and slowly pulled them down, scratching her skin while her guests looked away.

"Too bad we don't live in Europe or North America, then maybe you would have a firsthand experience of how real men treat their wives and how the law supports women!" Nasrin replied, rolling her eyes at her husband while she noticed her guests glancing uncomfortably at one another.

"Yeah, real men; don't you boys pay attention to this," Hooshang said to his sons. "The men over there don't know the first thing about being men. They had their nuts surgically removed at birth." Hooshang and his colleague once again chuckled.

"I actually have to go soon," Poorya said. "I have to … I mean, Payam and I are meeting a couple of friends at the café down the street." Poorya swallowed hard as he stood up, followed by his younger brother; both partially hung their heads and left the room, having said their farewells to their guests.

"We should get going as well," Sarah said, soon after Nasrin's boys left the apartment; she glared at her husband, who rolled his eyes at his wife before standing up.

"Yes, we should go; Mom is coming over for a visit tomorrow, and we better get going," Masoud said as he glanced at his hosts.

"But you just got here," Nasrin said. "At least have some more pastries and tea, maybe some fruits." She turned to her lady guest, who had already put on her head scarf.

"Perhaps next time, dear, but thank you so much for having us over; you two have to come over to our place one of these days," Sarah said as she put on her *manto* (overcoat).

After their guests had left, Nasrin confronted Hooshang. "How dare you talk about my dead father," she said, "especially after the way you refused to ever let him and my mother come over here for a visit?"

Ignoring her, Hooshang walked back to the living room and turned on the television.

"I had to go across town, just so I could see my father on his deathbed!" Nasrin continued as she stood in the doorway to the living room. Hooshang leaned back in his seat and channel surfed.

"My dad didn't owe you or me anything; get that in your head, Hooshang!" Nasrin added as he rolled his eyes at her.

"No, he didn't," he said. "I guess that's why your worthless brothers are getting more than you," Hooshang responded with a smirk, as he quickly glanced at Nasrin and then back at the television set.

Grinding her teeth and glaring at her husband's smirk, Nasrin stormed out and headed to the kitchen. The evening sun now gone, she stood in front of the window and stared at the bright street light, a rare sight that was not blocked by the thick black metal bars. She felt her stomach burning while the temperature of her skin rose. She wanted to scream at him and tell him that she hated everything about him. But his reaction would have been the same stupid smirk, which would have pushed her even closer to the edge.

She had been there before, just over a year ago, when her father was hospitalized with leukemia. She leaned over the window and grabbed the bars tightly with her hands as the heated memories of those days flashed before her eyes. She remembered how Hooshang refused to go to the hospital to see his father-in-law; he also prohibited his two sons from seeing their grandfather. Payam refused and stood defiant to his father, who reacted with aggression and force against his younger son. Screaming, Nasrin interfered and shielded her son, only to come in contact with her husband's swinging arm. Overhearing the domestic disturbance, one of her neighbors must have called the police, who arrived at their apartment only to make a speech about the negative effects of spousal abuse and how Hooshang should try to keep a cool head.

She released the bars and poured herself a tall glass of cold water and returned to her spot by the window before drinking the entire glass in one attempt. Nasrin looked outside at the street light again and thought about the upcoming court date she had with Moradi. A positive ruling from the judge could result in 300,000 tomans being monthly added to her father's estate, and even though her share in the estate was less than her brothers, nevertheless, the additional money meant that she wouldn't have to confront her husband every time that she needed money.

Nasrin spent the next forty-eight hours avoiding her husband. Ignoring one another had become a usual habit over the past few years, for the two spouses went for days without saying much to each other. They had also slept in different rooms ever since a major argument led Hooshang to leave the couple's bedroom and sleep in the living room. Nasrin always felt that their aggressive behavior toward one another, along with the climate of hostility in their home, had negatively impacted her sons, who seemed to desire spending time away from their parents through attending university in distant provinces and staying over at their friends' houses.

Plus, it seemed that every time she and Hooshang got into an argument, her sons acted colder. While the two boys would converse and laugh among each other and with their friends, they hardly spent any time with their parents and preferred to pass their times with their friends or in their rooms behind their computers.

Nasrin got up extra early on the day of her court hearing, even though the hearing wasn't till midafternoon. Unable to afford a lawyer, Nasrin looked through stacks of files and legal textbooks covering her small kitchen table underneath her window. Nasrin once again looked out her window while thinking about the events of her previous court hearing. About three months ago, she sat behind the desk designated for the plaintiff. The judge, a tall and skinny mullah, wearing traditional religious clothing, walked in and glanced at the two parties before staring at Nasrin. He then warned Nasrin that her hair sticking out of her scarf was an insult to the court and the piety of the Islamic Republic. He then questioned her judgment to approach the courts in a dispute over property without one of the male inheritors from her family present.

The black bars restraining her field of vision, Nasrin went over the rest of her previous proceeding. She had explained to the judge that her brothers lived outside of Iran. She thought that he was a reasonable man who would understand her situation and sympathize with her standing on her own. Instead, the judge told her that despite her brothers being out of Iran, she should nevertheless approach the court with a male companion like her husband or a male lawyer. Refusing to hear any more reasoning from Nasrin, the mullah flipped through her documents and told her that she was missing several important pieces of evidence. Ignoring her pleas for leniency and assistance, the judge then ruled in the favor of the defendant, who smirked at Nasrin and put on an over-the-top display of celebration outside of the courtroom as a humiliated Nasrin made her way out. She appealed the decision, which enabled the tenant to pay a fee determined nearly twenty-two years ago when her father bought the commercial property.

With the morning sun sneaking its way into the kitchen, Nasrin glanced away from the window and looked at her files. This time, she was prepared. She even tracked down the original contract that her father and Moradi made just fourteen months ago, before her father fell ill. Nasrin accidentally came across the new contract, written on a folded piece of paper, which was buried in one of her father's poetry books. It was the evidence that she needed to ensure that Moradi, who had treated Nasrin with nothing but contempt since her father died, would pay the fair fees indicated by the contract.

She sat down back at her seat and went over the files along with highlighted passages in the contract and property law textbooks she had bought from the university bookstore after her last hearing.

A few hours later, Nasrin set out for the bus stop. She wanted to get to the courts at least half an hour earlier. Wearing flat bottom shoes, thick black socks, a pair of old gabardine trousers she used to wear to work, followed by a long and gray *manto*, a black scarf, and even a black chador, which covered her entire body with the exception of a triangular shape that exposed her eyes, nose, mouth, and chin. She wanted to make a good impression on the new judge, who like most judges in Iran was a cleric.

Tehran's scorching July sun beat down on the unfazed Nasrin; she marched her way toward the bus stop and waited for her bus to arrive. This was the first of three buses that she had to take in order to get to the courthouse.

The images of no longer having to beg her husband for money in the back of her mind, Nasrin wiped down the sweat on her brow with the edge of her chador while going from bus to bus, finally arriving at the courthouse. Her attire along with her chador soggy and sticky from perspiration, Nasrin approached the main entrance of the courthouse, where an armed guard stood. Presenting her documents, the guard inspected Nasrin's appearance before looking over her court paper and granting her entrance.

Entering the courtroom, she noticed Moradi sitting in the respondent side of the room, along with his male lawyers. She quietly took her seat and placed her files in a binder in front her; when the tenant noticed her, he and his lawyers made dirty looks and quiet, rude chatter, which she ignored. Despite wanting to arrive earlier, it seemed that Nasrin had just made it in time, as shortly after her arrival, the judge entered the courtroom and all the parties began to rise. As Nasrin stood up, she cinched her chador tightly. The judge looked to be in his late fifties as he approached the bench, removed his traditional robe, and draped it behind his chair. He then partially removed his white turban in order to wipe the sweat sitting above his brow before restoring the cleric head guard. The mullah quickly glanced at both parties before informing them that they could take their seats. He removed a pair of reading glasses from a case in his pocket and proceeded to put on the wide, thick, and rosy tinted frames on his face and began reading the papers sitting in front of him.

Nasrin swallowed hard; she had always been critical of Iran's religious figures and strongly believed that the notion of having clerical men as judges created controversy and bias, as she felt they ruled in favor of the religious ruling classes and those who aided and supported the collective system. With that in the back of her mind, the mullah looked over at Nasrin again; he squinted at her attire before speaking.

"I see we have the pleasure of having you as our guest again, Mrs. Nasrin Etemadi," the judge said as Nasrin forced an awkward smile. "We are here in order to resume the property dispute between the estate of Mr. Jampour [Nasrin's father] and Ali Moradi. I hope you are more prepared this time than you were last time, Mrs. Etemadi," he added as he squinted back at Nasrin.

"Yes, Your Honor, I have everything in order," Nasrin quickly replied as she laid her right palm flat on the binder sitting in front of her while still clinging tightly to her chador with her left hand.

"Your Honor, if I may say something before we begin," the tenant's attorney said, "my client has received no support from the estate of Mr. Jampour; the two male successors of the estate are not even in the country, Your Honor!" Moradi squinted his eyes and stared down Nasrin, making her feel the contempt in his eyes.

"Your Honor, my brothers are out of the county, but I have obtained a power of attorney from both of them," Nasrin replied, as she flipped open the binder and yanked out a piece of paper, handing it to the bailiff, who then gave it to the judge.

"This will suffice; there is no need to have the other successors available, although for future proceedings, it would be more beneficial to have male successors present, as it will strengthen your case, Mrs. Etemadi," the judge said, tilting his head toward Nasrin and glancing at her over his glasses. Having heard that before, Nasrin slowly nodded and partially hung her head.

"Very well, now let's not waste the court's time any more and get down to the real reason that you have brought this poor man back here again," the judge said, as he glanced away from the set of papers sitting in front him and looked back at Nasrin.

"He is not paying the agreed amount of rent, Your Honor," Nasrin replied, nearly raising her voice.

"That is a lie, Your Honor! This woman doesn't know what she is talking about!" the tenant shouted as he stood up, faced the judge, and pointed his finger at Nasrin.

"Order! Order in the court!" the judge said, raising his voice. He stared at the tenant while his lawyer stood up, placed his arm around him, and advised him to calm down.

"Mrs. Etemadi, do you have any evidence proving your claim?" the judge said, facing Nasrin as the other side returned to their seats.

"Your Honor, Mr. Ali Moradi has been renting my father's store and the office unit located in the back of the store for twenty-two years," Nasrin said as she flipped through her binder, taking out several pieces of documents. "The original agreement set then was for him to pay a fee of 10,000 for the store and 5,000 for the office on a monthly basis; however, just last year and right before my father's sickness, a new contract was drafted which raised the rent to the amount of 200,000 per month for both the store and the office unit." Nasrin held up her hand and waved the new contract in the air before handing over the documents to the bailiff, who proceeded back to the bench.

"How much rent is the tenant paying your father's estate now?" the judge asked Nasrin as he looked over the documents.

"I'm paying them what is reasonable, Your Honor!" the tenant interrupted, raising his voice again as he stood up and stared down at Nasrin; his attorney quickly got up and restrained his client.

"Order! Mr. Ali Moradi, this is your final warning. I will kick you out if you interrupt the proceedings again!" The judge raised his voice as the two men returned back to their seats.

"He was paying the agreed 200,000 while my father was alive, but as soon as my father passed away six months ago, he went back to paying the fee that was agreed upon in the original contract, which is 15,000!" Nasrin said.

"That is preposterous, Your Honor, my client has no recollection of ever agreeing to this contract that is nothing but a cheap forgery, a fabrication, and an attempt to stain the reputation of this honest and innocent man!" the attorney claimed, pointing his finger at Nasrin, who glanced at the attorney and then back at the judge with her eyes wide in alarm.

"These are genuine documents, Your Honor," she said. "They are the documents that the court requested at the conclusion of the previous trial; I went through hell just so I could locate them, Your Honor!" Nasrin stood up quickly from her seat, nearly losing her grip on her chador while her jaw hung open in the air.

"Fabrication of documents is a serious accusation, counselor. Do you have any proof of this?" the judge asked the attorney of the tenant as he squinted his eyes at Nasrin's documents.

"Your Honor, my client has no reason to lie about the amount of rent he pays; he is a good man, a devoted Muslim who helps various charities and donates money to his neighborhood mosque on a regular basis," the attorney said as he opened his briefcase sitting on the desk, taking out documents as his client smiled and slowly nodded.

"We have a letter from the imam of his neighborhood mosque," the attorney said, "acknowledging Mr. Ali Moradi's charitable contributions." He handed several pages to the bailiff, who handed them over to the judge. The judge partially smiled as he flipped through the papers and studied them.

"Among those papers is also a letter signed by all of the neighborhood merchants who knew Mr. Jampour and have indicated that the rent between both parties have always been the 15,000 set out over twenty years ago and not a penny more!" the attorney continued as he glanced back at Nasrin for a mere second and then back at the smiling judge, who remained focused on the recent pages handed to him.

"This is nonsense, Your Honor! What would the neighboring merchants know about a private contract between my father and his tenant?" Nasrin raised her voice while quickly standing up. Not paying attention to her, the mullah continued to look over the pages that Moradi's attorney had provided.

"This is ridiculous, a taxi ride from here to uptown and back costs 15,000 these days, Your Honor! No self-respecting property owner in Tehran would charge rent this low!" she shouted, slamming her fist on the desk while breathing heavily. She glanced over at the respondent table and noticed the smirks on the faces of Moradi and his attorney.

Her stomach began to turn as she felt the burning sensation return to her belly once again. Nasrin felt heavy as her warm skin began to attach itself to her damp clothes. She felt like she was being weighed down. Her chest puffing in and out, Nasrin grinded her teeth and looked to the judge, who remained smiling while still going over the pages.

"Calm down, Mrs. Etemadi, you're getting hysterical; we're here to solve issues without raising our voices," the judge replied after a momentary pause. Nasrin stared at him.

"The court will assign an agent from the Department of National Revenue to appear at this store, and based on Mr. Ali Moradi's income, taxes paid, and the size of the property, the agent will determine the right amount of rent that needs to be paid. End of session!" the judge said as he stood up and reached for his robe. Moradi and his attorney smiled and shook hands. Screaming on the inside, Nasrin's chador flew off her head as she ran over to the mullah.

"Your Honor, please hear me out, just for a minute!" Nasrin pleaded before pulling her head scarf further down on her forehead while the judge began putting on his robe. Her hands wrapped around each other, she quickly added, "The financial state of my mother and I is in a poor shape. I beg you to please reconsider and raise the rent based on the evidence that I provided."

"The judgment is final, Mrs. Etemadi," he said. "Now please be at the location of your father's store a week from now, when the agent will appear and set the record straight." The judge gathered his papers and stood away from his bench while Nasrin froze to her spot. Cold sweat ran down the back of her neck as she stared at the smiling Moradi.

"And may I suggest that next time you convince your brothers to attend court proceedings, or at least obtain a male representative. A courtroom is no place for a lone woman," the judge said before walking away from Nasrin, who stood still while slowly dropping her head. Her mouth wide open, she slowly slouched toward her seat. After picking up her chador and binder, Nasrin headed out toward the bus stop in similar fashion.

The heat bearing down on her, Nasrin stood hanging on to the metal rail of the bus in the crammed back, among a horde of women. She felt dwarfed as she pictured the tenant, his lawyer, the judge, and even her husband towering over her while their giant heads mocked her and laughed at her. Giant drops of drool slipped out of their mouths and landed on the terrified Nasrin, who soon pictured herself drowning in a sea of the men's saliva.

She started to breathe deeply as once again her sweat-soaked attire began to weigh her down. Her head began to slowly spin as her vision blurred. Losing her grip on the hot metal rail of the bus, Nasrin leaned against the window. *How could the judge ignore my documents, a valid contract signed by the tenant?* She kept asking herself. Instead the judge focused on a sympathetic letter written by a mullah. This was the only thing that scared her, but she would have never thought that Ali Moradi would stoop this low to avoid paying his fair share of the rent. There was no secret about it; her father never did get along with the neighboring merchants, who would have most definitely supported Moradi's claim, but why would the judge put stock into what they thought the rent should be? It didn't make sense to Nasrin, who went from bus to bus thinking about what had just happened.

Her head still spinning, Nasrin arrived home in the evening hours and immediately headed to the kitchen sink, where she splashed some cold water over her sticky face before downing a full glass of the cold beverage. The giant faces of the men in her life still towering over her, Nasrin sat down under the open kitchen window and stared in between the metal bars at the clouds moving slowly through the blue sky. There was a silver lining in the mullah's judgment, she thought. After all, the rented commercial properties around her father's store were all paying rents around 200,000 to 300,000 a month. At the very least, the revenue agent will have to take the entire situation into consideration and declare an amount that without question would be more than Moradi was paying now. The warm summer breeze gently caressing her face, Nasrin looked at the scattered clouds moving in the blue sky again. Ever since her father had passed away, she found herself taking on the responsibilities of his estate, and since her mother had relied on him for funds, Nasrin had also been looking after her. She sighed. It would be nice if she had some time to herself and with her family, who she felt were drifting apart slowly.

During the next six days, Nasrin spent time with her boys. She laughed with them as they looked at old family albums. Her boys even taught her about social media and helped her open her own Facebook account. She taught cooking to Payam, who was planning on moving away for school. Nasrin even began to talk to her husband, who for the first time in a while spoke to Nasrin's mother and actually invited her to their apartment for Friday lunch. The lunch marked nearly twenty years since her family, including her husband, sat down to a meal with one of her parents. Smiles were all around at the lunch as her boys shared jokes and stories with their grandmother, who looked to be enjoying herself for the first time since the death of her husband. Nasrin even wore makeup and styled her hair for the first time in years; she sat next to her husband, who held her hand and smiled. At the conclusion of their lunch, Hooshang made a surprise announcement and informed the four of them that he was planning on renting a cottage along the coast of the Caspian Sea for a week before the summer was over.

Finally, the big day arrived; Nasrin stood over her kitchen table and placed her files into her binder. Holding a cup of tea, she looked out her kitchen window. Gone were the blue skies, replaced instead with gray and black clouds. The street light across the street was still on as Nasrin gazed upon it while slowly sipping her warm tea. Looking at the light, she realized that for the first time, she had not noticed the metal bars obstructing her view. She smiled, drank the rest of her cup, and prepared to head out to her father's store. She put on the same outfit she wore last week to the courts, minus the black chador, and this time instead of taking buses to her destination, Nasrin called for a taxi and made sure to arrive early.

Her father's property was not far from where she and her family lived. The neighborhood was a colorful mix of residential and commercial businesses ranging from furniture shops to fast foods and grocery stores. Keeping a close eye on the nearby stores, Nasrin requested the driver to stop and drop her off nearly a block away from her father's store. Having paid her taxi fare, Nasrin stood on the edge of the street and looked up and down the block. The streets were coming to life as shopkeepers rolled up the metal partitions of their stores and opened up their doors, while housewives and busy shoppers buzzed through the sidewalks in the search for fresh goods. With sounds of the busy street playing the background, Nasrin walked up the block toward the store.

Standing outside of Ali Moradi's grocery and fruit store, Nasrin quietly peeked in. The first thing she noticed was the skinny son of the tenant standing behind the register; Moradi was standing in the center of the store. With sweat staining his underarms, he was haggling over the price of fruits with a prospective customer. From what Nasrin could see, the store was alive and busy as customers inspected different fruits before placing them in their baskets and lining up at the register.

She wanted to go in; after all, this was her father's store, the one remaining memento that he had worked hard all of his life in order to purchase, in the hopes that one day his two boys would operate it. Her two brothers had long ago moved away, one to Australia and the other to England. Nasrin imagined what it would have been like if the two never left and instead aspired to live up to their father's dreams. She pictured the two of them running the store. Her younger brother, who was always good with math, would have been standing behind the register while the more social sibling would have been walking around the store, helping customers. She even pictured how her two sons could have made some money on the side while working at the grocery store during their summer holidays.

As she stared blindly at the mounds of fruit displayed just outside of the store, Nasrin noticed her name being repeatedly called. She turned around and saw a tall man in glasses standing just a few feet behind her. He wore a black suit along with a blue collar shirt and held onto a briefcase. Taking out papers with the headings and emblems of the courts and the Department of Revenue, the man introduced himself as Mr. Abbassi, the agent. A smile on her face, Nasrin greeted the man with partial bows as the two entered the store. Walking in front, Nasrin headed straight toward the register; Moradi's son noticed her.

"What the hell do you want here, lady? The goddamn rent isn't due for another week," he said loudly as he slammed the cash register shut and stared Nasrin down.

"I'm here to speak to your father," she said. "We have an appointment." Nasrin's smile quickly faded away as her nostrils flared.

"He's not here," he said, "and if you don't mind, I'm busy, so please feel free to get the hell out of our store!" The son of the tenant raised his hand and pointed to the door.

"Excuse me, I'm Mr. Abbassi from the Department of Revenue," the agent said. "I have a court order to inspect Mr. Ali Moradi's tax records and income-related documents." He stepped from behind Nasrin and held out the papers in his hand. "I suggest you go and get your dad, unless you want me to report him for failure to cooperate."

"Just a minute, I think he is in the back office," Moradi's son replied as he quickly turned around and headed toward the large space located behind the store. After a few short minutes, Moradi slouched through the office door and emerged with the same sweat-stained appearance that Nasrin saw earlier. He walked up to the register and glared deeply at Nasrin, who turned her attention back to the piles of fruit sitting on flat tables in the store.

"Are you Mr. Ali Moradi?" the agent asked.

"Yes, I have the documents you came for in my office, so just follow me," Moradi said as he turned around and slouched his way back to the office. Nasrin and the agent followed him.

"Here are my taxes and the income the store has had ever since I have been doing business here," Moradi said. "There are also letters from the imam of my mosque, indicating all of my charitable contributions."

"Charitable contributions ... pooffff," Nasrin sighed, while rolling her eyes; the agent and Moradi turned their attention toward her. His nostrils flaring, Moradi stared down Nasrin, who this time replied with a glare of her own.

"This should be enough to get this disobedient woman off my back!" Moradi said as he handed the papers to Abbassi.

"You son of a bitch!" Nasrin said. "How dare you call me disobedient when you're the one not paying his rent!" Moradi flashed a smirk at her, a smirk that she was far too familiar with and detested.

"Mrs. Etemadi!" Abbassi said, his mouth held open as Nasrin took a step back while Moradi continued to smirk at her.

"I mean, you don't know how difficult this man has been toward my father, my mother, and me; he has made our lives hell!" Nasrin said as she held up her arms and looked at the agent.

"I think it would be best if you went home, Mrs. Etemadi," Abbassi replied. "I can take care of the rest by myself." Nasrin tilted her head forward, her mouth agape in suprise.

"But I just got here," she said. "This is my property. I have a right to stay and observe the process, plus I brought all the documents you need." Nasrin pulled her binder out of her bag.

"I've got his documents," Abbassi said, "and now I can take your documents. There is nothing more here for you to do; your presence may interfere with my work, so please feel free to leave. You will receive our evaluation in a few days." Nasrin stood there, frozen to her spot, as Moradi snickered.

She slowly turned around and walked out of the office with her head down. On her way out, she passed Moradi's son, who laughed and uttered remarks that she didn't bother to listen to. Despite the high humidity and the gray clouds looking like they were about to burst, Nasrin decided to walk the rest of the way home.

Once she arrived, she headed to her kitchen and turned her kettle on as the sound of thunder echoed just outside of her window. Her cup in her hand, she stood by the window and watched the heavy rain stream down from the skies. She noticed the rain splashing and bouncing off the street light. She held out her nimble hand and passed it through the metal bars as the raindrops hit her palm.

The last time Nasrin and I communicated was August of 2010; she said that the revenue agent had set the price of rent at 90,000 tomans per month for the store and the office space. Voicing her dissatisfaction, Nasrin added that she was in the process of appealing the set amount. She strongly suspected that Ali Moradi had bribed the revenue agent once she left the store on that humid July morning. Nasrin also said that she had contracted the services of a male attorney and was hoping that for once, justice would be on her side.

While researching this story, I spoke to many women like Nasrin, and although each had their own stories and points of view with regard to life in Iran under the Islamic Republic, they all agreed that women in Iran deserved more equality in areas of employment, public sphere, and legal proceedings. In addition, all of the women, regardless of their age, agreed that they should also have complete autonomy over issues such as clothing, marriage, child care, sex, and contraceptives.

These demands were echoed during the demonstration following the disputed election of 2009 and in the recent "Arab uprisings," which saw government changes in Tunisia and Egypt.

Although many women that I spoke to admitted that they took to the streets and revolted against the shah in order to achieve a society based on human rights and higher dignity for women, the overwhelming majority believe that through the Islamic Republic, many rights that women had during the shah's reign have been diminished, along with the concept of respect and dignity.

The popular belief among the women in Tehran is that the climate of oppression and discrimination toward women would only improve with a complete regime change and the introduction of a secular and democratic system that places greater emphasis on rights, equality, liberty, and freedom of expression.

Chapter 13.
Shahram: Insidious Demons

In a June 2001 press conference, Iran's head of the welfare organization, Dr. Gholam-Reza Ansari, expressed concerns regarding the country's dramatic rise of drug addicts. According to him, there were around six million drug users in Iran, 10 percent of the country's population.[42] In the same press conference, Ansari indicated that out of the total number of users, around 1,200,000 were serious drug users and addicts that mostly used class A narcotics such as heroin.[43] Even more alarming, Ansari added that the numbers of narcotics users was increasing at a rampant rate of 600,000 annually.[44] This rise has been mostly among young Iranians, with three times more women than men among the new drug users. It is estimated that Tehran alone consumes around five tons of opium on a daily basis.[45]

Even though Ansari did not provide any particular reasons for the dramatic rise in the number of users, there are several obvious reasons for the epidemic that is sweeping across the nation. Many place the culpability on Iran's geographic proximity

---

42   http://news.bbc.co.uk/2/hi/middle_east/1407638.stm.

43   Ibid.

44   Ibid.

45   Ibid.

to Afghanistan, the world largest producer of opium, along with the low costs and high accessibility. The reality, however, seems to be the government's inadequate resourcing of rehab clinics, followed by the refusal of religious leaders to take the same tough stance on narcotics as they have on alcohol.[46] Many Iranians, especially those who are addicts, place the blame squarely on the shoulders of the government, as they believe that the high levels of unemployment (which unofficially stands at 35 percent), lack of fundamental freedoms, shortage of access to drug education, life below poverty for almost one third of the population, and living in a closed and censored environment have created an atmosphere of depression, where narcotic dependence has become inevitable. Based on my research and interviews, many Iranians also believe that the high numbers of addicts is solely attributed to the regime, which is overflowing the narcotic markets with inexpensive drugs simply to sedate and dull out the masses in order to ensure conformity.

These views were certainly shared by an unfortunate lost soul with the name of Shahram Azizi and his family. Shahram passed away just a few days before his twenty-sixth birthday from a heroin overdose; he had desperately struggled to hold down several jobs in order to provide for his family. The oldest of four children, Shahram, along with his mother and father, resided in a one-room flat in south Tehran's slum neighborhood. His father was a simple car mechanic who was in debt for most of his life; he died of heart failure when Shahram was only fifteen. The death of his father, along with the family's remaining debts, forced Shahram to take up work and give up on his education. Although Shahram wasn't the brightest student, he did desire to learn the trades of photography and photo development and wanted to attend college after graduating from high school, with the hopes of someday running a photo studio.

With the passing of his father, Shahram's mother, Zahra, also began to work as a housemaid so that the family could survive. Shahram took up work as an assistant in the same mechanic shop

---

46 http://news.bbc.co.uk/2/hi/middle_east/1407638.stm.

where his father had worked. The owner of the shop was a friend of his father and also one of the individuals the family had owed money to.

Shahram's father was no stranger to narcotics; he was an opium addict for most of his life. Shahram and his sister Soraya, who provided most of this story, recalled that after a long day at work, their father would come home, go to the corner of the room, and smoke opium out of a long pipe with his back turned to his wife and kids. She also recalled that their mother would also try to shield her children by situating herself between her husband and her children; she would usually use her white chador to screen the children from seeing what their father was doing. As you can imagine, their father was not the type of man who would spend much time with his kids. He would usually pass out in the corner of the room soon after finishing his smoke. Nevertheless, both siblings believed that their father was an honest man who desperately tried to ensure his family had the bare essentials, but unfortunately, at the end of the day, his addiction got the best of him. His heart failure was attributed to his heavy addiction to opium, hashish, marijuana, and tobacco. The death of his father came as a huge shock to Shahram, who was not ready to bear the load of being the main breadwinner, but at the same time, Shahram's pride didn't allow him to expect his sister and Sohail and Saalar, his two younger brothers, to leave school and work.

So even though working as a "grease monkey" (as he jokingly called it) in a mechanic shop did not come naturally to him, taking care of his family and stepping into his father's shoes did. And just a few months after starting work at the shop, Shahram took up smoking cigarettes. At first, he hid it from his family and his boss, but within less than a year, he was smoking a pack a day, and it was no longer concealed. Whenever the topic of cigarettes came up, Shahram would go out of his way to remind everyone that the main reason he was smoking was due to the stress of life, his job, and being the bread winner, but deep down inside, the real reason Shahram started to smoke was it made him feel more mature. He wanted to take on the persona of "the man of the house," the serious adult who stepped into his father's shoes and gave up his dreams so that his younger brothers and sister might get the chance to go to college. In fact, smoking made Shahram look like an adult, it made him look independent, and most importantly, it inspired confidence in himself.

By 2004, Shahram had successfully learned the trade and became a dependable mechanic. He also managed to pay most of the family debt and even paid for Soraya's dowry, which although it was nothing extravagant, for a low-income family, it was more than modest. At the end of the day, there was not much left for savings, but Shahram ensured that there was a roof over their heads by paying the rent on time, and along with his mother's maid salary, the family had enough food on their plates as they continued to live in the one-room flat.

Despite his heavy schedule, Shahram still kept his interest in photography and often took pictures with an older camera, which was one of the only two relaxations that he would spend time and money on. The other, of course, was his narcotic addiction. Shahram wouldn't really say when or why he began to take drugs, and most often his excuse for getting into the habit was "bad friends and good dope." Soraya, on the other hand, believed that Shahram started taking drugs once he thought that he had figured out his life, which for Shahram was a cycle of barely making ends meet, something that he was content with until life became difficult. It was at that point that addiction came with the territory; the surrounding circumstances transformed drug use into an addiction of necessity. As his depression deepened, Shahram took harder drugs, which eventually led to his death.

One of those surrounding circumstances was a skinny, light-haired boy named Davoud, who was Shahram's age. Similar to Shahram, he had dropped out of school and worked at a nearby mechanic shop. Davoud was the oldest of five and embodied the rough streets of Tehran at a young age. He was a small-time hustler who knew the underworld players, and while he associated with them, he was too smart (or too scared) to ever want to enter a life of crime. Davoud dropped out of school and entered work before

Shahram, and although Davoud's father was still alive, his reasons for choosing work over education were similar to Shahram's. Davoud's father was a cook, and although his salary paid the rent and ensured adequate food was provided, there were extra costs of life that the family couldn't cope with. Davoud's youngest sister had severe diabetes, and both she and Davoud's mother suffered from a rare blood disorder, which required stints in the hospital and blood transfusions. Davoud tried to make it as a cook like his father, but instead he found himself working his way up from an apprentice to a mechanic by the age of twenty.

In order to compensate for his lack of size and to prove his strength, Davoud would often find himself in dodgy situations such as getting into fights, reeking of marijuana and carrying a switch blade with him most times. Shahram and Davoud saw in themselves images of each other, and the two became not just best friends but brothers of the same struggle. Shahram would often talk about photography to Davoud, while Davoud would teach Shahram about the rules of the mean streets of Tehran. Davoud's frequent habit of pot smoking eventually passed to Shahram. At first, the two would smoke a joint together at the end of the week, which soon became at the end of every work day. Before they knew it, both were smoking three to four joints per day, whether they were together or not. Soon after Shahram's twenty-second birthday, they began to experiment with opium and often smoked the drug at the mechanic shop long after everyone was gone. As the years went by, Shahram found his own connections for drugs and no longer relied on Davoud to purchase them. Nevertheless, both would always keep time open for the other, especially when it came to smoking.

For Shahram, his life was not perfect, but it was more than adequate. He had a job that paid enough to keep his family fed and off the street, and he had a friend who shared the same struggles as he did. However, this all came to a crashing halt on one early November afternoon in 2010.

The late autumn winds blew against the two closed gates of the south Tehran mechanic shop as Shahram, wearing his usual gray jumpsuit, sat on a thick tire among his colleagues and ate lunch. There was grime underneath his fingernails, and his fingers were black and greasy. Shahram held onto the foil wrapped around his sandwich and dipped his cold-cut sub into a jar of mayonnaise before stuffing it in his mouth. Looking at Shahram, his gray-haired boss, Javad, along with the other two mechanics burst out into laughter. Nearly choking on the sloppy piece of bread and meat going down his throat, Shahram giggled as well while reaching for the cola bottle next to his leg.

He wiped away the sweat on his brow with his fingers, smudging his forehead while the grease from under his nails and fingers mixed with his perspiration and ran down his already darkened and sticky eyebrows. He set down the empty bottle and reached back for his half-eaten sub sitting on his lap. But before he could dip it again into the jar of creamy white mayonnaise, his cell phone in his pocket began to vibrate. He set down the sandwich and wiped his palms against his pants before reaching deep into his pocket. His sister's name appeared on the screen as he flipped open his phone using his chin instead of his other hand.

Shortly after saying hello, he immediately jumped up, knocking over the jar of mayonnaise along with dropping his sandwich onto the grimy floor of the shop. Javad asked Shahram what had happened after he closed his phone. His lips quivering and his eyes still wide open, Shahram told his boss that his mother had collapsed at work and was taken to a nearby hospital. Javad pushed back his gray hair and quickly reached for his car keys. He drove Shahram to the hospital, dropping him off at the emergency entrance before looking for a parking spot. Shahram quickly ran into the crowded entrance and walked toward the administration section. The lady at the desk informed Shahram that his mother was admitted into the public hospital and was given a bed in a ward room on the sixth floor of the hospital.

Not wanting to wait by the crowded elevator, Shahram jogged up the stairs, passing two or three steps in one leap at a time. This was the same hospital where his father was brought in when his heart gave out; he was pronounced dead in the emergency room. His greasy and sweaty palms slipping off the handrails of the staircase, images of that late June evening began to flash before his eyes.

He had been only fifteen years old and sat with his science textbook in his hands, preparing for his yearly finals. His mother had been sitting in the usual spot in the middle of the room, going over her younger children's homework while keeping an eye on their electric kettle. His eyes peeking over the top of his book, Shahram looked over at his mother and dad, who was also in his usual spot, right next to the folded blankets and pillows, holding his long pipe in his left hand. Soon he inhaled; slowly leaned his head back with his eyes closed, and slowly exhaled a ball of the tantalizing smoke. He repeated this two or three more times as Shahram continued to gaze upon his father. But this wasn't like the other times. With a grunt, his father had dropped his pipe. The sound now echoed in Shahram's ears as he ran up the stairs, sweat coursing its way from his hairline and over his brow. He recalled running in a pair of slippers along with his sister to the nearby hospital, where the ambulance had taken his motionless father. Tears rolled down his face, washing a clear stream between the grime and grease.

He yanked open the door of his mother's room, walking past the first three beds, separated by curtains; each bed contained a female patient along with grieving relatives hanging on the edge of the bed. Shahram heard Soraya's voice over the curtain of the fourth and last bed in the ward room.

"Mom?" Shahram called out as he swung the curtain to the side; his mother was resting on the hospital bed while his sister sat next to the bed. "What happened?" Shahram asked as he walked past the bed and glanced at his mother before looking over at his sister, who swallowed hard and lowered her head.

"It's nothing, Shahram," his mother replied, slowly lifting up her head and glancing at her son with dull eyes before smiling.

Shahram reached for her arm and held her hand before looking over at Soraya, who lifted up her head.

"She passed out at work," she said. "The doctors think that it might be from exhaustion; they are running a set of tests on her."

"I was cleaning the bathroom and must have stood up too fast," his mother said. "It's nothing, dear, no need to worry about me. I'll be okay." She slowly stroked Shahram's greasy sleeve. His lips trembling, he glanced back at his mother.

"I keep telling you to quit that goddamned job!" he said. "You need to rest and stay at home, Mom. I make enough money for all of us." Shahram held back his tears as he gazed upon his mother's dull and tired eyes.

"Listen to him, Mr. Big Shot makes enough money to take care of his mother and two younger brothers," Soraya said, rolling her eyes while Shahram turned his attention toward her. "I got news for you, Shahram, without Mom's salary, there wouldn't be enough food on the table for you, Sohail, and Saalar!" She glared at Shahram, whose nostrils flared while his grip on his mother's hand tightened.

"That's enough, both of you ... I don't want to hear you two argue over money and who pays for what!" his mother said, nearly raising her voice as Shahram nodded. He could hear the sound of footsteps approaching the set of curtains that separated his mother's bed from the other three patients in the room.

"Are you the eldest son?" asked a man wearing a long white coat and stethoscope. Shahram slowly nodded.

Soraya stood up and introduced Shahram to the doctor. Wiping his right hand against his chest, Shahram shook hands with the doctor, who said he had news regarding their mother's health and wanted to speak to them in private. With the noise of moans, overhead calls for doctors, and wheels of stretchers squeaking in the halls, the doctor led the two siblings to the quiet staircase that Shahram had climbed just minutes ago.

"Are you aware of the condition that your mother is in?" the doctor asked, looking at Shahram, who looked at Soraya before shaking his head.

"The patient had blood in her sputum when she was brought in; does your mother smoke?" the doctor asked.

Shahram stared back at him before shaking his head again.

"She doesn't smoke, but Shahram smokes at home, as did my father when he was alive," Soraya said.

"Well, that explains a lot," the doctor said. "We took a scan of her lungs, which showed the problem. I'm afraid her left lung contains a mass, and it may be cancerous." The doctor removed an X-ray scan from the large envelope and showed it to the two siblings.

Shahram's head began to spin while the images in the scan blurred over his eyes. Pictures of his fifteen-year-old self, screaming his father's name as his body was being eased into his grave swirled around his mind. He began to breathe deeply as cold sweat trickled slowly down the back of his neck; his eyes remained fixed and unblinking, looking at the X-ray. His heart pumped in his chest as he fathomed the sour thought of his mother's body, wrapped in a white cloth, being eased into a dark grave. Grinding his teeth while clenching his fists, he felt like slapping himself and screaming. He didn't want to lose her too. It took him nearly a decade to fill the void that was left by his father; he didn't want to do the same again.

"At this point, we're not able to confirm whether the mass is benign or malignant," the doctor said. "We would have to do a biopsy, but given my experience and based on what I've seen in the scan, I'm afraid to say that it doesn't look too promising." He shook his head before placing the scan back into the envelope.

The term "malignant" rang inside Shahram's spinning head; he swallowed hard and looked at the doctor before asking, "Does she need surgery? We'll do anything, Doctor; just tell us what we have to do!"

"Like I said, we're not sure whether it is cancer," he repeated, "but after the biopsy we will have a better idea. In the meantime, I would like to keep her here."

"What do we do if it's ... cancer?" Shahram asked, his lips quivering.

"My suggestion would be chemotherapy," he said, "that is, again, if the biopsy shows it is malignant; if it's not, then we would need to operate on her in order to remove the mass in her lung."

"Chemotherapy? How much would that cost?" Soraya asked.

"Well, at this stage I'm really not sure, but I should be able to have a clearer answer within the next few days and after the biopsy," the doctor replied.

"But if you would have to guess, I mean, on average, how much does chemotherapy cost?" his sister asked as Shahram rolled his eyes as her.

"I apologize, Doctor, we lost our father not too long ago," Shahram said, "and my sister just wants to know so we can do whatever we can for our mother ... whatever it takes!"

"Well, there are four particular medications for chemotherapy made in Iran, and the costs are relatively the same. However, the major factors with regard to costs that you have to take into consideration is whether we'll be treating her as an inpatient or an outpatient," the doctor replied.

"I guess she would qualify as an outpatient, right?" Soraya asked as Shahram looked back at her, this time glaring at his sister with his nostrils flared.

"No, she would not," the doctor said, "especially given her condition and her symptoms. As I said, she should be admitted at least until we've a better understanding of what we're dealing with."

"So how much would an extended stay cost?" Soraya asked; Shahram continued to glare at his sister, this time grinding his teeth while his nostrils remained flared.

"Listen, I know you're concerned about your mother and you want to do the best for her," he said, "but I still recommend that she be admitted; in the meanwhile, you'd best discuss this among yourselves. Lung cancer is very serious, so take your time and talk to the administration department when you have made your decision. Now if you'll excuse me, I have other patients to attend to." The doctor began to walk past them.

"Wait, Doctor, be honest with me ... what are her chances?" Shahram asked as the doctor held the door open.

"If it is in fact lung cancer, then her chances are not good, but with chemotherapy, some luck, and a lot of prayer, then perhaps she can beat it. I'm really sorry, but I have to go," the doctor said as he left the floor.

"First it was Dad, now it's Mom," Soraya said. "I don't know if I have the strength to lose her." She sat on the first set of stairs while a gentle stream of tears ran down her face.

"Outpatient, Soraya? Outpatient?" Shahram asked. "Are you fucking serious?"

"Yeah, I said outpatient! Excuse me for looking at all the options!" his sister shouted back as more tears ran down her face.

"Please! Other options? Save that kind of talk for when you want someone to feel sorry for you, Soraya. We both know you're worried about your own pocket!" Shahram said, raising his voice as he continued to glare at his sister.

"How dare you talk to me that way? Did you ever stop to think that she is here because you and dad puffed that shit smoke in her face every day of the year for the past twenty *fucking* years?" Soraya shouted back as she stood up and faced her brother, who clenched his fists.

"You weren't complaining about me smoking when I was working my ass off to pay your dowry so you could marry that worthless loser, who has never offered to help this family, never! Not once have I heard him offer to pay some of the rent, our debts, not even the goddamned water bill!" Shahram shouted back before punching the metal door of the staircase. His sister took a step back and stood next to the first set of stairs.

Silence fell through the already quiet stairs, as both siblings hung their heads. Breathing heavily, Shahram remembered his father's funeral again, recalling how his sister held him as he screamed for his father while she cried next to him. He turned his back as tears once again streamed down in between the grime and grease on his face. The thought of anything happening to his mother sent blinding jolts into his head, but Soraya had a point, one that he could not ignore. Although this was a public hospital and the costs of admission were far less than a private hospital, his family did not have health insurance, nor did they qualify for a government grant, which would help pay the majority of the hospital costs. But most importantly, they didn't have the kind of money that an extended stay in a hospital required.

"I'll talk to Farhad tonight," Soraya said, referring to her husband. "We'll figure something out, Shahram. It will be okay. I'm sure Allah isn't going to take her too … at least not now."

She wiped away the tears from her eyes using a napkin while Shahram stood with his back turned to her and blindly stared at the floor.

"Listen, I'm going to go and be with Mom," Soraya said as she walked up and hugged her brother from behind before leaving the staircase; Shahram stood motionless, still gazing at the floor.

Wiping his face and smudging more grease and grime over the thin, clean stream left by his tears, Shahram sat down on the step where his sister was sitting. Cupping his palms over his face, Shahram wondered if it was, in fact, his and his father's smoking that was the main cause of his mother's condition. Besides a seasonal dry cough, his mother seemed healthy and never previously complained about her health. Could it be that deep down inside, she knew that the family could not afford to have her treated? He started to rub his temple as questions and feelings of guilt began to enter his mind.

It had to be it, he said to himself as the painful jolts throbbed over his temple. His mother must have known about the blood in her cough, and the only reason she kept it from him was because she knew the family could not afford to hospitalize her and pay for her treatment. He imagined his mother sitting in the middle of their flat with a warm smile on her face, along with her white chador draped over her head and her arms spread around her kids, who laughed as they worked on their notebooks. He might have done a somewhat adequate job of replacing his father, but there was no way he could do what his mother did. And it wasn't just the role that she played at home; without his mother's salary, the family would not have food on the table.

His nose began to run as the tears returned to his eyes and rolled down his face. He lifted up his head, got on his knees, and held out his palms, pleading with God to not take his mother away from them. He begged God to spare her and let them at least keep her a little longer, until his younger brothers were older. He wanted his brothers to grow up with the hopes of attending college, not to experience the scarring sight of burying a parent while facing the harsh, depressing reality of getting a job. This depression had led him to abuse narcotics as a sedative.

Leaving the hospital that night, Shahram promised himself that he would do anything in his power for his mother. Deep down inside, he knew that the money they needed would not be easy to obtain, plus he had to make sure that the rent, bills, and other expenses were paid for during this time.

The hospital administrator informed them that their mother's stay cost 100,000 tomans per night (approx. US$100), and two days later, Shahram and his sister received the news they were dreading. Speaking to them privately again, the doctor told the two siblings that the biopsy indicated that the mass in her lungs was malignant; even worse, the cancer had rapidly expanded through her left lung and required immediate chemotherapy treatment for ten weeks. This would cost 1.5 million tomans per week (approx. US$1,500); bringing it to a total of 2,200,000 per week.

Breathing heavily, while his heart slammed against his chest, Shahram nearly reached a point of suffocation; he made just over 1.15 million tomans a month. But the images of his mother being wrapped in a white cloth while his younger brothers leaned back and puffed the gray scent of opium sent him into a darkness that he didn't ever want to see. The painful jolts throbbing over his head, Shahram went back and sat by his mother's side. Swallowing hard, he brought a smile to his face and held her hand as she opened her dull eyes and smiled back at her son.

Shahram wasn't going to give up; he spent that night going over numbers and figuring ways that he could pay for his mother's medical expenses. But he wasn't alone, and just when it seemed that it was impossible to raise the money, his friends and family came to his aid. His boss Javad, who looked at Shahram like his son and was so impressed with Shahram's work, especially with his efforts in paying back his father's debt, agreed to loan Shahram the sum of 3 million tomans. Javad also lent his car to Shahram during the evenings so he could use it as a makeshift taxi and make some more money.

Davoud also lent him a few thousand tomans, along with his motorcycle, which Shahram used in order to deliver pizza and fast food after his taxi shift. Shahram would sleep every night at the mechanic shop, working there from eight o'clock until four o'clock; then he would take Javad's car and pick up passengers in Tehran's busy streets until ten o'clock, just after the rush hour came to an end, and finally he would deliver food until one o'clock. On Fridays, when the shop was closed, he spent the entire day delivering food. His sister and brother-in-law, despite being in the same poor financial state as Shahram, also chipped in with the hospital expenses.

His two younger brothers would go to their sister's house for food or eat at the hospital, where the staff would give the boys leftover food and extra meal trays. Shahram would visit his mother every chance he would get, but given his work schedule, he was limited to seeing her once or twice a week. His landlord, who the family had been renting from ever since Shahram was born, gave Shahram a break over the rent, telling him that he would only charge them rent once his mother was out of the hospital.

With such an insane schedule, Shahram did not have much time to eat; he would often stuff his pockets with sandwiches and snacks, which he would gulp down either behind the wheel of Javad's car or when he was underneath the hood of a car during his shop hours. As far as staying hygienic went, Shahram often used the sink in the shop to wash off the grease and grime, and he took a shower on Fridays in a public bath house a block away from the shop.

He bought a cheap picture frame and placed one of the few photos of his mother in it, placing it next to the makeshift bed he had made in Javad's office. All he had to do for inspiration was to look at the picture every day, despite the poundings in his head, the crackling and soreness of his bones, and the blurriness of his vision. Shahram's only sedative came in the form of inexpensive hashish, which he would smoke every night. He would lie on his mattress and, with his mother's picture turned around, puff the soothing black smoke out of his lungs, just before his head would hit the pillow. Nevertheless, for the first three weeks, everything seemed to come through, as Shahram was just barely able to pay his mother's medical expenses.

When the fourth week began, Shahram was driving Davoud's motorcycle back to the shop after his last delivery of the night. The chilly late November winds blew against his face, but they could not keep him from yawning, and his eyes slowly began to close and open. The bike began to drift toward the sidewalk; the drowsy Shahram nearly ran over a stray cat, which through its screech snapped opened his eyes just before the motorcycle collided with a trash bin in the street. Hurled into the plastic waste collection box, Shahram grunted and held onto his back in pain. If he had not collided with the trash box, he surely would have ended up hitting a parked car and landing on a much rougher area instead of soft plastic bags filled with garbage. Picking up the twisted and smoldering motorcycle, Shahram limped into the dark and cold night and walked the rest of the way back to Javad's shop.

With only scratches on his face, legs, and back, Shahram woke up early the following morning and called Davoud, arranging to bring the cycle to his friend's shop. Although Shahram was more than capable of fixing the bike himself, doing so would have taken time away from his actual job (and more importantly, his pay). Plus, Davoud was a skilled motorcycle mechanic and had forgiven Shahram before after a similar run-in with his bike.

"What the fuck did you do to my bike Shahram?" Davoud asked when he saw the condition of his motorcycle.

"I had a little run-in … nothing that can't be fixed," Shahram answered as he glanced back at the bike.

"What did you have a run-in with, a fucking tank?" Davoud asked as he stomped on his cigarette, while Shahram shook his head.

"No, jackass! I was delivering pizza and must have shut my eyes for a second or two," Shahram replied. Davoud walked toward the bike, kneeled down, and began staring at the busted parts.

"Shut your eyes?" Davoud asked while continuing to look over the damaged parts of the bike.

"Davoud, listen, I can fix it, but it's going to take me the whole day, and I wouldn't get to do my work," Shahram replied.

"So you thought you'd get that sucker Davoud to do it, as if I don't have shit to do!" Davoud said, lifting his head and glaring at Shahram.

"I need your help, Davoud; I wouldn't have asked if I didn't," Shahram replied. Davoud sighed, shook his head, and stared back at the bike.

"Come on, man," Shahram said. "If I don't show up tonight, I'll lose my delivery gig; you know I need the money!"

Davoud said, "*Need*? Yeah, that's the word I was just thinking about too!" Davoud pushed his light brown hair out of his face while rolling his eyes and shaking his head again.

"What the fuck is that supposed to mean?" Shahram asked, raising one of his eyebrows and glaring at Davoud.

"It means lately you only call when you need something, Shahram! We used to hang out, have a smoke, relax and blow off some steam; now you never call," Davoud replied.

"I'm sorry for not being around, Davoud, I really am. Without your help, it would have been impossible for me to afford my mother's medical treatment … but you know what it's like. You've been in the hell that I've been living in for the past four weeks." Shahram walked up to Davoud and placed his hand on his friend's shoulder.

"Okay, I'll take a look at it," he said, "but I can't promise anything. I'm sure it's going to take a miracle for this tin can to work again."

Davoud turned around and smiled, and then the two friends embraced each other.

"As for your sleep problem," he added, "I might have something for you that can help. I'll come by your shop around four and give it to you along with the bike. That is, if it's fixed by then," Davoud added as Shahram smiled and nodded before limping back to his shop.

The day went by rather quickly, and before Shahram got a chance to scratch his head, he noticed Davoud standing with the bike in the alley behind the entrance to Javad's shop. From what he could see, the bike was running and looked better than ever.

"Holy shit ...you fixed it up, Davoud," Shahram said with a big grin as he wiped his hand against the side of his pants and embraced his friend, who smiled back.

"It's not 100 percent," Davoud replied, "but it'll do the job. That doesn't mean you can push peddle to the metal on her yet; be gentle and give her a bit of time to warm up."

"I don't know what to say; this means the world to me," Shahram said as he embraced the skinny, brown-haired Davoud.

"Okay, okay, just be careful next time," Davoud replied with a smile as Shahram stepped away and looked closer at the bike and the repaired parts.

"By the way, about your sleep issues, I got something you can use, something that will help you stay up," Davoud said, looking around the quiet alley before reaching into his pocket and producing a small clear plastic bag with an elastic band tied around it; the bag contained small bits of clear crystal.

"Is that *shishe* [crystal meth]?" Shahram exclaimed, nearly raising his voice. Davoud quickly returned the bag into his pocket before looking around again.

"Shh, keep your voice down," he warned. "Yeah, it's *shishe*."

"Where did you get it?" Shahram asked as Davoud took out the bag again and handed it to him.

"I got it from my guy, you know, Mehdi Khakrobe [Garbage Mehdi]," Davoud answered, referring to a shady drug dealer that Shahram was familiar with. Silence swept across the alley as the evening winds swirled and picked up the small trash sitting behind the shop. Shahram continued to stare at the small bag while Davoud reached for a cigarette.

"Listen, don't sweat over it. It's not all that different from what we've smoked before … it just keeps you up and gives you that bit of energy you need," Davoud said in between taking puffs from his cigarette. Shahram continued to look at the bag closely.

"Just put some in a piece of aluminum foil, heat it, and inhale the smoke using a tube, you know, like … an emptied pen casing," Davoud added.

"You've done this before?" Shahram asked.

Davoud slowly nodded. "Yeah, I've done it once or twice before. Take my word, this stuff works like a charm; you'll be energized like never before, have a concentration level like never before, and the best part, you can hump like never before," a giggling Davoud said as his eyes nearly lit up. Shahram smiled and rolled his eyes while slowly shaking his head.

"I'll think about it, Davoud. I gotta get going and hit the rush-hour crowd," he said. "I'll talk to you tomorrow." Shahram pocketed the bag, hugged Davoud one more time, and rolled the motorcycle into the shop.

The bag of crystal meth sitting in his pocket, Shahram hit the roads in search of passengers, but all he could think about was what Davoud said about the effects of the meth and how it could help him stay alert and energized. The truth was he had heard about meth before and thought about taking it just a few days before banging up Davoud's motorcycle. The past three weeks had exhausted him, and despite all of his efforts, he was barely making his mother's medical payments. He couldn't afford to miss any one of his paychecks.

Just before ten at night, after finishing his taxi route, Shahram arrived back at the mechanic shop. He headed toward Javad's office, where he and Davoud often smoked hashish, marijuana, and opium, next to the window facing the alley. He looked into the office trash can and pulled out a crumpled piece of aluminum foil. He smoothed out the foil over the office desk, reached into his pocket, and pulled out the plastic bag. He paused and stared at the bag before looking at the picture of his mother sitting on the edge of the desk, right next to where he slept. Biting his lower lip, Shahram reached across and flipped over the frame, making sure it lay face down. He sighed, pinched a few crystals out of the bag, and set them in the middle of the foil before removing the ink tube out of a clear pen. He reached for his lighter and inhaled the smoke through the empty pen.

Shahram felt as if someone had hit the fast forward button of his life; over the next three and a half weeks, he flashed in between his three jobs without ever having to take a rest. At first he would only smoke after he was done with his taxi shift, en route to his delivery gig. Then it became twice a day, and before he knew it, he was smoking in between meals. Whenever he ran out, he would call Davoud, who through his contacts would buy Shahram the colorless crystals.

One evening in December, roughly seven weeks into his mother's hospital stay and chemotherapy, Javad asked Shahram to drop off his car, as he needed his vehicle. Having just smoked his evening dose of crystal meth, Shahram drove to his boss's house with some reluctance; he had a world of respect for Javad and did not want his boss to find out about his narcotic addiction.

Reaching the apartment building where his boss lived, Shahram rang the buzzer and informed Javad that the keys were in his vehicle, parked right outside of the building. Before he could leave, though, Javad called down and insisted through the buzzer that Shahram come in and have tea with him. Hanging his head, Shahram agreed and entered the gates of the building; Javad came out of the entrance to meet him. The two headed down the stairs to a small basement of the building, where his boss along with his family resided.

"My wife will be down with tea and dates shortly," Javad said. "Have you had dinner yet?" The two sat on a wooden bed in the dim basement.

"Yes, thank you, I had a sandwich just after work," Shahram quickly replied, hoping the tea would arrive soon while avoiding Javad's eyes so his boss did not notice he had smoked crystal meth. Javad's wife soon arrived with a tray containing two cups of tea, dates, and small pastries. After greeting Shahram and inquiring about his mother's condition, she left, and Javad closed the basement door.

"So how's the whole taxi biz treating you?" he asked. "Is it getting you the cash you need?" Javad picked up a cup of tea while keeping his eyes fixed on Shahram.

"Yes, it is," he said. "I mean, I'm very grateful to you and your family for looking after me all these years, and now you're lending me money and your car … I don't know how to repay you." Shahram looked at the tray as he lifted a cup of tea along with a pastry, trying to occupy his hands so he wouldn't scratch the acne that had rampantly developed over his face ever since he began smoking meth.

"You're working, what … seventeen, eighteen, nineteen hours a day?" his boss asked as he continued to gaze at Shahram.

"Yes, I would say an average of eighteen hours every day," Shahram answered before taking a handful of dates from the tray and stuffing them, one by one, into his mouth.

"My God, eighteen hours? How are you able to do it?" Javad asked. "I mean, if it was one of my sons, they would have given up after the first day!"

Shahram looked at him through the corner of his eyes before swallowing hard.

"Well, you know what they say, when there is a will, there is a way," Shahram replied as his heart began to beat faster.

"You can stop bullshitting me, boy," his boss said as he slammed down his cup on the thin metal tray sitting in between them.

"I swear, Javad, I'm getting money honestly!" Shahram replied, breathing heavily as he noticed Javad's flared nostrils, raised eyebrows, and unblinking eyes staring down at him.

"You think I was born yesterday? That I'm some fool? You think I don't notice the scratch marks and scabs all over your face? The dark colors of your teeth? Good God, boy, you've lost nearly ten kilos in two weeks! Just look at yourself!"

Shahram began to slowly hang his head while getting choked up.

"Your poor father started working for me when you were in diapers, and even after all those years of being an addict, he had the decency not to show up to work drugged out of his mind!" Javad shouted, pushing his hair away from his face. Staring at the floor with his head down, tears soon began to run down Shahram's face and dropped onto the cold tiles next to his feet.

"You're like a son to me," Javad continued. "I closed my eyes whenever you and that idiot Davoud smoked grass and opium in the store or in the fucking alley behind the store and I would find you the next morning passed out over my desk, with the whole store smelling like drugs!" Javad pushed the tray out of the way while leaning over toward Shahram's ear.

"Well, no more! No more, goddamn it! I can't stand by and do nothing anymore!" Javad shouted with tears in his eyes.

Shahram broke down and began to sob. "Mr. Javad, please understand, my mother's going to die. I have to get the money and pay for her treatment; for the love of God, please understand," Shahram said while sobbing and wiping his running nose.

"Your poor mother wishes she was dead every time she takes a look at your face! Just look at what you have become, boy!" Javad replied loudly as tears rolled down his eyes. "You're supposed to give the poor thing emotional support and lift her spirit, not show up at her bedside looking like a street junkie!"

Shahram got down to his knees and grabbed Javad's legs while burying his head in the old man's lap. "What can I do?" he asked. "Please help me, please!" He looked up as the tears streamed down his eyes; Javad placed his palm over Shahram's head and slowly stroked his hair.

"You owe it to yourself to get clean; heck, you owe it to that poor woman to get clean. God forbid if anything was to happen to her, let her at least remember you as her son, as Shahram, and not some lowlife junkie!" his boss replied.

Shahram nodded his head while wiping the tears away from his face.

"Just have faith, son," he continued. "Show your mother that she has raised a worthy son, and I'll help you."

Shahram leaned back next to the fallen tray and tea cups.

"How much money have you made this week?" Javad asked.

"Around 700,000," he said. "I was hoping to make another 300,000 by week's end and my brother-in-law is supposed to make up the rest." Shahram wiped away the last of the tears, while Javad squinted his eyes and gazed at the low basement ceiling.

"I have around two million in the safe in my office," he said. "I can lend it to you but you have to promise me to get clean and stay clean!"

"That would come out to five million that you have loaned me," Shahram replied. "It will take me forever to pay you back!"

"It's all right, son, I will just take little by little from your wages until the money has been paid, once your mother is out of the hospital," Javad said while the tears came back to Shahram's eyes as he quickly embraced his boss.

"Now, I'm going to prepare this room for you," he said. "We'll put a mattress on this bed, and you'll spend the next 120 hours here, locked up in this room until you can kick this demon out of your system. My brother-in-law spent five days in this room, and now he's a free man, free from all that shit!"

Shahram leaned back and slowly nodded before wiping away his tears. "But what about my delivery job?" Shahram asked.

"You don't need that chump change," Javad said. "I have a client who brings trucks to the shop every now and then; you know him, Mr. Taheri. He is building kitchen cabinets for new complexes in Karaj, and he can always use a pair of good hands, once you've kicked your habit."

Shahram gazed back at him, quiet and unblinking.

"You can come to work first thing in the morning and then head out at three in the afternoon. He needs someone to work the second shift; you can sleep over there in one of the empty units and catch a ride to work in the mornings. It would work out perfectly, not to mention that the payoff is one million a week," Javad said. "But don't forget, Shahram, all bets are off if you don't do exactly what I say for the next five days; you understand?" Shahram quickly nodded.

After setting up a mattress over the old wooden bed, Javad tied Shahram's arms and legs to the four legs of the bed, and for the next forty-eight hours, he kept him tied while periodically checking up on him.

Besides the large amounts of methamphetamines that he had used the previous weeks, Shahram's body had grown a strong dependence to narcotics over the past five years; going cold turkey was awfully hard; he spent most of the 120 hours screaming and shouting in pain and craving. He was only given water and tea as his body began to show signs of withdrawal. Vomiting and urinating into a metal bucket set up next to the wooden bed became the main two acts that his body could handle. Shahram only began to tolerate and consume solid foods on the fifth and last day of his makeshift rehab, as his dependence on the narcotics began to come to an end.

He often recalled the last day of his ordeal as a proud moment for both him and Javad as the two sat down and ate together. He felt proud of himself and saw in his boss a father figure he had needed since his dad passed away. The meal was a quiet one, none of the two men engaged in conversation, but their spirits were high, smiles were all around and hope was returning to a young man who had not had a taste of it since his early teens. At last he was clean; his first stop was the hospital and a visit to his mother.

She was in good spirits despite the fact that her health was deteriorating. Although she began chemotherapy almost immediately after being admitted, doctors had warned that the cancer was rapidly taking over her left lung, and although the treatment had slowed down the spread of cancer, years of being exposed to secondhand smoke and traveling long hours to work in Tehran's polluted air had already done the damage. Shahram also learned that day that his mother had known of her condition for some time; her failure to seek medical treatment at an earlier time added to the deterioration of her health. Nevertheless, her doctor said that she had a fighting chance, and they were still hoping that she could walk away.

The family's spirits were high too as everyone was pitching in to help; even some of their neighbors, who had known the family for years, were gathering money to pay for her medications and treatment. Some of the women close to her even set up a prayer hour once a week, praying for a speedy recovery for the widowed mother of four.

Speaking to her son for the first time in over four weeks, his mother told Shahram that she was grateful for everything that he and others had been doing for her. She was proud of him and of how he seemed to have gotten himself together.

Her frail face lit up when she woke up and saw Shahram next to her bed. He reached over and took her hand as he asked his mother why she had not told the family about her sickness.

Her smile slowly fading away, she looked up at the ceiling of her room and began to tell her son that she had noticed blood in her sputum shortly after Shahram's father passed away; being well aware of the poor status of the family's income, she kept her illness a secret from her family.

Placing his forehead on the bedrail, tears filled Shahram's eyes. Lifting up her now bald head, his mother placed her palm on the back of her son's head and caressed him. She told him that everything was going to be all right and that Allah wasn't going to take away both his mother and father, at least until one of her children gave her the gift of a grandchild. She giggled as Shahram lifted up his head and smiled at his mother's bright face. Holding on to his hand, she told Shahram that he should never get down on life should the unthinkable happen to her. She wanted her son to stay strong and be a good role model to his two younger brothers, who she strongly believed looked up to him. Swallowing hard, Shahram smiled, stood up, and kissed her forehead as she embraced her son tightly. Tears running down both of their faces, his mother told Shahram how proud she was of him, who as a fifteen-year-old boy had dropped everything in his life and took on a demanding job in order to support his mother, sister, and brothers.

Chapter 14.
Shahram: Over the Edge

~~~~~ᨇᨇᨇ~~~~~

S hahram began his new work routine the very next day, as Javad had planned. After working eight hours in Javad's shop, he would take a taxi to the outskirts of Karaj, where the apartment complexes were being built. The work required Shahram to assemble cabinets and attach them to the kitchens. Having spent years as a mechanic and working with similar tools, Shahram began his new job brightly and was even praised by his new employer, who informed him that if he learned the trade quickly and worked well with others, they would surely include him in their next project, which would promise a higher salary. His new boss also loaned Shahram his own set of tools.

All seemed to go according to plan; Shahram was working steady, was getting enough rest, and making more than he was before. More importantly, he was doing all this without his previous chemical and narcotic dependence. He was proud of himself and even brought the framed picture of his mother to his new work site; he would lie next to it every night in his sleeping bag, in the middle of the empty units. During this time, his mother's health even began to improve, although by a small percentage; Shahram couldn't be happier than the way things had turned out for him. That was until about two weeks into his new job.

The late December wind howling in the unpaved roads of the complexes, Shahram tucked his head in between his shoulders and narrowed his eyes while walking in the dark hours of the early morning. He held onto his tool bag with his left hand, while his right hand held his paycheck in his coat pocket: a travelers' check for 1.7 million tomans. He planned to stop at the hospital during his lunch hour and deposit the money, which was due the following day.

The wind lashing against his rosy cheeks, Shahram closed one of his eyes and squinted at the quiet main road with his other eye. He glanced at his wristwatch; it was six o'clock, giving him about an hour to make it to the mechanic shop. Ever since Javad took Shahram in and helped him get clean, Shahram had raised his discipline at the shop and showed more respect to his old boss; he felt he owed him more than duty as an employee and treated the gray-haired Javad like a close family member.

Blowing his warm breath into his hands cupped over his mouth, Shahram noticed a black sedan driving up the main road. As the small flurries of snow began to blow against his body, Shahram put his shivering hand in the air and waved toward the vehicle, which slowed down and pulled up next to him.

"Where you headed?" the driver of the black vehicle asked as Shahram ducked his head and looked into the car.

"Azady Square," Shahram replied, looking at the driver and noticing three other men in the car.

"It's going to cost you 15,000," the driver said, looking at Shahram and the tool bag he was holding.

Shahram quickly nodded as the flurries along with the howling winds whipped across his face.

"Get in," the driver said, "but you have to sit in the middle as that gentleman is getting out before we reach Azady Square." The man sitting in the back opened the door, while Shahram quickly jumped into the car.

The driver began to drive as Shahram squeezed into the tight spot. He slowly closed his eyes and tilted his head back on the cold leather cushion of the car.

"Do you live around here?" the driver asked, looking at Shahram in the rearview mirror.

"No, I live in south Tehran," Shahram replied as his head rested on the cushion.

"What are doing around here?" the driver asked. "Do you work here or something?" The driver kept his eyes on Shahram while partially glancing at the road.

"Yeah," Shahram replied, slowly nodding his head.

"Do they pay you well over here?" the driver continued, as Shahram opened his eyes and looked at him through the rearview mirror.

"You looking for a job, man?" Shahram asked as he noticed that along with the driver, the passenger in the front and the two other men next to him had their eyes on him.

"Just curious bro, just wanted to know if you get paid well," the driver replied with a grin. Shahram raised his eyebrows and stared back at him through the mirror.

"Listen buddy, I've had a tough night, so do you mind just driving the car and not asking so many questions?" Shahram said while he held tightly to the handle of his tool bag.

"Working hard? So you must be getting paid well!" the driver replied with the same grin as he looked to the man sitting next to him, who also chuckled.

"Could you mind you own business, man? Just drive the fucking car already!" Shahram raised his voice and clenched his fist while staring down the driver through the mirror.

"Relax buddy, we don't want to waste anyone's time; we just wanna know if we're robbing the right guy," the driver said, as the front-seat passenger suddenly turned around and sprayed something in Shahram's eyes.

Shouting, Shahram quickly closed his eyes as the sprayed agent began to burn and sting his eyes and face. Letting go his grip on his tool bag, Shahram began to rub his watering eyes while the two men sitting on his sides clutched onto his arms and the driver yelled at them to quickly knock him out.

Struggling to open his eyes, Shahram wriggled his upper body as punches began to land on his face and head. Ducking his head, he squinted open his right eye and noticed the close proximity of his mouth to the hand of the man clenched around his right wrist. Opening his mouth, Shahram launched his gaping jaws forward and sank his teeth into the top of the man's hand. Forcing his teeth into the screaming man's hand, Shahram yanked his head back and ripped a piece of the man's flesh. Blood dripping around the corner of his mouth, Shahram spit out the tiny piece of flesh and pulled his arm out of the screaming man's clutches. Squinting his watery eyes open, Shahram quickly reached for his tool bag with his freed arm. He unzipped the bag and grabbed for his hammer as the blows against his head and face continued. The car swerved on the road as the driver continued to shout at the other three men; Shahram gripped tightly the handle of his hammer, but before he could remove it out of his bag, a crushing blow smashed against his arm.

Screaming at the agonizing pain in his right arm, Shahram grinded his teeth, lifted up his head, and squinted open his stinging and blurry eyes just before another blow came in from the front passenger, striking his temple and the side of his head. His head spinning as drops of blood trickled down his head and over his eyelids, Shahram closed his eyes and passed out.

Shahram slowly opened his eyes as the cold winds pierced the side of his body. His efforts to lift up his black and blue right arm only ended in shouts and screams of agony. Grinding his teeth, he slowly sat up. His head spinning and feeling heavier than usual, Shahram felt with his left index finger, gently going over his right arm before coming to the painful conclusion that the bones in his right arm were at the very least cracked or even broken. He bit his lower lips while rubbing the back of his left arm across his damp eyes, which while still a little blurry were nevertheless functional. With tiny pieces of gravel and dirt settling in the stinging gash above the corner of his right eyebrow, Shahram noticed that he had been dumped in a barren and remote area. Gone were his coat, jeans, shoes, and tool bag; all that he was left with were his briefs and a T-shirt.

With his head spinning, Shahram slowly got up. Dragging his arm by his side, he began to limp and slowly followed a set of tire tracks that led him toward the main road. Staring down at the cold, silent road, Shahram started to scream and shout for help. Tears soon began to run down his cold and bloodied face as the reality of what had just happened to him settled in. The money he so desperately needed, along with his cell phone and his boss's tool bag, had been viciously stolen from him. Shivering, Shahram tilted his head up and shouted, asking God why he was being treated this way, while more tears ran down his face.

It wasn't too long that a patrol car from a nearby police division drove by. The officers immediately rushed out of their car when they noticed the nearly naked Shahram stumbling on the side of the road. He passed out in the back of the patrol car as the officers took him to a nearby clinic.

The sound of a crying toddler ringing through the hallway, Shahram slowly lifted open his swollen eyes. His right hand was placed in a cast that ran from his wrist up to his biceps, while bandages ran around his forehead. Shahram noticed Javad standing at the foot of the bed, looking at him and holding his hand onto the side of his gray head.

"How you doing, son?" Javad asked; Shahram quietly moaned while trying to sit up.

"It hurts, my head," Shahram said, grinding his teeth as he reached over the dressing and around his temple with his left hand.

"That's because it's busted; same with your right arm, not to mention your two broken ribs," Javad said. Shahram slowly tilted his head and noticed the thick wrappings around his chest and ribs. "Those sons of bitches did a number on you. They must have felt that breaking your hand and head wasn't enough, so they kicked you in the side once they dumped you out of their car," Javad added.

Shahram began to slowly run his hand over the bandages on his ribs.

"Fortunately, you didn't suffer any brain damage," Javad continued, "but they had to give you sixteen stitches on your forehead."

Shahram quietly stared down at his lap. Tears began to stream down his puffy eyes as Javad swallowed hard and gazed at the sobbing Shahram.

"My money … the tools … they took it all," Shahram said as Javad shook his head, holding back the tears that lay in the corner of his eyes.

"What am I going to do now?" Shahram asked as his tears soaked through the blanket draped over his legs.

"It's going to be all right, kiddo," Javad said. "I'm going to take care of your bill here, and first thing tomorrow, I'm going to pick you up after you get discharged. I've also talked to your sister, and she is aware of what happened. I think the best thing for you to do is to come and stay with us. You should not visit your mother in this condition." He reached over and gently patted Shahram's ankle.

"I'm such a fucking burden," Shahram replied, sobbing and shaking his head.

"Nonsense," Javad said. "How many times do I have to tell you that you're like one of my sons? Now stop crying, it's late and you should get some rest. I'll see you tomorrow, Shahram."

The next day, as promised, Javad picked Shahram up after his discharge. While the puffiness around his eyes had come down and the large bandages around his head were replaced with a much smaller dressing, Shahram nevertheless still felt the stinging pain and the discomfort of having to walk around with his arm wrapped in a cast.

"Any news from the police?" Shahram asked Javad as they both got in his car.

"No, but if it helps, you're not their first victim," he said. "There have been six other people who got robbed just like you did!"

"You would think that after seven robberies and assaults, they would have caught a bunch of highway robbers," Javad said, shaking his head. "Instead, they go after people with satellite dishes and green shirts."

"By the way, don't worry about the tools, your boss owes me a favor. I'm sure I can work something out with him."

"Has Soraya said anything about this week's hospital costs?" Shahram asked.

"Not really," Javad replied. "She told me last night that she and Farhad are trying to put together the money; they plan on borrowing from friends and neighbors. Listen, kid, you know you're family and that I would lend you cash if I could, but the way things have been lately, with the bills and the rent, I'm afraid that I can't help you out here."

"You've done more than enough for me and my family," Shahram said. "I would be ashamed of myself if I took another toman from you." He looked into Javad's teary eyes as silence took over the car once again.

"Why don't you go by the mosque this afternoon?" Javad suggested. "You know, the one near your house; maybe you could talk to the mullah there."

"Mullah? What mullah?" Shahram asked, raising one of his eyebrows.

"Ever since your father passed away," Javad explained, "your mother has been going to that mosque and donating money, helping out in their charities and organizing events for the mosque's female congregation ... you know, as sign of a good omen, so that God will look after you and your brothers and sister. Just go there this afternoon and ask them for some financial help; it's the least they could do, especially since your mother has been helping them out for years." Shahram slowly nodded his head before looking out of the car's window.

That afternoon, Shahram headed out for the mosque after speaking to Soraya. She said that she and Farhad had struggled to put together around 750,000 tomans; they hoped that Shahram could somehow get the rest of the money that they needed to pay the hospital in order to keep their mother there.

His hand lying in the sling around his neck, Shahram walked in the gray and mild December streets of south Tehran while thinking about his mother's charitable contributions. He shrugged his shoulders and imagined how much money his mother had donated to the mosque over the years; he wondered whether her help and efforts actually brought the family any good luck. Just before entering the mosque, one last thought crossed his mind: he wondered whether his family would have been in the same financial troubles had his mother not made so many donations over the years and saved her money instead.

With that in the back of his mind, he walked into the mosque, going past the big prayer room and down a hallway. The mosque was very clean, and since it was past prayer time, there were not too many people around. The floors were decked out in what looked like marble and granite; the entire mosque was beautifully designed. Although it was only a few blocks away from his family's flat, this was Shahram's first time back since his father's funeral.

Shahram approached the end of the hallway and arrived at a door, where a man in a military uniform sat behind a desk.

"You can't be back here, boy," he said. "Get lost!"

"Please sir, I need to see the mullah," Shahram replied, gazing deep into the man's eyes.

"Mullah? Watch your mouth, you little punk! This is the holy imam of the mosque that you're referring to, plus his grace doesn't see hoodlums that wander off the streets!" the uniformed man shouted, staring at the sling around Shahram's neck.

"Please sir ... it's very important. My mother is dying and ... his holiness knows my mother!" Shahram further pleaded, holding onto the side of the desk the uniformed man sat behind.

"Go on, get out of here. Are you deaf? I said get lost!" As he stood up from his seat, the mullah opened the door of his office.

"What is going on here? What's all this noise about?" the mullah asked as he glanced at the uniformed man before looking Shahram up and down.

"It's nothing, sir," the soldier quickly said, standing up straight with his hands held behind his back while looking forward and past the mullah.

"Your holiness, please! I need your help," Shahram said. "It's a matter of life and death!" He got down on his knees as a few tears rolled down his face.

"What is it? I'm a very busy man," the mullah replied as Shahram quickly stood up.

"My mother's name is Zahra; she is a member of your congregation. Zahra Azizi!" Shahram quickly replied.

"Yes, sister Azizi," the mullah said. "Your mother hasn't been here in a while; has she forgotten us now?"

"She has been in the hospital with lung cancer for the past eight weeks or so," Shahram replied.

"Oh dear! Well, be sure to tell her that she'll be in my prayers," the mullah said as he stepped back toward his office.

"Please sir! Please just hear me out for two minutes! I really need your help! I lost my father; I don't want to lose my mother too!" Shahram nearly screeched as more tears rushed down his face. The mullah turned his head and gazed at him silently, still with one eyebrow raised.

"Don't do it for me," Shahram said, "do it for my two younger brothers, who will be orphans in the eyes of God soon; do it for them!"

The mullah sighed loudly and nodded his head before rolling his eyes.

"Let him through," the mullah said to the uniformed man standing a foot from him. Shahram smiled, wiped his face, and nearly jumped toward the door.

"But you only have two minutes, boy … understand?" the mullah said loudly. Shahram quickly nodded while closing the door of the office behind himself.

"God bless you, sir, you don't know what this means to me and my family," Shahram said with a smile.

"Stand in the corner, over there," the mullah said. "I don't want you to get grease on my rug." He pointed toward the tiled corner of his office while Shahram looked at his shoes before glancing at the burgundy-colored Persian rug on the floor.

"Now what's this about sister Azizi that you speak off?" the mullah asked as he took his seat right under large framed pictures of Khomeini and Khamenei.

"She has been diagnosed with lung cancer and requires chemotherapy, which she has been undergoing for the past seven weeks," Shahram said, while keeping an eye on his sneakers and the edge of the rug.

"Yes, you have already said that; get to the part that involves what I can do!" the mullah said loudly as Shahram quickly nodded, nearly bowing his head.

"Yes sir; my family and I have been paying for her medical treatment until now, but as you can see, my right hand is broken and I can no longer work," Shahram said, slowly lifting the sling that held his cast.

"I'm not blind, boy, I can see your bloody arm," the mullah snapped. "The mosque can give you a check for 500,000 tomans; now, this money does not require any interest, but it must be paid back within a year."

"Only 500,000! Your grace, we need at least 700,000 just to pay for this week's chemotherapy and hospital bed," Shahram replied.

"You should be on your knees, kissing my shoes and thanking God that I'm giving you this amount and not kicking you out of the mosque for looking like an addict!" the mullah said, raising his voice again.

Shahram hung his head and stared down at the rug.

"Now, 500,000 is the most the mosque can pay on loans," he continued, "and given that sister Azizi is one of our valued parishioners, I'm willing to put her ahead of a lot of other deserving people ... but she still needs to go through the application process."

Shahram lifted up his head and asked, "How long does this process take?"

"It takes time ... there are forms, procedures, a one-month waiting period. You don't think I'm going to hand 500,000 tomans to some kid off the street who is covered in a cast, bandages, and motor oil, do you?" the mullah replied as he once again looked at Shahram from head to toe.

"One month? But I have to pay the hospital fees today ... or at the latest tomorrow!" Shahram said, holding out his left hand with his eyes wide open.

"This is the best that I can do; you can take it or leave it!" the mullah replied as he pointed to the door before picking up his pen and going back to a stack of papers sitting in front of him.

"What about the charity boxes outside every mosque in this city," he asked, "the ones my mother has been stuffing with bills for years now? What about that money ... aren't those boxes labeled 'Charity for the needy'? Well, I'm in need, my mother is in need." Shahram's nostrils flared while he squeezed tightly his broken arm's fist as tears rolled down from his eyes.

"Boy, how in the name of Allah am I supposed to give you money from the charity boxes?" the mullah replied. "I don't even know where that money ends up. What I meant to say is, that money goes to the leader's office, and it is for him and his prominent staff to decide who is worthy enough to receive a segment of it."

Shahram continued to look at him with one eyebrow raised.

"You have taken enough of my time today," the mullah said. "If you want the loan, then take these documents and show them to brother Sajadi outside. He will give you more instructions on how you can file the documents and get the loan."

The mullah took out a few pieces of paper from a compartment in his desk.

"Now go and thank God that your mother is a valued member of the mosque and that she will be in our prayers; you yourself should also start coming to the mosque and pray for her. You can even help out like your dear mother used to do," the mullah said after he handed the papers to Shahram, who stood there gazing at the mullah.

His head hanging between his shoulders, Shahram walked out of the mosque along with a handful of papers. Slowly shaking his head, he reflected back on the question that he asked himself before he walked into the mosque. It seemed that not only had those questions remained unanswered, but now he was left with even more questions. He was never really the praying type and wondered whether God was punishing him for his lack of interest toward the mosque and the institution of prayer. He scratched his head and rubbed his fingers over his bandage. On the other hand, he had just found out that morning that his mother had regularly attended the mosque and helped in almost all facets of the mosque; then why, he wondered, was she the one to suffer from cancer? He sighed and shook his head some more before heading toward the offices where the uniformed man outside the mullah's room had instructed him to go.

Shahram spend the entire afternoon chasing down offices and finally managed to complete the required instructions of the mullah and put together the necessary documents before applying for the loan. And although the application process took over one month, he had no other choice but to apply for it, as he could use any help he could get.

After informing his sister of the situation at the mosque, Shahram decided to head over to his work district in the hopes that a familiar face would lend him a helping hand. It was around six in the evening, and most of the shops began to close down their gates for the day. Shahram walked over to Davoud's mechanic shop. He was hoping to run into Davoud's boss, who used to work with his father back in the day. Davoud's boss was always kind to Shahram, and this time was no exception. Seeing Shahram walk into his shop with his hand broken and his head busted up, the man got out his checkbook and wrote him a check for 500,000 tomans. Tears in his eyes, Shahram thanked him and promised to pay him back within the next few weeks.

Shahram hung back at the shop and waited to see Davoud, who he hadn't spent much time with lately. That evening, Davoud was sent out on a job to purchase parts and was in charge of closing down the shop.

"Holy shit, man, what happened to you?" Davoud asked as he walked into the shop and noticed Shahram's arm cast and bandages.

"It's nothing, Davoud; I fell down a ladder at work," Shahram said, swallowing hard.

"This happened at the construction site you're working at?" Davoud asked as he raised his eyebrows.

"Yeah, it happened there. Listen, I need a big favor from you, bro," Shahram replied as he reached into his pocket and took out a pack of cigarettes, offering a smoke to Davoud before taking one for himself.

"You need the bike again?" he asked. "I don't think it'll be a good idea to get on it with only one arm ... you might break the other one too." They both chuckled.

"No, I don't need to borrow your bike; I need some cash," Shahram said as he gazed at the red glowing tip of his cigarette.

"How much do you need?" Davoud asked.

"Around 300,000," Shahram replied, still gazing upon the cigarette.

"Shahram, you know you're like a brother to me," Davoud said, "and you know I'll help you no matter what, but my mom's in the hospital again, and my dad and I've been paying through the teeth. I can't lend you that much cash right now." Davoud dropped his head and stared at the floor while Shahram slowly nodded his head.

"I think I might know a guy you can borrow the money from," Davoud said, "but we gotta take a ride." Shahram quickly lifted up his head and nodded with his eyes stretched wide open.

The two got on Davoud's bike and Davoud rode them to a nearby area where a knocked-down apartment building lay in ruins. Shahram knew the area well and never really liked it, as it was notorious for heroin addicts and homeless junkies, who lived in the ruins.

Approaching the area where the wreckage was located, Shahram spotted a lonely figure standing by the side of the street, smoking a cigarette. It was Davoud's drug dealer, Mehdi Khakrobe (Garbage Mehdi), and while it was not clear to Shahram why he had such a nickname, the rumors on the street suggested that Mehdi's father had been employed as a city sanitation worker, and that's where the name apparently came from.

Getting off the bike a few feet from Mehdi, Davoud reminded Shahram not to call the drug dealer by his nickname, as not only did he resent the title, he would often get violent with those who used the nickname.

"Well, well, if it isn't my main junkie Davoud; back for a fix so quick?" the drug dealer said as Davoud nervously smiled and shook his hand.

"Hey Mehdi? This is my friend, Shahram," Davoud replied as he introduced Shahram, who proceeded to shake Mehdi's hand.

"So what is it that I can get you and your friend?" Mehdi asked.

"The thing is ... well ... you always liked my bike, right? So I wanted to give you the exclusive opportunity to buy it from me," Davoud said, moving aside so Mehdi could take a look at his bike, while Shahram's eyes and mouth stretched wide open as he quickly looked to Davoud.

"That banged up piece of shit? Why the fuck would I want to buy that?" Mehdi said as he spat on the ground right next to Davoud.

"Come on, man ... it's an original Honda. The thing is a babe magnate; you know you'll be fighting off chicks with a stick once you get on this bad boy!" Davoud said while Shahram continued to gaze at his friend with his mouth hanging wide open.

"Shut up, Davoud. So what do you want for it?" Mehdi replied before spitting again.

"Whatever is fair ... say 450 large," Davoud said.

"Are you fucking high? That piece of shit ain't worth more than 350, and I wouldn't pay you more than 300," Mehdi said, staring into Davoud's eyes.

"Can you at least make it 310? For old time's sakes," Davoud said, holding out his right hand. Mehdi eyed his hand before slowly nodding and rolling eyes.

"Okay, I'll give you 310; that's only because I know you're going to give it all back to me when your junkie ass comes back for a fix," Mehdi said with a chuckle before taking out a stash of bills and counting them. Davoud winked at Shahram, who continued to stay glued to his spot with his mouth hanging open.

"So what made you decide to sell your bike now?" Mehdi asked. "You need money or something?"

"No ... I mean, yeah; you know how it is, got family in the hospital," Davoud replied while trying to count the money the dealer had handed him.

"Why don't you sell one of your kidneys instead?" Mehdi asked, chuckling again.

"You can do that? I mean, how much can you get for a kidney?" Shahram asked.

"A kidney can run you around three or four million these days," Mehdi replied before lighting up another cigarette.

"But how does it work? Do you sell it to a hospital?" Shahram asked.

"Well, it depends," he said. "You gotta go to the hospital and line up a buyer who is desperate first, and then you have to play cat and mouse with them, tell them that the list of donors is long and you're healthy and willing to donate your kidney ... of course, for a price, that is," Mehdi replied, exhaling black smoke out of his lungs and toward the direction of Davoud.

"You know anyone who might be interested in buying a kidney?" Shahram asked.

"I might," he said, "if you're willing to pay a finder's fee, that is."

"I'll pay a finder's fee if you can find someone willing to pay four million ... and half of it in advance," Shahram said, as he noticed Davoud lifting up his head and staring at him.

"No sweat, kid. I'll call you once I hear from my contact; shouldn't take that long ... there are usually three or four losers like you two who sell their kidney to this guy every month," Mehdi said as he chuckled again.

"Now if you ladies excuse me, I have some business to do ... unless you want to buy some more heroin, Davoud?" Mehdi said as Shahram stared at Davoud in alarm after hearing the word *heroin*.

"What can I say? Every pain's got its own treatment," Davoud said as he dropped his head, reached into his pocket, and gave Mehdi a sum of money in exchange for the heroin wrapped in a piece of tinfoil.

With the early December sun setting, the two walked back toward Davoud's mechanic shop. After a few blocks, Davoud reached into his coat pocket and handed over the stash of money he had just gotten from Mehdi for his motorcycle.

"I can't believe you did that for me, Davoud!" Shahram said. "You loved that bike." He pocketed the money and looked back at Davoud.

"I'm sure you would have done the same for me," Davoud replied as he turned to his friend and smiled.

"But what about your mother; don't you need money to pay for her hospital stay?" Shahram asked.

"I'm getting paid by the end of the week, plus my dad works, so it makes things a little easier. Boy, I can't even imagine the hell you have been in the past eight weeks," Davoud said as Shahram glanced at the sling around his neck.

"I'll pay you back, Davoud. I promise ... you can even buy back your bike," Shahram said after a quick pause. Davoud smiled and slowly nodded.

The two walked the rest of the way in complete silence as small flakes of snow began to drop over the now dark streets. Entering the shop, the two headed straight for the office, where Davoud quickly turned on the kettle while Shahram took a seat next to the desk.

"When did you start doing heroin?" Shahram asked.

"It's like I just said; every pain has its own treatment, and I got a lot of pain that needs to be treated," Davoud said as he poured a few spoons of dried tea leaves in a tea pot, while Shahram looked back at him with silence.

"So are you set for money?" Davoud asked as he sat behind the desk while taking out his pack of cigarettes.

"For this week; next week is a whole other story. Well, at least I don't have to hold my breath until the money that the mullah sanctioned comes in the mail," Shahram replied, rolling his eyes and shaking his head.

Davoud raised one of his eyebrows before taking out two cigarettes for himself and Shahram.

"I forgot to tell you, I went to the mosque that my mom has been going to since forever and asked for their help," he explained. "The mullah there gave me an application for a loan of 500,000 that takes a month to go through!" Shahram said before shaking his head again while reaching for the cigarette. "I don't know, I might have to sell my kidney after all."

Shahram sighed as Davoud leaned over the desk with his lighter and lit his cigarette.

"You really are thinking about what the snake said earlier?" Davoud asked before lighting himself up.

"It has nothing to do with Mehdi Khakrobe," Shahram replied. "The truth is, before my dad died, he was going to sell his kidney so he could pay his debts. I overheard my mother telling one of the neighborhood women back then."

Davoud gazed at him silently.

"It's not even about the money that I need to pay next week, Davoud. It's about the fees that I have to pay the week after that, and the rent and my debts ... the groceries, my brothers, and who knows, maybe even more goddamned hospital fees!" Shahram raised his voice as he hurled his cigarette against the ground before stomping his foot on it.

Davoud continued to look at him silently.

"The whole fucking country is built on an oil mine," Shahram said, "and I have to beg some fat fucking mullah for money ... and get a fucking lecture on how my mom is in the hospital maybe because I don't pray enough or go the mosque enough."

Davoud quietly nodded while dropping his eyes and looking at the desk in front of him.

"Isn't it funny? I get judged by some fucking hypocrite who looks down at me as a junkie with one hand and speaks about God with the other, while he sits pretty in his fucking office with his Persian rug underneath his feet, with a bulldog guarding him and the money and blood of this nation in his pockets! All underneath the eyes of the two biggest crooks in the world [Khomeini and Khamenei]," Shahram said, still pushing his toe against the crushed cigarette.

"It's a joke," Davoud said. "That's what it is, a bad joke, played on us by a bunch of thieves who call themselves representatives of God."

He stood up and poured hot water from the kettle into the pot while Shahram nodded before looking at the twisted and crushed cigarette underneath his foot.

"So how long do you have to keep your cast on?" Davoud asked before pouring tea for himself and Shahram.

"Five weeks … at least that's what the doctor said," Shahram replied as Davoud handed him the hot beverage.

"What are going to do for money now?" Davoud asked as he sat back down behind the desk.

"I don't know, I can't work with a busted arm; might as well start begging on the street. At least that's where I'm headed for," Shahram said while holding his cup and blowing on the steaming surface. Davoud slowly shook his head before reaching inside his pocket and taking out the tinfoil containing the heroin he bought earlier.

"So, what's this I've been hearing about you getting clean?" Davoud asked as he took out a small syringe and set it down next to the foil. Shahram stared at him and the foil with his eyes stretching wide.

"Yeah, old man Javad helped me get clean," Shahram replied as his eyes continued to be locked on to the piece of foil.

Davoud retrieved a metal spoon from next to the stove.

"I don't know why you're messing with this stuff, man; this is the most insane shit there is, Davoud," Shahram said as he raised his twitching fingers and rubbed his stitches over the bandage covering them.

"Insane? This is the only thing that makes sense, Shahram. I can do it wherever I want, it doesn't have a smell, and no visible needle marks if you shoot it between your toes. Plus it lets me forget about all of this!" Davoud said as he looked straight into Shahram's eyes. "Like the fact that my poor mother and sister are going to be in and out of the hospital as long as they are alive! The fact that I have to work as a fucking grease monkey for the rest of my life! The fact that I could never afford to have a family, and even if I could, no one in their right mind is going to let me marry their daughter!"

Davoud raised his voice before shaking his head.

"For every pain there is a treatment, a painkiller, and my pain is so harsh that I have to heal it with this shit!" Davoud added as he lifted up the foil and squeezed it with his thumb and index finger.

Shahram looked at him silently, his eyes glancing in between Davoud and the foil he held between his fingers.

"What can I do, Shahram? Go to a psychotherapist and cry about how fucked up my life is? Or go to a mosque and pray to God that hopefully one day money will start to rain from the sky and my troubles will be over? No, Shahram, if you want my opinion, this is the only thing that makes perfect sense." Davoud slowly took the edges of the foil with his fingers and opened it up before pouring the milky substance onto the spoon.

Silence fell in between the two as the evening December winds rattled against the garage doors of the shop. Shahram continued to stare at Davoud with his mouth hanging wide open. Davoud held the spoon over his lighter until it all melted into a brown liquid. Davoud quickly reached for his syringe and fixed the needle on it before sucking up the liquid in the spoon with the syringe.

"I know you've gone clean and all," Davoud said, "but I'll leave a little bit of it in the syringe; just enough for a taste, in case you change your mind." Davoud looked into Shahram's eyes while rolling up his sleeve.

Shahram bit his lower lip as he watched his friend inject the needle into his arm, close his eyes, and then lean back into the chair after taking out the half-empty syringe. What Davoud just said about heroin making perfect sense began to broadcast over Shahram's ears. Davoud even hinted to revelations that Shahram had not even contemplated about; Shahram had never even thought about having a family or even life past the next few years. He felt that all that he had known up to that point was how to fix cars while his only possessions were an old camera along with a couple of old and wrinkled photography magazines.

This was perhaps the very same reason why his father had abused drugs ever since Shahram could remember. He stared back at the brown liquid lying inside the syringe, just about a few inches away from his reach. Shahram paused, looked at Davoud with his eyes closed while slouching in his seat, and reached over and grabbed the syringe.

Doing heroin that day took him back to when he first smoked marijuana. He felt light, like a small bird flying over the events that took place over his life. He flew over the black and white colored events of the day his dead father was laid to rest. He flew outside the window of the hospital where his mother was clinging to life. He flew over the tiny apartment that his family lived in and his skinny twelve- and fifteen-year-old brothers sitting in front of empty plates. He flew over Javad, his sister, and Davoud, who all looked up at him while he passed over them.

After spending the night in a euphoric daze, Shahram left the mechanic shop in the morning and headed over to Javad's shop. When he arrived, he saw that his coworkers were all gathered around Javad, whose face was wet with tears.

"There you are, my son," Javad said. "I'm so sorry." He paused and swallowed hard. "Your sister has been looking for you all morning; she tried to call you but your phone has been off. Your mother passed away a few hours ago."

Shahram felt dizzy and weak as the first waves of grief swept over him and knocked him to his knees. Tears gushed out of his eyes and he dropped to the ground.

—————

After the death of his mother, I lost track of Shahram; later, I heard about his subsequent death, just two weeks after his mother had passed away. According to his sister Soraya, Shahram's body was found in the same ruins where he had met Mehdi Khakrobe; the cause of death was attributed to a heroin overdose.

While I'm not able to tell you what went through Shahram's mind in the last days of his life, what I can tell you is that despite the fact that Shahram had a destructive relationship with narcotics throughout most of his adult life, he always gave his all when it came to providing for his family. He never wanted his brothers to inherit the same fate that he had been given; unfortunately, it looks like history will likely repeat itself, as Soraya informed me that the older of the two brothers was now working at the same mechanic shop where Shahram and his father had worked.

Soraya's final words during our interview were not that different from the wishes of other Iranians that I talked to during the process of writing this book. She wished to live in an Iran that provided hope instead of depression and drama. A place where narcotics were not the sanctuary for the millions of disenchanted and lost souls. She wanted her kids and the future generations to have access to alternative channels of expression, affordable education, rehab, better job opportunities, and a tougher government stance on narcotics. Lastly, she wanted to live in a society where addiction was not perceived as a personal illness but as a social problem that needed immediate care.

Appendix.
The Numbers behind Iran

~~~~~~ᘯᘯᘯᘯᗕᘯᗕ~~~~~~

Iran's General Statistics

Based on the *CIA Fact Book* and the government of Iran's recent census (July 2011), Iran's population stands at approximately seventy-eight million; two thirds of the population are estimated to be between the ages of fifteen and sixty-four.[47] Out of the two thirds of the population just mentioned, nearly 85 percent are aged between fifteen and thirty-one, meaning that nearly 60 percent of Iran's entire population consists of individuals who are below thirty-one, and more importantly, this population consists of individuals born after the 1979 revolution.[48] With regard to Tehran, official numbers indicate a population figure of roughly eight million.[49] However, the majority living in Tehran believe the official figure to be much higher—approximately eighteen million. Accordingly, the spike in the population of youths is more evident in Iran than in any other county, as the median age is estimated at only twenty-six years.[50]

---

47   https://www.cia.gov/library/publications/the-world-factbook/geos
     /ir.html.

48   Ibid.

49   Ibid.

50   Ibid.

Life expectancy in Iran, meanwhile, is estimated to be around seventy years, and although the nation has boosted its literacy rate to 80 percent, sadly the national expenditure on education is only estimated to be 4.7 percent of Iran's GDP.[51]

The country's GDP (purchasing power parity) is estimated around $818 billion, ranking twentieth in the globe.[52] However, the nation's GDP with regard to real growth rate is estimated at an insignificant rate of 1 percent. The GDP per capita stands at $5,493, putting Iran alongside war-torn Iraq rather than wealthy oil producers such as Saudi Arabia and Kuwait.[53]

The official state's unemployment numbers released in 2010 projected a percentage around 15 percent.[54] However, many in Iran believe the number to be much higher, near an astonishing 35 percent. It is estimated that each year, around 750,000 Iranians enter the labor market, which has only been adding about 300,000 new jobs annually.[55]

Although Iran exports nearly 2.5 million barrels of oil per day, making the country one of the richest nations on the planet, the reality is that nearly 20 percent of its population lives below the poverty line. Excluding oil production, the country's industrial growth rate stands at a shocking negative 1.4 percent, ranking Iran's industry 154th among other nations. Despite the increasing price of oil, based on 2010 figures, Iran's national debt stands at $14.5 billion, while the official state numbers have placed inflation at 10 percent.[56]

---

51   https://www.cia.gov/library/publications/the-world-factbook/geos /ir.html.

52   Ibid.

53   http://www.forbes.com/sites/danielfisher/2011/07/05/the-worlds -worst-economies/2/.

54   https://www.cia.gov/library/publications/the-world-factbook/geos /ir.html.

55   Ramin Jahanbegloo, "The deadlock in Iran: Pressures from below," *Journal of Democracy,* 2003.

56   https://www.cia.gov/library/publications/the-world-factbook/geos /ir.html.

Again, actual figures in Iran have placed the inflation much higher, ranging around 20 to 50 percent on a weekly basis. This astonishing figure has largely been attributed to the nation's low productivity, unemployment, high cost of living, and skyrocketing prices of real estate.[57] The economic situation has become so dire that in a recent *Forbes* magazine article, Iran's economy was placed among the top ten worst economies on the planet.[58] Further, at the time of writing this book, the current exchange rate is 1,045 toman to US$1,[59] an astonishing figure given that the exchange rate in 1978, just a few months before the revolution, was approximately 7 toman for every US$1.[60] This is more proof of what many people in Iran (and especially Tehran) believe: living standards of Iranians are now much lower than what people used to enjoy before the 1979 revolution, under the Pahlavi monarchy.

On the other hand, the Islamic Republic's lack of spending on educational facilities, rampant unemployment, and high costs of living have resulted in distressing social costs such as drug addiction, prostitution, depression, crime, and even higher rates of suicide. Nowhere have these social ills been felt more than at the youth levels, who as well are suffering from disenchantment about life in Iran, especially in the aftermath of the controversial elections of 2009.

Additionally, the lack of public schooling has led to the creation of private schools and universities, which nevertheless have a higher price tag, which restricts many families from affording to put their children in schools and universities. Even the population that can afford schooling is faced with the daunting reality of unemployment once they graduate from school.

---

57   Ramin Jahanbegloo, "The deadlock in Iran: Pressures from below," *Journal of Democracy*, 2003.

58   http://www.forbes.com/sites/danielfisher/2011/07/05/the-worlds -worst-economies/2/.

59   http://www.gocurrency.com/.

60   http://www.farsinet.com/toman/exchange.html.

Regime's Clothing Restrictions

The overwhelming response that I received from younger Iranians was that the regime along with its ultra conservative nature—has not only turned its back completely on the demands of the youth, but through oppressive policies and draconian measures, it has nearly criminalized the welfare of the youth. The regime's policies not only affect significant issues such as fundamental rights such as freedom of expression and association, the regime also controls trivial matters like clothing, hairstyle, music, dancing, and even dating, which directly affect the lives of the young.

As part of the clothing policies that have carried on since the early days of the revolution, women and girls older than seven are required to wear clothing in public that cover their hair and entire bodies, along with wearing a *manto*, an overcoat-like garment that conceals their shape. The only exception is that women are not required to cover their faces and hands. Men and boys over the age of seven, on the other hand, are also required to wear clothing that cover their entire bodies with the exception of hair, hands, and face. The punishment for failing to obey the clothing guidelines usually results in arrests, prison sentences, and even lashings.[61]

In recent years, especially after the controversial presidential election of 2009 and the wide demonstrations in its aftermath, the regime's newly revamped "moral police" (including 70,000 forces appointed by the supreme leader, Khamenei) have upped the ante in "making sure that the state's Islamic values, including the strict dress codes, are followed and that decadent Western values are abolished."[62] Some of their recent policies include arresting women who wear loose-fitting head scarves that expose the front side of their hair and tight-fitting overcoats that expose the shape of their bodies.[63]

While for men, arrests and even lashings have taken place for anyone wearing necklaces or sporting a glamorous hairstyle.

---

61   Wright, *The Last Great Revolution,* 2000, p. 136.

62   http://www.guardian.co.uk/world/2011/jun/14/necklace-ban-men -tehran-police.

63   Ibid.

And while again this is all done under the heading of upholding "Islamic values" and "addressing public concern," the majority of Iranians are all aware that the recent clampdowns are merely attempts by the regime to spread panic and fear and control the society through what is mostly described as burly and bearded thugs who arrest and beat up anyone who looks remotely anti-regime or is dressed inappropriately.[64]

Regime's Censorship and Restriction on Music, the Internet, and Satellite Television

In addition to clamping down on clothing and hairstyles choices, which affect mostly the youth, the regime has additionally placed similar restrictions on publications, music, movies, the Internet, and anything that the regime considers a threat to their existence; they combine these offenses under the heading of "Western and anti-Islamic influences."

Similar to the clothing restrictions, the regime places a strict ban on most foreign (especially American) publications, movies, and music. Additionally, any domestic publications, motion pictures, or music that criticizes the regime is also banned, and producers and writers end up in prison or even face execution. The organization Reporters Without Borders ranks Iran's press and censorship as "very serious," which is their worst ranking on their five-point scale.[65]

With regard to the Internet, the regime has severely clamped down; many bloggers and online activists living in Iran face jail time, abuse, and even death sentences. Following the recent periods of unrest and demonstrations, the regime has called for Internet disconnections, filtering almost all foreign and opposition media and news-related pages and jamming telephone lines.[66]

In May 2010, Ebrahim Jabari, one of the commanders of Iran's Islamic Revolutionary Guard Corps (IRGC), confirmed the creation of a "cyber army." By January 2011, it had shut down

---

64   Ibid.

65   http://en.rsf.org/.

66   http://en.rsf.org/internet-enemie-iran,39777.html.

221

online networks and arrested many of the country's Internet users who circumvented the state's filters or used social media in their fight against the regime.[67]

With regard to the Internet, the regime has legitimized censorship under a so-called "committee of experts," citing content "contrary to the morals of society," "contrary to religious values," "contrary to security and social peace," and "hostile toward government officials and institutions." Additionally, the Iranian Parliament passed a law prohibiting selling or using filter circumvention software.[68] The regime's propaganda machine also uses the above reasons to censor human-rights pages and news networks.

This "committee of experts" includes the Ministry of Communications and Information Technology, the Ministry of Culture and Islamic Guidance, the Ministry of National Security, and Tehran's public prosecutor.[69] The same "experts" have also prohibited accessing social media sites such as Facebook and Twitter, labeling the popular networks as "Iran's hidden enemies," charging they are being used to recruit members against the regime. Further, the regime has claimed to have hacked opposition networks such as Voice of America, Twitter, and many other blogs and new sites that deliver news and messages in Farsi (Iran's official language).[70]

Music, especially popular Western music, has similarly been placed under the umbrella of "contrary to Islam and Islamic values."

In the late 1980s, during his presidency and before being promoted to the status of supreme leader, Ayatollah Khamenei banned all Western music.[71] Today, while Western music is still

---

67   http://en.rsf.org/internet-enemie-iran,39777.html.

68   Ibid.

69   Ibid.

70   Ibid.

71   http://www.smh.com.au/world/irans-supreme-leader-seeks-music-ban-20100804-115xn.html.

demonized, it is the actual playing and recording of music that has faced much harsher treatments.

Since the late 1980s, getting a recording license from the Ministry of Culture and Islamic Guidance has proved to be an extremely difficult and frustrating task, while underground gigs, recording studios, and raves are constantly raided by the moral police and radical militias.[72]

The struggles of Iran's musicians along with Tehran's underground music scene was wonderfully described by the talented new wave director Bahman Ghobadi, whose motion picture *No One Knows About Persian Cats* won the special jury prize at the 2009 Cannes Film Festival.[73]

Music and musicians in Iran have taken on a persona that is more like a fugitive on the run. This image continued under the presidency of Ahmadinejad, who shortly after becoming president in 2005 banned all forms of "Western and decadent music."[74]

While there are no actual set laws in Iran's legal codes with regard to music, the subject is similar to many other forms of expression; it remains highly controversial and, at most times, taboo. Nevertheless, similar to many other bans and restrictions, Iranians (especially the youth) have found ways to break through the barriers of these restraints and have managed to flourish in establishing underground music, circumventing the regime's Internet filters, and even creating underground fashion runways.[75]

June 2009 Demonstrations

On June 12, 2009, in an unprecedented turnout, 42 million voters—approximately 65 percent of the entire population of

72   http://www.guardian.co.uk/music/2010/mar/20/no-one-knows-about
-persian-cats.

73   http://www.npr.org/templates/story/story.php?storyId=125993739.

74   http://www.guardian.co.uk/music/2010/mar/20/no-one-knows-about
-persian-cats.

75   http://www.thedailybeast.com/newsweek/2009/09/17/sewn-in-secret
-iranian-designers.html.

Iran—went to the polls with a distinct goal: to send a clear message to Iran's supreme leader Ayatollah Khamenei and President Ahmadinejad that they wanted reform, basic human rights, freedom of expression, and a more accountable government. What took place just days after the elections were atrocities that can only be described as severe human rights violations. Just hours after the polls were closed, and despite strong allegations that 14 million ballots were missing, Iran's state media reported that President Ahmadinejad had won a majority government. It was not long before legitimate cries of election fraud began to spread throughout the country, and masses of devastated voters took to the streets to display their outrage. Instead of calling for an investigation into the elections, the regime reacted by sending out riot police, disciplinary forces, and *basij* militias, who carried out savage beatings and arrests; they even fired on unarmed and innocent demonstrators, resulting in a numbers of deaths. Those who were arrested found themselves in Tehran's notorious Evin and Kahrizak prisons, where security forces used torture and rape on the arrested population, which also led to numerous deaths.[76]

Some of the most notable victims of the brutality of the regime in the aftermath of the 2009 disputed elections were twenty-six-year-old Neda Agha-Soltan, who was shot and killed in plain sight during the demonstrations by members of the *basij*; nineteen-year-old Sohrab Aarabi, who was also shot in the chest by security forces, and whose body was not returned to his family for nearly a month;[77] and twenty-eight-year-old Taraneh Mousavi, who was arrested by plainclothes officers for attending the gathering of mourners for the martyrs of the postelection protests and died after reportedly being sexually abused and raped by security officials while in custody.[78] In a June 2011 article in the *Guardian*, a story broke with regard to security forces using mass

---

76   http://www.timesonline.co.uk/tol/news/world/middle_east /article6839335.ece.

77   http://articles.latimes.com/2009/jul/14/world/fg-iran-sohrab14.

78   http://www.huffingtonpost.com/shirin-sadeghi/the-rape-of-taraneh -priso_b_233063.html.

rape as a weapon against male and female activists and members of the opposition.[79] The article even suggested that prison guards were giving condoms to criminals and encouraging them to rape imprisoned political activists.[80]

Marriages

In June 2009, just a few days before the Iranian presidential election, *Time* magazine published an article outlining the "marriage crisis" in Iran.[81] The article described the poor state of the Iranian economy and its effects on the institution of marriage.[82] According to official figures, there are between 13 and 15 million Iranians of marrying age, and in order to keep the figure steady, around 1.65 million marriages should be registered yearly; however, the actual figure is about half that number.[83]

The article attributed the decrease to several liberal trends that have swept over Iran, such as the fact that more women than men were attending universities and seeking jobs, fewer were marrying at young ages, and premarital sex was no longer considered taboo.[84] However, Azadeh Moaveni, the author of the article, indicated that the real reasons behind the marriage crisis in Iran is the government's "mismanagement of the economy, high inflation, unemployment rates, and soaring real estate prices."[85]

More and more men are finding their marriage proposals turned down by women, who simply are afraid of getting into a marriage when there is barely any room for necessities let alone luxuries. The author further argued that the unbelievable increase in real estate prices under Ahmadinejad, where housing prices—

---

79   http://www.guardian.co.uk/world/2011/jun/24/jailed-iran-opposition-activists-rape?INTCMP=SRCH.

80   Ibid.

81   http://www.time.com/time/world/article/0,8599,1903420,00.html.

82   Ibid.

83   Ibid.

84   Ibid.

85   Ibid.

especially in Tehran—increased by 150 percent (in four years), also played a huge role in pricing out many men from the marriage market.[86]

The controversial procedure of temporary marriages (also known as *"sigheh"*) dates back to the day of the Prophet and pre-Islamic Arabia. Historically, it is indicated that the Prophet himself made the practice permissible during one of his journeys, in which it was stated that when Muslim men were away from their wives and passing their time in much discomfort, the Prophet gave them permission for fixed-term marriage.[87]

After being introduced, the practice for the most part had mixed responses. On the one hand, many young unmarried couples who wished to travel together in Iran and wanted to stay in the same hotel rooms and avoid arrests by the moral police found the concept of *sigheh* beneficial. However, today the overwhelming majority of Iranian women feel that the medieval practice is not only degrading to women but also a social diease that renders the tens of thousands of children born under temporary marriages as illegitimate. It is no longer young couples who obtain a *sigheh* but middle-aged men who are already married and take younger women as their temporary wives.

As mentioned, due to the poor state of the Iranian economy, the institution of temporary marriages has gained an unfortunate popularity, as the concept of *sigheh* represents access to luxuries that many women have limited or no access to. The practice has been promoted mostly by men for women as an easy ride, filled with cars, apartments, and jewelry, courtesy of an older man in exchange for companionship and sex. The reality, however, is it causes the breakup of families, mistrust between fathers and children of the original marriage, and an inevitable conflict between wives and temporary wives.

Many women have also bought into the stereotypical method as a way of having someone to take care of them while avoiding the dramas and emotions that married life entails. Divorced

---

86   http://www.time.com/time/world/article/0,8599,1903420,00.html.

87   http://www.al-islam.org/al-serat/muta/.

women favor temporary marriages, as the divorce laws under the Islamic Republic do not provide much in terms of spousal support and alimony payments. In fact, in a divorce, men are almost always granted the children and the property and possessions that they brought into the marriage. Hence, in temporary marriages, divorced women find someone who will provide them with at least some of the things they had when they were married.

Call it right or wrong, call it humble adultery or purified prostitution, nevertheless this medieval tradition is slowly becoming the norm in Tehran, especially among Tehran's rich and powerful. Temporary marriages also benefit the ruling mullahs. They celebrate the practice not only as "casting away the modern and Western-driven principles of marriage" between two partners by providing models for marriages from the seventh century, and they also make a hefty profit from it, since the process requires paying a mullah for his services.

Prostitution in Iran

Prior to the 1979 revolution, prostitution was legalized; however, it was confined to a designated zone in the southern part of Tehran called "Shahr-e No," which offered brothels and prostitution to its clientele behind closed doors.[88] This district was surrounded by walls on each side, and its entrance was guarded by authorities, who made sure that peace was maintained within the district at all times and that minors were kept out.

However, under the Islamic Republic, prostitution became a zero tolerance taboo, and the punishments for taking part in the practice ranges anywhere from lashes to even executions for repeat offenders.[89]

In a report in the year 2000, the head of Tehran's cultural and artistic affairs, Mohammad Ali Zam, indicated that the average age of prostitutes had dropped from twenty-seven to twenty,

---

88   Ibid.

89   http://www.slate.com/id/2189816/.

while placing the culpability on poverty in addition to neglecting religious obligation.[90]

Prostitution aside, the report also indicates that as the gap between the rich and poor deepens and unemployment and the high cost of living increases, other social ills such as drug use and suicide have begun to rise to unprecedented levels.[91]

Besides the medieval punishments of lashing, imprisonment, and execution in the rare cases, the regime has not really implemented any policies in order to combat the increase of prostitution.

Instead of attacking the real causes of the problem and resolving the rampant inflation, unemployment, staggering levels of poverty, and a degrading quality of life, the regime has promoted the practice of temporary marriages for prostitutes and their clients in order to insure that prostitutes are kept off the streets.[92]

While the concept of *sigheh* was discussed earlier, the regime's poor choice of a loophole in the Islamic laws has backfired, because temporary marriage contracts can be set anywhere from one hour to ninety-nine years. Under this concept, men can acquire the services of a prostitute by legally marrying her for the amount of time that they plan to satisfy their sexual needs,[93] after which the marriage contract most likely will come to an end and the woman finds herself back on the streets, doing what she was doing just hours before her temporary "marriage."

Nevertheless, the practice of getting a *sigheh* with regard to prostitutes is becoming popular among men, and although the process of attaining it takes time out of the working hours of prostitutes, in order to avoid arrests, many clients are insisting that their "dates" be prepared to temporarily "take the plunge" by making a visit to a registry office and obtaining a temporary

---

90   http://news.bbc.co.uk/2/hi/middle_east/822312.stm.

91   Ibid.

92   http://www.slate.com/id/2189816/.

93   Ibid.

marriage from a cleric.[94] In that sense, it is a win-win for the religious establishment, who not only demonizes prostitution but also requires an oath to be administered by a cleric for a fee. Makes you think why pimps in the rest of the world get a bad name.

Ironically, Iranian officials like to promote the country under their rule as a land of chastity and righteousness, but the reality is far from this. In a recent sting operation in the northern city of Neka, several government officials and security officers were arrested for trafficking and operating as many as five brothels.[95] And while the now disgraced former police chief of Tehran has become the face of dishonor and corruption, the reality is that in recent years, other officers of Iran's state security forces and the Islamic Revolutionary Council have all been arrested in brothels.[96]

Besides the dreadful stigma, the disenchantment, and the depression that many prostitutes in Tehran face, there is yet another tragic consequence that awaits them. With the rampant increase of prostitution and drug use, there has been a spike in the increase of HIV/AIDS.[97] In a country where there is minimal education and HIV awareness, there is no doubt that the rate of infection will rise even more.

Homosexuality in Iran

In Iran, homosexuality is not only forbidden, it is punished by imprisonment, corporal punishment, and even execution under the Islamic penal system.[98]

It is noteworthy to mention that despite the taboos and negative stereotypes, homosexuality ironically has been a somewhat mainstream concept in Persian society for many centuries. Classic

94　Ibid.

95　Ibid.

96　Ibid.

97　Ibid.

98　http://www.independent.co.uk/news/world/middle-east/brutal-land-where-homosexuality-is-punishable-by-death-792057.html.

Persian literature includes tales about sexual relations between two males.[99]

In today's popular culture, Iranians quite often make references of homosexuality and the city of Qazvin. This reference has over the past century transformed into frequently told jokes that depict men from Qazvin as lovers of young boys. In present day Iran, being gay is often stereotyped along two popular depictions: *bachebaz* and *evakhahar*. The former is widely described as a vicious, sex-crazed child molester, while the latter describes a gay man who is effeminate.

During the reign of the shah and before the 1979 revolution, homosexuality was also similarly declared illegal, although it is important to note homosexuality behind closed doors was slowly gaining a degree of tolerance; there were even talks of creating gay right organizations similar to the "gay liberation movements" of the 1970s.[100]

Nevertheless, even with minimal tolerance, it is fair to say that regardless of the political climate in Iran, homosexuality has remained a highly controversial topic. There has been no education, support groups, or organizations to provide guidance and support to those who are homosexual or suffer gender confusion. As a result, it would be a fair assessment to say that homosexuality in Iran doesn't exist in dialogue; however, it is nevertheless a topic that nearly every Iranian shares an opinion about.

With regard to dealing with homosexuality, since the Islamic Republic has banned all sexual relations outside of a heterosexual marriage, the regime has come up with a makeshift policy that offers sex change operations for homosexuals, who then as transsexuals can engage in what the regime calls "heterosexual" relations.

This policy has stretched back to a fatwa declared by Ayatollah Khomeini. As per the fatwa, homosexuals and bisexuals are

---

99   http://www.kirjasto.sci.fi/sadi.htm.

100   http://en.wikipedia.org/wiki/LGBT_rights_in_Iran#cite_note -gaycitynews.com-6.

pressured into undergoing a sex change in order to live without legal and social persecution.[101]

In 2008, it was reported that Iran is the second largest nation (Thailand being the first) in carrying out sex change operations, with the regime providing up to half the cost for those who require financial assistance while issuing new birth certificates.[102]

This enforcement has been mostly detrimental to gay men rather than beneficial, as many gay men who have undergone the operation face greater rejection from their families and their lovers. Many struggle to figure out their new life as they try to fit what are the norms in the society. Many who have undergone the operation admit that they would have never considered having their sex changed had they not been forced to.[103]

The punishments for refusing to undergo sex change operations and carrying on with homosexual relations have been outlined by the Parliament of the Islamic Republic approved under Articles 108 through 140.[104]

Under the articles, engaging in consensual sodomy among adult men is punished by death while consensual sodomy among nonadults is punished by seventy-four lashes. As for women, consenting adult females who engage in lesbian sex are punished by a hundred lashes, and if the act is repeated three times, upon the fourth time the individuals face the death penalty.[105]

Just a few days before finishing the first draft of this book, Iran's state-run news agency reported that three men were executed under Articles 108 and 110 for engaging in sodomy and acts that are against the Sharia laws of the country.[106]

---

101   http://www.ecoi.net/file_upload/mv100_cois2001-irn.pdf.

102   http://news.bbc.co.uk/2/hi/7259057.stm.

103   Ibid.

104   http://www.unhcr.org/refworld/country,,IRBC,COUNTRYREP,IRN,,3 ae6a8170,0.html.

105   Ibid.

106   http://www.huffingtonpost.com/2011/09/06/gay-men -hanged_n_951162.html.

Women in Iran

Pre-Islamic Iranian women were involved in many aspects of society such as the economy and the marketplace, while many women during the Sassanid Empire were recruited in the army; they even fought against the Roman armies alongside their male counterparts.[107] Persian women have also historically been the subject of art, paintings, literature, and sculptures.[108]

In the twentieth century and under the Pahlavi dynasty (1925–1979), women were introduced to many areas of reform. The early phases of the Pahlavi reforms were introduced with force, as the government of Reza Pahlavi ordered the compulsory unveiling of women and the removal of traditional Islamic dress codes.[109]

During the same period, Iranian women began to join the workforce, as many in mostly urban centers took jobs in the education and administration sectors. With the increase in jobs, the level of literacy also began to rise, which led to the emergence of women in even higher positions such as ministerial, medical, and even judicial occupations.[110]

Reza Shah's son and successor, Mohammad Reza Pahlavi, introduced even more reforms that affected women. In 1963, he granted female suffrage and the right to vote. Shortly after, women began to run for office and were elected to the Majlis (the parliament), to the upper houses, and even as cabinet ministers.[111] The year 1967 introduced the Family Protection Act, which aimed in improving the status of women in society by promoting equality

---

107 Dodgeon M. H. and Lieu, S. N. C. *The Roman Eastern Frontiers and the Persian Wars (AD 226-363); A Documentary History*. London: Routledge, 1991, pp. 24, 67, 184, 197, and 307.

108 http://www.iran-bulletin.org/art/CINEMA2.html.

109 Pappé, Ilan. *The Modern Middle East*. London: Routledge, 2005, p. 237.

110 Ibid.

111 Ibid.

between men and women and giving women far more rights in areas of divorce and child care.[112]

The act also reformed the archaic divorce laws; husbands were required to obtain a decree of divorce from the courts instead of simply declaring divorce verbally three times, as was stipulated by Sharia law. Women could now apply for divorce, and unlike the previous stance in Sharia law, which automatically granted child custody to men, under the newly established family protection, courts would make the custody decisions. Additionally, by 1975, the minimum age that a woman could marry was raised from fifteen to eighteen.[113]

Following the 1979 revolution and the transformation of Iran into an Islamic Republic, Iranian women lost many of the rights that they had gained under the Pahlavi regime.

Practically all the laws that empowered women previous to the 1979 revolution were reversed, starting with restrictions placed on women's dress codes, with the introduction of mandatory *hejab* (Muslim head covering) and loose-fitting coats (*manto*) designed to cover the body in order to avoid exposure to men.[114]

During the early phases of the Islamic Republic, the *hejab* was only mandatory for women who appeared on television. Shortly after that, women working in government buildings were required to bear the *hejab* or risk losing their jobs. A few months later, the *hejab* became mandatory and women appearing in public were required to wear the head scarf or the chador (a full-length cloak).

Shortly after, the enforcement of the *hejab* began to take place in a severe fashion, as women who failed to adequately cover their hair or other body parts in public became subject to punishments of up to seventy lashes or imprisonment of sixty days.[115]

During the early phases, the regime in addition began to encourage women to stay at home and not seek employment.

---

112   Ibid.

113   Wright, Robin B. *The Last Great Revolution*, 2000, p. 156.

114   http://www.letsgoiran.com/iran-women-dress-code.

115   Wright, Robin B. *The Last Great Revolution*, 2000, p. 136.

This policy, however, began to change once the Iran-Iraq War began and women's employment became needed.[116] Although it is important to note that now women make up 30 percent of Iran's work force, while as of 2007, it was reported that 70 percent of the country's science and engineering students were women.[117]

During the rule of President Khatami (1997–2005), women gained more breathing room in terms of dress codes and social activities. However, based on the overwhelming response, it seem that with the presidency of Ahmadinejad (2005–present), there has been a shift toward the early days of the Islamic Republic.

Dress codes aside, under the Islamic Republic, the legal status of women also began to change, as the new wave of Sharia law began to take over Iran's judicial system. Under the Islamic Republic's codes of law, testimony from two women in court was held to be equal to the testimony of one man, while with regard to inheritance, women were entitled to half of the inheritance of the men.[118]

Family law also became subject to greater changes. Gone were the days of the Family Protection Act, as under the Islamic Republic, a man no longer required his wife's consent in taking on a second marriage.

Divorce is also granted only at the husband's consent, and many women argue that the current divorce laws have only given rise to a higher rate of spousal abuse and spiteful marriages. When a decree of divorce is granted, custody of the children is granted to mothers until a child has reached the age of seven, upon which the custody exclusively goes to the father.[119] This is a slight

---

116   Keddie, Nikki. *Modern Iran: Roots and Results of Revolution*, Yale University Press, 2003, p. 257.

117   http://www.law.harvard.edu/students/orgs/jlg/vol28/halper.pdf.

118   http://www.payvand.com/news/08/feb/1170.html.

119   http://www.aljazeerah.info/News%20archives/2003%20News%20 archives/November/30n/Iranian%20women%20win%20improved%20 child%20custody%20rights.htm.

improvement from previous codes, which automatically granted fathers custody regardless of their qualification as a parent.[120]

With regard to spousal support, at the time of marriage, a man must offer some property or gift to his future wife, who can request this upon divorce or even take delivery during the course of the marriage.[121] This is known as *mahr* (or "dowry" in English) and is usually agreed upon in gold coins. One significant aspect to note is that although now the price of gold coins is set in accordance with inflation, women who were married years ago find their *mahr* to be fairly inadequate and a tool of confinement that keeps them remaining in the unhappy marriage.

In sports, women are still prohibited from entering soccer stadiums where men are playing, while women athletes are also banned from taking part in any sport where a male referee or coach would come into contact with them.[122] In addition, women who represent Iran in sporting events such as the Olympics must wear uniforms in line with the state's Islamic codes and cover hair, necks, arms, and legs.

This requirement led to the dismissal of the Iranian women's soccer team by FIFA, the international football association, who decided that the head scarves that woman players wore in order to cover their hair broke the association's dress code.[123]

In an August 2010 speech, conservative cleric Ayatollah Ahmad Khatami, while persuading Iranians to stop watching satellite programming, declared that women should in particular refrain from watching male sports altogether, as sports such as swimming and wrestling exposed women to men who are *haram* (forbidden) to them.

---

120   Ibid.

121   http://www.international-divorce.com/iran_divorce.htm.

122   http://www.adnkronos.com/AKI/English/Sport/?id=1.0.1687961175.

123   http://www.washingtonpost.com/sports/united/olympics-2012-fifa -bans-headscarves-for-irans-women-soccer-team/2011/06/06/AGzT1JKH _story.html.

Opium in Iran

is important to note that narcotic use has been a problem in
an for many years now, as the epidemic dates back to the 1800s
hen colonial powers, especially the British, began to cultivate
pium poppies in Iran.[124] Opium soon became the country's main
ncome, and before the discovery of oil, opiates had a significant
art in making up Iran's gross national product.[125]

The smoking of opium has long been a tradition as a painkiller
and an alternative to alcohol, which is forbidden under Islam.
As such, addiction to opium has historically been interpreted
as a personal disease rather than a social stigma. Many actually
turn to religious figures and institutions for a "cure" to their
addiction, rather than rely on alternative sources, such as rehab
and medication, which are for the most part expensive and
infrequently available.

---

124   http://www.unodc.org/unodc/en/frontpage/responding-to-drug-use
-and-hiv-in-iran.html.

125   Ibid.

Last Words

———～⟶～———

I t is for you to decide what kind of regime the Islamic Republic is, both on a domestic scale and an international scale. My intention in writing this book has been to shed light on the extreme difficulties that the people of Iran face on a day-to-day basis in dealing with life under the regime, and while my hopes are that one day the place that I used to call home will have an accountable and responsible government, it is nevertheless for the people of Iran to come to this decision.